Quitting the Sex Trade

This anthology of original studies focuses on why and how sex workers and sex market facilitators, including pimps, quit the sex trade. There is extensive literature on 'desistance' with different theories explaining why people quit crime. There is little research about sex market facilitators' 'desistance,' and aside from some notable studies, few are about sex workers' quitting. The studies in this anthology explore a spectrum of quitting the sex trade from voluntarily stopping, 'drifting,' and retiring, to intervention-based or coerced stopping due to influences and impositions by programs and specialized courts.

This book provides insight into the meaning of this work; how people in the sex trade view their engagement in licit/illicit spheres; and it will inform providers who interface with people from these communities regarding how to support desistance. Further this book may help those engaged in emerging topics related to the sex trade, including (1) global trends in sex work decriminalization and human trafficking criminalization; (2) the recent emergence of human trafficking intervention courts in the USA; and (3) the development (and impact) of new laws, policies, and intervention programs designed to reduce human trafficking (globally, regionally, country level) and more localized efforts to support desistance among participants in the sex trade.

The book will be of interest to academics, researchers, and advanced students of Criminology, Sociology, Law, Policy, and Psychology. It was originally published as a special issue in the journal *Victims & Offenders.*

Amber Horning is Assistant Professor in the School of Criminology and Justice Studies at the University of Massachusetts, Lowell, USA. For the last decade, they have researched commercial sex markets and human trafficking. Dr Horning has led one of the largest studies on sex market facilitators in the United States.

Quitting the Sex Trade

Why and How Pimps and Sex Workers Leave the Business

Edited by
Amber Horning

Routledge
Taylor & Francis Group
LONDON AND NEW YORK

First published 2021
by Routledge
2 Park Square, Milton Park, Abingdon, Oxon, OX14 4RN

and by Routledge
52 Vanderbilt Avenue, New York, NY 10017

Routledge is an imprint of the Taylor & Francis Group, an informa business

British Library Cataloguing-in-Publication Data
A catalogue record for this book is available from the British Library

ISBN13: 978-0-367-69526-2

Typeset in Minion Pro
by codeMantra

Publisher's Note
The publisher accepts responsibility for any inconsistencies that may have arisen during the conversion of this book from journal articles to book chapters, namely the inclusion of journal terminology.

Disclaimer
Every effort has been made to contact copyright holders for their permission to reprint material in this book. The publishers would be grateful to hear from any copyright holder who is not here acknowledged and will undertake to rectify any errors or omissions in future editions of this book.

Contents

Citation Information

The chapters in this book were originally published in the *Victims & Offenders*, volume 14, issue 5 (July 2019). When citing this material, please use the original page numbering for each article, as follows:

Introduction

Quitting the Sex Trade: Keeping Narratives inside the Debates on Prostitution Policy and Legislation
Amber Horning
Victims & Offenders, volume 14, issue 5 (July 2019) pp. 533–539

Chapter 1

A Safe Harbor Is Temporary Shelter, Not A Pathway Forward: How Court-Mandated Sex Trafficking Intervention Fails to Help Girls Quit the Sex Trade
Misty Luminais, Rachel Lovell, and Margaret McGuire
Victims & Offenders, volume 14, issue 5 (July 2019) pp. 540–560

Chapter 2

Harlem Pimps' Reflections on Quitting: External and Internal Reasons
Amber Horning, Lyndsay Thompson, and Christopher Thomas
Victims & Offenders, volume 14, issue 5 (July 2019) pp. 561–586

Chapter 3

The Recursive Relationship between Substance Abuse, Prostitution, and Incarceration: Voices from a Long-Term Cohort of Women
Ronet Bachman, Samantha Rodriguez, Erin M. Kerrison, and Chrysanthi Leon
Victims & Offenders, volume 14, issue 5 (July 2019) pp. 587–605

Chapter 4

Uncovering Intentions to Exit Prostitution: Findings from a Qualitative Study
Andrea N. Cimino
Victims & Offenders, volume 14, issue 5 (July 2019) pp. 606–624

Chapter 5

"It's like Being an Electrician, You're Gonna Get Shocked": Differences in the Perceived Risks of Indoor and Outdoor Sex Work and Its Impact on Exiting
Kathleen Preble, Karen Magruder, and Andrea N. Cimino
Victims & Offenders, volume 14, issue 5 (July 2019) pp. 625–646

Chapter 6

Self-Narratives of Persistent Pimps and Those Anticipating Desistance: Emotions, Conventional Work, and Moral Profitability Calculus
Loretta J. Stalans and Mary A. Finn
Victims & Offenders, volume 14, issue 5 (July 2019) pp. 647–669

For any permission-related enquiries please visit:
http://www.tandfonline.com/page/help/permissions

Contributors

Ronet Bachman Department of Sociology and Criminal Justice, University of Delaware, Newark, USA.

Andrea N. Cimino Danger Assessment Training and Technical Assistance Center, School of Nursing, Johns Hopkins University, Baltimore, USA.

Mary A. Finn School of Criminal Justice, Michigan State University, East Lansing, USA.

Amber Horning School of Criminology and Justice Studies, University of Massachusetts Lowell, USA.

Erin M. Kerrison School of Social Welfare, University of California, Berkeley, USA.

Chrysanthi Leon Department of Sociology and Criminal Justice, University of Delaware, Newark, USA.

Rachel Lovell Begun Center for Violence Prevention Research & Education, Mandel School for Applied Social Sciences, Case Western Reserve University, Cleveland, USA.

Misty Luminais Independent Contractor.

Karen Magruder School of Social Work, University of Texas, Arlington, USA.

Margaret McGuire Begun Center for Violence Prevention Research & Education, Mandel School for Applied Social Sciences, Case Western Reserve University, Cleveland, USA.

Kathleen Preble School of Social Work, University of Missouri-Columbia, Columbia, USA.

Samantha Rodriguez Department of Sociology and Criminal Justice, University of Delaware, Newark, USA.

Christopher Thomas Department of Criminal Justice, CUNY Graduate Center/John Jay College of Criminal Justice, New York, USA.

Lyndsay Thompson Department of Criminology and Justice Studies, University of Massachusetts Lowell, USA.

Loretta J. Stalans Department of Criminal Justice and Criminology, and of Psychology, Loyola University Chicago, USA.

INTRODUCTION

Quitting the Sex Trade: Keeping Narratives inside the Debates on Prostitution Policy and Legislation

Amber Horning

Recently, the public heard intimate details of powerful men in the U.S. buying sex, e.g., the case of New England Patriots owner Robert Kraft charged with soliciting prostitution, possibly from sex trafficking victims. These sex scandals sometimes raise questions about whether the sex worker is acting voluntarily, under pimp-control, or due to force, fraud or coercion. These scandals also generate conversations about how such cases are handled and how similar situations can be prevented. There are generally a few interrelated questions 1) is it voluntary? 2) how can supply and demand be reduced? 3) can policies or laws accomplish this by inciting buyers, sellers and sex market facilitators to quit? 4) what other factors will prompt these social actors to exit the market? All of the questions are important; however, the answers are generally interdependent.

Sex scandals, such as the one discussed, raise some awareness about social actors within the sex trade, but the public is not very informed about their perspectives. There are many policies and laws that try to encourage, incite or force sex workers or pimps to quit the sex trade. These policies and laws are rarely evidence-based. The perspectives of different social actors in the sex trade, particularly their reasons for slowing down or quitting, should be given more weight in the crafting of prostitution policy and legislation.

The anti-trafficking movement has gained momentum with some academics hoping to abolish prostitution because they view it as inherently coercive and inextricably linked to sex trafficking (see Farley, 2004; Hughes and de Compostela, 2004) to those with harm reduction perspectives to those who are critical of the reductive and harmful impact of the anti-trafficking movement (see Bernstein, 2012; Blanchette & Da Silva, 2012; Weitzer, 2007). Many prostitution policies are created to disrupt business to decrease its prevalence. Sweden crafted the Nordic Model in 1999, which is a legal policy where buying sex is criminalized, and sex work is decriminalized (Leander, 2005). This model does not account for sex workers' voices (Jordan, 2012) and it pushes typical buyers out (Dodillet & Östergren, 2011). In Sweden, there are indications that sex workers face more danger because on the street their exchanges are rushed and the remaining street buyers are "crazy." Alternatively, some rely on sex market facilitators in indoor brothels (Dodillet & Östergren, 2011) According to Skilbrie (2019), the Nordic Model is also geared towards changing the publics' attitudes about masculinity and sexuality. In Sweden's plight to change public opinion, sex workers are in harm's way. Recently, the Nordic Model is spreading as it has been adopted by many other European countries, as well as Canada and Israel.

In 2018, the U.S. passed anti-trafficking legislation, that is, Fighting Online Sex Trafficking Act (FOSTA) and the Senate bill, the Stop Enabling Sex Traffickers Act

(SESTA) that target online sites where sex is sold, such as Backpage, by making these sites responsible if third parties post ads for prostitution, including consensual sex work. This legislation has adversely affected independent sex workers because it drives them to street-based work and it has given legitimacy to pimp-controlled sex work (Chamberlain, 2019). Prostitution policies geared towards curbing buyers or sex market facilitators or disrupting how buyers and sellers meet often produce 'occupational risks' or dangerous work conditions as discussed by Preble and Cimino (2019) in this special issue. These occupational risks may incite quitting for some, but at what cost to human life? These types of policies force sex workers to seek dangerous and possibly lethal alternative routes to labor, such as hiring a pimp or trafficker or accepting risky clients. Preble (2019) calls for more awareness of occupational risks that are physical, emotional or legal.

In the U.S., sex traffickers face lengthy sentences, from 15 to 25 years. However, we know that deterrence based on sentence length rarely reduces rates of illegal activities (Tonry, 2012), especially in illicit markets (Dorn & South, 1990). In the U.S., some states have adopted the Human Trafficking Initiative Courts (HTIC), where if victims of sex trafficking successfully quit, then prostitution charges and related charges are expunged. These problem-solving courts are well-meaning, but there are not quantitative studies showing that they work. In this special issue, Luminais & Lovell (2019) conduct qualitative research on a juvenile HTIC in Ohio, and they find that court staff discusses poor success rates and successive admissions. According to Luminais and Lovell (2019), the court's idea of "success" should be re-assessed.

In some countries, such as New Zealand, legalizing prostitution has led to increased employment, health and safety rights for sex workers (Abel, Fitzgerald, Healy, & Taylor, 2010). In the U.S., sex work as a labor movement is gaining momentum. Some groups in the California sex trade, such as exotic dancers are debating whether they want to unionize. The regulation of indoor markets may not be the safe or correct solution (see Sanders, 2007). There is a drive to legalize voluntary sex work in the U.S. (aside from Nevada where it is already legal). Some researchers have found that legalizing prostitution increases sex trafficking (e.g., Cho, Dreher, & Neumayer, 2013) and others have fond that it reduces trafficking (Abel et al., 2010). Cunningham and Shah (2017) found during the decriminalization of prostitution in Rhode Island that there were overall reduced rates of sexual assault and sexually transmitted infections (STI's). Several studies have found that decriminalizing sex work brings stability and safety to sex worker lives (e.g., Brents & Hausbeck, 2005; Harcourt et al., 2010).

Within academia, why sex workers quit has been documented by researchers, such as Baker, Dalla, and Williamson (2010) and Oselin (2014), but there have been only a few studies about domestic minor trafficking victims (e.g., Clawson & Goldblatt Grace, 2007) or pimps quitting the sex trade (i.e., Davis, 2017). There are many studies on the perspectives of minor sex trafficking victims (e.g., Dank, 2011; Horning, 2013; Marcus et al., 2014; Williamson & Prior, 2009) and a few about pimps (e.g., Dank et al., 2014; Horning, Thomas, Marcus, & Sriken, 2018; Stalans & Finn, 2016). The time frame or the historical moment and current legal/policy changes, e.g., the War on Drugs, the Crack era, or SESTA/FOSTA contextualize accounts of quitting. The context can influence individual reasons for quitting, such as detrimental changes in markets increasing occupational risks or increases in sentencing heightening fear of punishment, yet as illustrated in this special issue there are other crucial reasons. These reasons are individual, such as life course reasons and they often involve cognitive changes that are related to participants' values or identities.

This special issue contains primarily qualitative studies where sex workers, domestically trafficked minors or pimps within the sex trade where interviewed. Generally, in studies about quitting, there are debates about who qualifies as a desister, with some researchers having rigid criteria, e.g., Farrington & Hawken, 1991) to some with less lengthy qualifications, e.g., Maruna, 2001. The earlier stages or states of quitting are just as relevant as stopping for more extended periods or "forever." This special issue contains studies about those in the sex trade in various stages of quitting. Most of the studies do not profess to detail the accounts of desisters; however, many rely on desistance theories to explain quitting that may or may not be desistance. The more common type of quitter may not be committed to stopping and this can be explained by "drift" (Matza, 1964; 2018) or haphazardly moving in and out of crime or as part of "yo-yo-ing" (Oselin, 2014) or having the idea of returning to crime, or life-course or routine activities reasons, which are initially more external (Laub & Sampson, 1993; Sampson & Laub, 1993).

A few studies in this special issue address how shifts in the illicit marketplace, such as the Crack Era or the War on Drugs can incite people to temporarily or permanently quit or at the least it contextualizes quitters' reasons for stopping. In Bachman and Kerrison's study, *The Recursive Relationship Between Substance Abuse, Prostitution, and Incarceration: Voices from a Long-Term Cohort of Women* they analyze the narratives of drug-involved women who also worked as sex workers with a focus on this nexus of drugs and sex work. Their participants were released from prison in the 1990s and were re-interviewed in 2010/2011. They find support for Paternoster and Bushway's 'Identity Theory of Desistance' where participants imagine a "feared" self who is often one who "ended up dead" and a viable "possible" self. Both exist in their quitting accounts. Overall, personal reasons that involve identity work mattered more to them. However, most of their participants entered the sex trade to support drug habits during the Crack Era. Due to stringent criminal justice policies during that iteration of the War on Drugs meant that they spent long stretches in prison. That Era shaped their "feared" selves and contextualizes perceptions of occupational risks and it also adversely influenced their experiences within the criminal justice system, which did not prompt their quitting.

In Cimino's (2019) study, *Uncovering Intentions to Exit Prostitution: Findings from a Qualitative Study*, she also tests a process-oriented model of intentions to exit sex work called the Intention to Exit Prostitution (or Sex Work). The reasons include glamorization, risk-recognition attitudes, stigma from significant others, one's own resilient self-efficacy beliefs, and agency. She finds that participants' weigh the risks and rewards and that quitting is a cumulative process. Cimino also finds support for the "Identity Theory of Desistance" because those who could not imagine a feared self with a dangerous fate persist.

Occupational hazards increase or decrease depending upon changes in open air illicit markets (Curtis and Wendel, 2007) with heightened danger in drug markets spilling over into sex markets. In Preble and Cimino (2019) study, *"It's Like Being an Electrician, You're Gonna Got Shocked": Differences in the Perceived Risks of Indoor and Outdoor Sex Work and its Impact on Exiting*, she explores how perceptions of risk vary depending upon whether sex workers' labor indoors or outdoors. Occupational risks increased during the Crack Era, and this influenced their decisions to exit. Horning, Thompson and Thomas's study *Harlem Pimps' Reflections on Quitting: External and Internal Reasons* analyzes 43 ex-pimps' accounts, also finding that those who worked during the Crack Era feared the violence and volatility of that illicit marketplace. They express great concern about what could happen to them and their workers. Additionally, ex-pimps in their sample had a lot of trouble managing workers who were using crack.

Despite increases in U.S. sex trafficking sentences and law enforcement's crackdown on prostitution, fear of punishment or prison are not principal reasons for pimps' quitting in these samples. Horning, Thompson, and Thomas (2019) find that some younger ex-pimps fear sex trafficking sentences because they tend to work with women in their age bracket, including those under eighteen (also see Horning, 2013). Stalans and Finn's (2019) study, *Self-Narratives of Persistent Pimps and Those Anticipating Desistance: Emotions, Conventional Work, and Moral Profitability Calculus*, show that persisters continue to do legitimate work to avoid arrest. They safeguard the risk of arrest and punishment as opposed to quitting the sex trade.

Luminais and Lovell's study, *A Safe Harbor is Temporary Shelter, Not a Pathway Forward: How Court-Mandated Sex Trafficking Intervention Fails to Help Girls Quit the Sex Trade*, explores the Human Trafficking Intervention Court (HTIC) for juveniles in the State of Ohio. Most strikingly, these researchers are unable to get many young people to participate in the study. They speculate that many did not identify as trafficking victims or the program did not resonate with them. This problem-solving court that is supposed to be victim-forward has only a handful of graduation parties thrown by court staff for minors who finish the program. This type of court may not be the best solution for these young people who may not identify with the trafficking victim label, and who may feel stigmatized by it.

This special issue includes two studies about pimps quitting the sex trade. These studies document the gamut of quitting from those only considering quitting (Stalans and Finn, 2019) to those who have stopped for a long time, but who have never entirely given up the pimp identity (Horning et al., 2019). In Horning at al. (2019), they found that most ex-pimps accounts are interdiscursive and can include external, e.g., occupational, environmental or policy reasons and life course, and internal, e.g., moral reasons for quitting. Stalans and Finn interview 49 active pimps or drivers managing sex workers and ask them questions about why they persist and discuss anticipated desistance. Those with "double lives" discuss work as financial security and enhanced social identity, whereas the persisters value legitimate work as a strategy to avoid arrest. These typical "hooks for change" incite staying or quitting depending on social relationships and contexts. It is moral and emotional dilemmas in line with McAdams (2013) that prompt thoughts of quitting. Davis (2017) applies how ex-pimps never fully leave the "pimp" mindset. In part, this is due to pimping being a high-point and a glamorized part of their lives, which is a well-documented pull (Dank et al., 2014; Davis, 2017; Horning et al., 2018) and this is reflected in Horning et al.'s article where the "bad ass" me theme or the theme where pimps reflect on pimping as their "golden years" or as "high status" is prevalent in the majority of accounts.

In this special issue, the themes that are similar across studies are risk and stigma. The theme of risk is not a surprise because many of these samples are lower-echelon social actors who were involved in street-based work. Another recurrent theme is stigma related to worrying about family members, especially children knowing how they make money and judging them. On the flipside of stigma, some of these participants stay for the glamor and money or reminisce about it, though this is primarily evident with ex-pimps. Across studies, participants' reasons for quitting are cumulative, that is they often involved a series of external, life course or internal reasons and they tend to be interdiscursive with multiple themes present in single accounts.

Policies and laws that aim at decreasing the sex trade should take into account social actors' perspectives within the sex trade. Overwhelmingly, these participants do not stop primarily due to changes in policy or law. Some participants quit due to occupational hazards created due to changes in illicit markets that draw other members of the sex trade into more dangerous or even lethal situations. Creating dangerous and uninhabitable markets is never a viable policy angle. Accounts from the participants in this special issue contain many personal reasons for quitting, such as life course changes, e.g., having a child or internal reasons related to cumulative dissatisfaction with that lifestyle. Many of the life course or internal changes require cognitive and identity work where participants grapple with processing new ways of feeling and being. Any policy or legal system attempting to curb social actors' participation in the sex trade needs to focus on the quality of the participants' self-described changes and the long-term processes of quitting rather than on creating dangerous, punitive or stigmatizing approaches.

Disclosure statement

No potential conflict of interest was reported by the author.

References

Abel, G., Fitzgerald, L., Healy, C., & Taylor, A. (eds). (2010). *Taking the crime out of sex work: New Zealand sex workers' fight for decriminalisation*. Bristol, UK: Policy Press.

Baker, L. M., Dalla, R. L., & Williamson, C. (2010). Exiting prostitution: An integrated model. *Violence against Women, 16*(5), 579–600. doi:10.1177/1077801210367643

Bernstein, E. (2012). Carceral politics as gender justice? The "traffic in women" and neoliberal circuits of crime, sex, and rights. *Theory and Society, 41*(3), 233–259. doi:10.1007/s11186-012-9165-9

Blanchette, T. G., & Da Silva, A. P. (2012). On bullshit and the trafficking of women: Moral entrepreneurs and the invention of trafficking of persons in Brazil. *Dialectical Anthropology, 36* (1–2), 107–125. doi:10.1007/s10624-012-9268-8

Brents, B. G., & Hausbeck, K. (2005). Violence and legalized brothel prostitution in Nevada: Examining safety, risk, and prostitution policy. *Journal of Interpersonal Violence, 20*(3), 270–295. doi:10.1177/0886260504270333

Chamberlain, L. (2019). FOSTA: A hostile law with a human cost. *Available at SSRN 3314708*. doi:10.2139/ssrn.3314708

Cho, S. Y., Dreher, A., & Neumayer, E. (2013). Does legalized prostitution increase human trafficking? *World Development, 41*, 67–82. doi:10.1016/j.worlddev.2012.05.023

Cimino, A. (2019). Uncovering Intentions to Exit Prostitution: Findings from a Qualitative Study. *Victims and Offenders*

Clawson, H. J., & Goldblatt Grace, L. (2007). *Finding a path to recovery: Residential facilities for minor victims of domestic sex trafficking.*

Cunningham, S, & Shah, M. (2017). Decriminalizing indoor prostitution: implications for sexual violence and public health. *The Review of Economic Studies, 85*(3), 1683–1715.

Curtis, R., & Wendel, T. (2007). "You're always training the Dog": Strategic interventions to reconfigure drug markets. *Journal of Drug Issues, 37*(4), 867–891. doi:10.1177/002204260703700407

Dank, M. (2011). *The commercial sexual exploitation of children.* El Paso, TX: LFB Scholarly Publishing LLC.
Dank, M. L., Khan, B., Downey, P. M., Kotonias, C., Mayer, D., Owens, C., ... Yu, L. (2014). *Estimating the size and structure of the underground commercial sex economy in eight major US cities.* Washington, D.C: Urban Institute.
Davis, H. (2017). Exit from the Game: Ex-pimps and desistance in the USA. In Horning, A., & Marcus, A (Eds.),*Third party sex work and pimps in the age of anti-trafficking* (pp. 111–129). NewYork, NY: Springer.
Dodillet, S., & Östergren, P. (2011, March). The Swedish sex purchase act: Claimed success and documented effects. *Conference paper presented at the International Workshop: Decriminalizing Prostitution and Beyond: Practical Experiences and Challenges. The Hague* (Vol.3).
Dorn, N., & South, N. (1990). Drug markets and law enforcement. *The British Journal of Criminology, 30*(2), 171–188. doi:10.1093/oxfordjournals.bjc.a047988
Farley, M. (2004). "Bad for the body, bad for the heart": Prostitution harms women even if legalized or decriminalized. *Violence against Women, 10*(10), 1087–1125. doi:10.1177/1077801204268607
Farrington, D. P., & Hawkins, J. D. (1991). Predicting participation, early onset and later persistence in officially recorded offending. *Criminal Behaviour and Mental Health, 1*(1), 1–33. doi:10.1002/cbm.1991.1.issue-1
Harcourt, C., O'connor, J., Egger, S., Fairley, C. K., Wand, H., Chen, M. Y., ... Donovan, B. (2010). The decriminalisation of prostitution is associated with better coverage of health promotion programs or sex workers. *Australian and New Zealand Journal of Public Health, 34*(5), 482–486. doi:10.1111/j.1753-6405.2010.00594.x
Horning, A. (2013). Peeling the onion: Domestically trafficked minors and other sex work involved youth. *Dialectical Anthropology, 37*(2), 299–307. doi:10.1007/s10624-012-9289-3
Horning, A., Thomas, C., Marcus, A., & Sriken, J. (2018). Risky business: Harlem pimps' work decisions and economic returns. *Deviant Behavior*, 1–26. doi:10.1080/01639625.2018.1556863
Horning, A., Thompson, L., & Thomas, C. (2019). Harlem Pimps' Reflections on Quitting: External and Internal Reasons. *Victims and Offenders.*
Hughes, D. M., & de Compostela, S. (2004, July). Prostitution: Causes and solutions. In *Paper delivered at the Conference on Female.*
Jordan, A. (2012) The Swedish law to criminalize clients: A failed experiment in social engineering. Issue paper 4. Program on human trafficking and forced labor, center for human rights & humanitarian law. Retrieved from: http://rightswork.org/wp content/uploads/2012/04/Issue-Paper-4.pdf
Laub, J. H., & Sampson, R. J. (1993). Turning points in the life course: Why change matters to the study of crime. *Criminology, 31*(3), 301–325. doi:10.1111/crim.1993.31.issue-3
Leander, K. (2005). Reflections on Sweden's measures against men's violence against women. *Social Policy and Society, 5*(1), 115–125. doi:10.1017/S1474746405002794
Luminais, M., & Lovell, R. (2019). A safe harbor is temporary shelter, not a Pathway Forward: How Court Mandated Sex Trafficking Intervention Fails to Help Girls Quit the Sex Trade. *Victims and Offenders.*
Marcus, A, Horning, A, Curtis, R, Sanson, J, & Thompson, E. (2014). Conflict and agency among sex workers and pimps: A closer look at domestic minor sex trafficking. *The ANNALS of the American Academy of Political and Social Science, 653*(1), 225–246.
Maruna, S. (2001). *Making good* (pp. 86). Washington, DC: American Psychological Association.
Matza, D. (1964; 2018). *Delinquency and drift.* US: Routledge.
McAdams, D. P. (1993). *The stories we live by: Personal myths and the making of the self.* New York, NY: Guilford Press.
McAdams, D. P. (2013). The psychological self as actor, agent and author. *Perspectives In Psychological Science, 8*(3), 272-295.
Oselin, S. S. (2014). *Leaving prostitution: Getting out and staying out of sex work.* NYU Press.
Preble, K., & Cimino, A. (2019). It's like being an electrician, you're gonna get shocked: Differences in the perceived risks of Internet-facilitated and street-based sex work and its impact on exiting. *Victims and Offenders.*

Sampson, R. J., & Laub, J. H. (1993). Structural variations in juvenile court processing: Inequality, the underclass, and social control. *Law and Society Review*, 285–311. doi:10.2307/3053938

Sanders, T. (2007). No room for a regulated market? The implications of the co-ordinated prostitution strategy for the indoor sex industries. *Safer Communities*, *6*(1), 34–44. doi:10.1108/17578043200700006

Skilbrei, M. L. (2019). Assessing the power of prostitution policies to shift markets, attitudes, and ideologies. *Annual Review of Criminology*, *2*, 493–508. doi:10.1146/annurev-criminol-011518-024623

Stalans, L., & Finn, M. (2019). Harlem Pimps' Reflections on Quitting: External and Internal Reasons. *Victims and Offenders.*

Stalans, L. J., & Finn, M. A. (2016). Defining and predicting pimps' coerciveness toward sex workers: Socialization processes. *Journal of Interpersonal Violence*, *37*(6) 0886260516675919.

Tonry, M. (2012). *Punishment and politics.* Willan.

Weitzer, R. (2007). The social construction of sex trafficking: Ideology and institutionalization of a moral crusade. *Politics & Society*, *35*(3), 447–475. doi:10.1177/0032329207304319

Williamson, C., & Prior, M. (2009). Domestic minor sex trafficking: A network of underground players in the Midwest. *Journal of Child & Adolescent Trauma*, *2*(1), 46–61. doi:10.1080/19361520802702191

A Safe Harbor Is Temporary Shelter, Not A Pathway Forward: How Court-Mandated Sex Trafficking Intervention Fails to Help Girls Quit the Sex Trade

Misty Luminais, Rachel Lovell, and Margaret McGuire

ABSTRACT

Results from an evaluation of a juvenile human trafficking court are presented to explore the ways in which tensions between (a) human trafficking rhetoric, (b) a legal framework that cannot resolve the conflict inherent in the victim-delinquent identity required by Safe Harbor legislation, and (c) the lived experiences of youth in the program do not support youth actually quitting the sex trade. Practical hurdles to implementation of the program are also discussed, and recommendations on how other jurisdictions might approach the issue are offered.

Introduction

As human trafficking receives more attention and funding in the United States, whole classes of behaviors that were previously classified as illegal have been reclassified as something "other than illegal." According to the Trafficking Victims Protection Act (federal statute 22 USC Chapter 78), anyone engaged in selling sex under the age of eighteen is a victim of human trafficking. Ohio (the state where this research was conducted) has a similar statute (ORC §2905.32) – a Safe Harbor law that forbids charging youth under the age of sixteen with prostitution. Youth in the sex trade between the ages of sixteen and eighteen may be considered victims of trafficking if there is demonstrable force, fraud, or coercion (the same standard in place for adults). "Safe Harbor" juvenile dockets are the outgrowth of this statute with the goal of diverting youth from the juvenile justice system by substituting treatment and other interventions in lieu of incarceration. However, the existing research on the process and efficacy of specialized dockets in addressing juvenile sex trafficking is limited.

Discussions about and reactions to the subject of human trafficking are often emotionally charged and tend towards the bombastic, frequently characterized by oft-repeated and oft-disproven guesses instead of scientifically-based research. In this charged arena of research, we provide a case study that details the process and outcomes for the Safe Harbor Project – a specialized docket for minor victims of human trafficking in Cuyahoga County, Ohio. By examining the process and outcomes of the docket, our study provides nuance to the larger discussion around human trafficking by arguing that the language used to describe human trafficking reflects a conception of the world that can speak past the lived experiences of youth identified as having been trafficked. The language and framework of the criminal justice system further complicate these interactions as the people employing this lens have a different perspective on what role youth play in the circumstances that brought them to the attention of the juvenile justice system. The histrionic political rhetoric deployed in popular discussions of human trafficking comes into conflict with the precise legal framework needed to assign blame, hold offenders accountable, and protect the community. Both legal and political frameworks ignore how youth (who are disproportionally young women) interpret their actions, and the unarticulated mishmash of the two competing frameworks can result in juvenile justice interventions that fail to help the youth in question leave the sex trade. Tension exists between the juvenile justice system's need to identify a clear victim/offender, political rhetoric's desire for uncomplicated victims in need of rescue, and youths' desire to define themselves as actors with agency in a complicated situation. This article is a direct response to Weitzer's call for a micro-level analysis of human trafficking that illustrates the complexity of individuals' lived experiences (2015).

This paper details the results of an evaluation of the Safe Harbor Project in Cuyahoga County (Cleveland, Ohio, USA) by elucidating upon the struggles of an emerging safe harbor docket situated in a particular political context. Specifically, we detail the key challenges at each phase in the process (identification, intake, engagement, and discharge/graduation) and how conflicting worldviews complicate the process. Although the docket identified a sizable number of youth as trafficked or at risk of being trafficked, the vast majority of the youth were not enrolled in the docket, and only a few successfully graduated. Results also indicate that the docket has yet to be successful in helping the youth quit the sex trade. We posit that the court has not accomplished this in large part due to the court's conflicting framework that defines youth as both victims and delinquents. We recommend elucidating and implementing a new definition of success that explicitly includes: desistance from the sex trade, incremental progress, and the voices of those served by the court. We present these findings to highlight the difficulty of serving this population via a criminal justice setting and make suggestions for other jurisdictions considering this route.

Background

Specialized court dockets

The problem of children in the sex trade, while not a new issue, is a serious social and public health problem that has received much greater social awareness in recent years (Lutnick, 2016). Even the different terms for it invokes questions of agency, e.g., commercial sexual exploitation of children, youth in the sex trade, human trafficking. Recent increased awareness of this issue through the term "human trafficking" has brought heightened momentum across the country to tackle the issue, and jurisdictions across the country have begun to respond through the use of specialized juvenile court dockets, including dockets in Beaumont, Texas (Flahive, 2015), New York City, New York (Lippmann, 2013), and Reno, Nevada (Deruy, 2016).

Specialized court dockets have been widely used for decades as a way to judicially address the needs of specific types of offenders, such as defendants with drug addiction (Sevigny, Fuleihan, & Ferdik, 2013), defendants with mental illness (Barber-Rioja, Rotter, Schombs, & Barber-Rioja, 2017), defendants suffering from homelessness (Huck & Morris, 2017), and even veteran offenders (Yerramsetti, Simons, Coonan, & Stolar, 2017). Specialized court dockets are meant to provide a more a therapeutically-oriented judicial approach to court supervision and treatment (Supreme Court of Ohio, 2016).

Diversion programs specifically for minors have been found to decrease recidivism and increasing well-being, particularly for defendants with drug addiction and mental health challenges (Collins, Lonczak, & Clifasefi, 2017; Kretschmar, Butcher, Flannery, & Singer, 2014; Kretschmar, Tossone, Butcher, & Marsh, 2018), although Mears et al. (2016) argue that in general, diversion programs can lead to police "net-widening" without an empirical foundation of rigorous evaluation. Shields and Letourneau (2015), specifically focusing on the application of diversion as directed by various state Safe Harbor laws, state "It is unknown whether diversion policies have effectively achieved their goal. Further, there are no scientific assessments of unintended consequences, positive or negative, associated with diversion policies" (p. 4).

Adapting a specialized court docket model to human sex trafficking, in particular, human sex trafficking of minors, is particularly challenging for a couple of reasons. First, other diversion courts broadly rely on a disease/disorder model, where therapy or treatment for a particular issue is thought lead to positive outcomes, such as reduced recidivism. For example, veterans courts are based on the idea that veterans share a particular set of characteristics that can be treated (such as PTSD, head injuries, and substance abuse). Dockets that primarily serve indigent and homeless defendants accused of misdemeanors or some low-level felonies related to their economic situation (Pope-Sussman, 2015) are often predicated on treating what seems to be the root of a person's homeless status, such as addiction and/or mental illness.

Second, a fundamental tension exists in the framework of the juvenile criminal justice system that presents several challenges for the court in serving victims of human trafficking. On the one hand, they often have extensive histories of trauma (similar in some ways to veterans), and on the other, suffer the effects of poverty, substance abuse, and other mental health issues (similar to those suffering from homelessness), all of which is compounded by their status as juveniles (Lutnick, 2016). According to federal and state legal statutes and popular discourse, victims of minor human sex trafficking are, by definition, victims. Yet, the court is designed to define these victims of human trafficking (those charged with criminal complaints) as delinquents.

Within the disease/treatment model, the cause and effect relationship between drug addiction and some types of crime (the addiction drives the person to steal to maintain their habit) is well-understood. The same can be said for someone living at the edges of society – being homeless makes it almost impossible to hold a job which leads one to steal in order to eat, or more directly, not having a home can lead to sleeping outdoors and violating anti-camping ordinances. In these cases, there is a genesis to the problems that, in some way, can be addressed. However, in the case of human trafficking, the cause-and-effect is less clear. The genesis of the problem is often thought to be the person exploiting the youth. However, there is frequently no clear exploiter ("trafficker") who is compelling (via force, fraud, or coercion) an underage woman to engage in the commercial sex trade, according to the traditional and legal definition of trafficking. Instead, there are more ambiguous types of "trafficking" such as youth who are "involved in the life" arranging "clients" for other girls "involved in the life," or girls termed "self-trafficked" because they sell nude photographs of themselves. Even in the less ambiguous cases where there was an identified pimp who exploits a girl for material gain, how does the court contextualize the issue of exploitation using a disease model when the girl does not define her relationship to the pimp as exploitative? Is it reasonable to define this as an addiction? Addition to a person? A lifestyle? What is the treatment for that? Rhetorically, this may be an appealing metaphor, but it leads to imprecise practices.

As stated previously, the court is designed to see people in terms of victims and offenders – people who have been injured by crimes and people who commit crimes. The trafficking framework demands that court personnel see the youth on the docket as inhabiting those two roles *simultaneously*. The argument is that the victimization has led directly to the commission of the crimes under consideration, like in the case of a person experiencing an alcohol/drug problem shoplifting, where the defendant is asked to be accountable for their actions, even when driven by addiction. In the case of trafficking victims, they are, at the same moment, supposed to be accountable for their actions and supposed to acknowledge how exploitation and victimization have brought them to this point, removing any agency they feel for their actions. The court itself is designed as a punitive system, set up to assign blame and punish the guilty.[1]

Research on human trafficking dockets

Human trafficking dockets are a relatively new phenomenon and, therefore, there is limited research to inform best practices. Evaluations that include the voices of current and former sex workers tend to be more critical of court intervention (White et al., 2017; Yale Global Health Justice Partnership, 2018a, 2018b), while research that is focused on service providers and court actors are more likely to stress positive outcomes (Center for Court Innovation, 2015; Gibbs, Hardison Walters, Lutnick, Miller, & Kluckman, 2015). For example, an evaluation of Queens Court in New York by the Red Umbrella Project (Ray & Caterino, 2014), a sex-worker led advocacy group, found that despite the intentions of the court, arrest and court involvement did not end victimization or address economic justice. Furthermore, Ray and Caterine note that in one instance, the lack of interpreters in the court extended the time a Mandarin person was in the system by five to six months. Yet, an evaluation of Minnesota's Safe Harbor practices across the state, which include but are not limited to court diversion, note positive results for participants in that they learned about personal safety, how to identify abusive relationships, and how to find safe and affordable housing (Shcauben, Atella, Imberston, Turner, & Highum, 2017). Another study based in Minnesota (Golke, 2011) finds that victims may not report victimization due to fear of their exploiters or previous bad experiences with law enforcement, but this study does not explore whether or not that group of youth consider themselves as victims.

Existing literature on human trafficking dockets (adult and juvenile) also finds that the court and key stakeholders often fail to incorporate feedback from the victims regarding what resources and services they need. Thus, well-intended efforts often fail to secure the resources and services that victims are most in need of, mainly housing and employment

(Lutnick, 2016; Ray & Caterino, 2014). In human trafficking courts that serve adults, social workers within the criminal justice system have been criticized for using coercion and downplaying self-determination of the persons they are serving (Bergquist, 2015). Dank, Yahner, and Yu (2017) found that most adults served by trafficking courts in New York were more frequently treated as defendants, rather than as victims, by both police and courts.

In terms of examining the role the courts play in desistance from sex work, the results often point to a lack of effectiveness. A three-year evaluation of a diversion program in Dallas found failure rates as high as 84%, due in part to the disconnect between the clients' motivation to participate in a specialized docket to avoiding criminal charges and the courts desire to have participants quit sex work ("leave the life") (Preble, Praetorius, & Cimino, 2015). Cimino (2017) argues that because people have different paths to entry into different types of sex work, a one-size-fits-all court-driven approach is less successful than approaches motivated by the individual's desire to leave, which are also diverse. Additionally, what is found to be effective or not effective in one jurisdiction cannot necessarily be uniformly applied to all jurisdictions, as each jurisdiction implements a local court response to human trafficking (Malangone, Mazur, & Goodman, 2015). Studies that use other measures of effectiveness, such as the evaluation of the Franklin County human trafficking court (Miner-Romanoff, 2017), show reductions in behaviors without complete desistance in most cases.

Safe harbor project

In May 2015, the Cuyahoga County Court of Common Pleas Juvenile Division (Juvenile Court) began a specialized docket (the Safe Harbor Project) to address youth who have been or are at risk of being trafficked and have a pending complaint ("charge"). In Ohio, several courts are experimenting with the application of Ohio's Safe Harbor law (ORC §2905.32), including the juvenile court in Summit County (Restore Court) and adult courts in Franklin County (Empowerment Program) and Cuyahoga County (Human Trafficking Specialized Docket), since the law's adoption in June of 2012. The state has followed the lead of the federal government in strengthening penalties against traffickers and allowing some leeway for victims of trafficking accused of crimes. The legal statutes are broad, with room for interpretation, and the newness of court-based intervention in response to the shift in the legal landscape means there is a marked deficit in established best practices for developing, implementing, and sustaining a specialized docket for minor victims of human trafficking.

Soon after the formation of the docket, court staff reached out to the first and second authors to ask for assistance with an outcome evaluation. They recognized that traditional outcomes for specialized dockets, namely compliance with conditions of their probation (yes or no) and abstinence from the activity that lead to criminal complaints (yes or no), would likely be insufficient measures for their purposes. They had already been working with this population for some time and knew that the youth often went "AWOL" (absent without official leave – or capias/disengagement with the court/runaway), often returning (or attempting to return) to their exploiters/pimps/sex work. The court staff asked for help in developing outcomes that would reflect the amount of incremental progress being made by the youth and the extensive efforts expended by the court to help youth obtain incremental progress. Early conversations with the court staff revealed the court staff's concerns with the "victim-delinquent" issue. Probation is designed to hold the youth accountable for their actions (as delinquents), but a victim-centered, trauma-informed framework meant stakeholders should understand violating probation by going AWOL as a trauma response, not as a deliberate criminal act.

We should note that while we use the term "docket" in this paper to refer to the Safe Harbor Project, it is a not officially a docket, as recognized by Ohio's Supreme Court. Docket certification through Ohio's Supreme Court is a rigorous process that demands clear metrics and strict participation guidelines. The court staff felt remaining uncertified gave the program more leeway to handle a larger set of cases, unconstrained by criteria that might not reflect the diverse circumstances facing girls in the program. The court uses the term human trafficking among stakeholders and the public, but we should clarify that the docket only handles cases of human sex trafficking and not labor trafficking.

Methods

Over a year, the first and second authors investigated how the project had been planned and implemented through a process evaluation and attempted to study the impact on youth through an outcome evaluation. At the outset, the authors intended for the process evaluation to analyze case flow to determine how youth moved through the system. However, very little data was being collected systematically by the court about when and why youth were failing to proceed in the process. However, the first and second authors did review data collection practices, archived materials, and case files. With this limitation in mind, the authors relied more heavily on qualitative data than was their original intention of a mixed-method design. The judge and bailiff (who was primarily responsible for the administration of the project at one point) were interviewed for about ninety minutes each. The advisory board participated in a two-hour focus group with both the first and second author. The initial research design recognized the importance of including the perspectives of youths and families served by the Safe Harbor Project. Multiple barriers arose which made including them difficult, including scheduling around emotionally tense court hearings, youth going AWOL, and child welfare's lack of response to repeated inquiries about interviewing children who were wards. The authors compensated participants for interviews ($25 gift cards), but the small stipend was not a sufficient motivation when stacked against other challenges. One author interviewed one youth, while the other author interviewed the youth's guardian. These interviews took place immediately following the youth's successful graduation from the program. Despite the stated barriers, the authors were able to hear the youth speak for themselves at hearings. Participant observation took place in the form of attendance at monthly advisory board meetings, at meetings of other groups concerned with human trafficking in the county, and court hearings. Although the original research design called for the authors to attend court every time a youth had a hearing, court staff were more willing to share scheduling information for graduations (successful completions) and "promising" victims. Often, the authors only learned about difficult cases afterward. Because there was no set schedule for Safe Harbor hearings, it was difficult to predict when youth would be in court, i.e., Safe Harbor did not have a specific day on the court's docket. Over the year, the authors attended eight hearings that lasted between half an hour to one and a half hours. Both authors attended advisory board meetings and court hearings, writing memos afterward and then debriefing together. Interviews and focus groups were recorded and transcribed then iteratively coded using *a priori* codes based on the literature. Memos were also thematically coded.

Working as a researcher in a court setting brought about its own challenges. The authors were simultaneously considered colleagues with expertise and as outside evaluators. Most of the time, the authors only observed interactions in meetings and people appeared comfortable sharing their unfiltered opinions in their presence. However, this closeness may have inadvertently translated to the youth and guardians that the researchers were affiliates of the court despite their stated independence.

The process[2]

Early on, it became evident that the docket's process was complicated and not well understood or elucidated by key stakeholders. Therefore, along with an outcome evaluation, a process evaluation was also included. Evaluation activities began in August of 2016. This is the general process by which the youth proceed through the main phases of the docket: identification, intake, engagement, and discharged/graduation. This process varied by the individual and even throughout the evaluation, as discussed below.

Youth were identified as "possibly trafficked" by law enforcement, court staff (such as other jurists, probation officers, magistrates, bailiffs, detention center workers), rape crisis staff, hospital staff, child welfare workers, or social services staff. When a youth was identified as possibly being a victim of human trafficking, the youth was brought to the attention of the Safe Harbor Project manager or bailiff (this shifted over time), who requested an assessment be conducted by rape crisis counselors using the Loyola Tool (called the Rapid Screening Tool for Child Trafficking) (Center for the Human Rights for Children, Loyola University Chicago, & International Organization for Adolescents, 2011). All assessed youth were included on a list of possible victims and eligibility was assessed by primary members of an advisory board, who met face-to-face monthly but regularly communicated via email, phone, and text. The advisory board was primarily composed of interested law enforcement (including members of the FBI Human Trafficking Task Force), probation officers, service providers, public defenders, guardians ad litem, child welfare workers, social workers from behavioral health agencies/therapists, and others who had demonstrated an interest in juvenile human trafficking. This cross-disciplinary group shared insights into a particular youth's behavior and history with the court and/or child welfare and made recommendations specific to that individual close to when she (all on the docket were cisgender girls, discussed in detail later in the paper) would be seen by the judge for the first time.

After the identification phase, the intake process began with an assessment to determine whether the youth qualified for the Safe Harbor docket. To qualify the youth needed to: (a) screen positive for trafficking according to the assessment, (b) have a pending criminal complaint that was in some way related to their trafficking experience, and (c) agree to participate (both the youth and guardian). In exchange for participating in the Safe Harbor Project, youth were offered essentially the same services offered to all alleged delinquents in juvenile court – mainly individual or group counseling (sometimes both), family therapy, and support groups. They would enter a plea in abeyance, which meant that they pled guilty to their charges, but if they successfully completed the program, the charges would be dismissed, sealed, and expunged. The terms of compliance were also comparable to other youth involved with juvenile court – youth agreed to random drug tests and were assigned a probation officer, a case manager, guardian ad litem, and/or a public defender and also agree to remain in compliance with the programs set forth by these groups. Youth were usually required to attend school physically or online and/or obtain part-time employment or volunteer while attending all court hearings and mandated treatment sessions. The additional benefit not offered to others in juvenile court was that after successfully completing the program, Safe Harbor youth had their records expunged immediately.[3] Furthermore, most of the providers who offered services had familiarity with trafficked youth and were trained in trauma-informed practices.

After intake, the youth moved to the engagement phase, which typically lasted between 90–270 days (but legally no more than 270 days). In this phase, they must meet the conditions of the court. If they abided by the conditions of the court and did not engage in "risky behavior" (primarily this means not engaging in the sex trade but can also mean not using illegal substances or running away), they could successfully graduate and have the criminal complaints under consideration immediately expunged. Youth who did not stay in compliance, in some cases to a higher or lesser degree, would be discharged as unsuccessful. Because they had already pleaded guilty to their charge, they would return to the regular juvenile court process, usually sentencing. While this was the general process and phases of the docket, as discussed below, the process was often modified.

Results

Over the course of the year study, approximately one hundred youth were identified as possibly trafficked, the court maintained approximately twenty active cases, and four girls had completed the program from its inception in May of 2015 – the court's strictest definition of success. Of the four girls that successfully graduated, one girl was known to have returned to the sex trade, based on a subsequent criminal complaint she incurred during the evaluation period. Given such large attrition rates at key phases in the process – identification, intake, engagement, and discharge – below we detail the significant issues related to attrition at each of the phases in order provide a more contextual understanding as to why the Safe Harbor docket had, up to this point, not been successful in getting the girls on the docket to quit the sex trade.

Identification: defining trafficking and "criminal complaints related to trafficking"

The "growing pains" of the docket meant definitional changes in the identification phase of the process. For example, throughout the evaluation, the core concept of "victim of trafficking" changed. At times, a strict definition of trafficking was employed, requiring a clearly identified trafficker who victimized girls. At other times, the definition expanded to include those at risk of trafficking. For example, there were conversations about charging one girl with a felony for selling nude photos of herself online for being a "self-trafficker," partly to compel her participation in the program. In terms of self-identifying as a victim of trafficking, youth were intentionally not asked whether or not they defined themselves as victims of human trafficking. This was thought to be a term/label they did not use or would reject outright. Defining oneself as a victim of trafficking was considered a process the youth needed assistance with.

Additionally, there was also a lack of agreement and consistency in what qualified as a "criminal complaint related to the youth's status as a victim of trafficking." Complaints like truancy could more easily be tied to being a victim of trafficking, while others were more difficult to tie to their trafficking. For example, theft of a motor vehicle was once considered to be "related" to one girl's trafficking, but shoplifting was not related to another girl's trafficking. Essentially, the advisory board and court staff would attempt to persuade the prosecutors that almost any criminal complaint was related to their status as a victim of trafficking in order to offer them the broadest scope of relief, but prosecutors had to agree before youth was admitted to the docket. What was considered a qualifying criminal complaint greatly varied over time.

Intake: balancing the "carrot and the stick"

As with any specialized docket, clients must weigh the rewards of the program (the carrot) against the possible punishments (the stick) of the program. The benefits of the program were that youth who successfully completed the program had their records related to the trafficking expunged immediately, received counseling that was tailored to survivors of human trafficking, and were provided a more hands-on approach by their case managers and team. To complete the program, youth must meet the conditions of the court, which often required a great deal of effort from the youth and their guardians. For some guardians, meeting these conditions was not feasible, leading them to decline participation on behalf of their children. The entire family would be under court surveillance for an extended period of time, which could certainly be interpreted as the stick portion of the equation. Additionally, during the evaluation period, to be on the Safe Harbor docket, the youth had to make an admission to the criminal complaint, which was held in abeyance upon successful completion of the program. If unsuccessful, the youth could be adjudicated on the complaint.

Youth with status criminal complaints (such as unruly or violating curfew) had even less incentive to participate in the Safe Harbor Project, even if they were being trafficked, as the amount of supervision required by the court greatly exceeded what the youth would generally receive if their complaint moved forward in a non-specialized docket in juvenile court. As with most specialized dockets, those with more serious complaints have much greater incentive to participate, and the court has an incentive to upcharge to compel participation. The court did not document the reasons why the youth and/or the guardians declined to participate and/or the complaints for all identified youth, so we were unable to examine this relationship empirically. However, our observations in court and attendance at advisory board meetings suggest that youth and/or their guardians felt the benefits did not outweigh the amount of effort required or possible repercussions of failing the program, and thus, declined to participate.

Race, gender, and class identification

Race, class, and gender also play a role in identification. According to the advisory board and court staff, the preponderance of youth flagged as trafficked were African American, cisgender girls who lived in poverty, had extensive histories of trauma (physical, emotional, and sexual abuse), and prior child welfare and/or juvenile court involvement. Some had developmental disabilities. However, most did not have severe mental health conditions/diagnoses (e.g., mood disorders, schizophrenia) or substance dependency issues. It is unclear from our evaluation whether this points to African American girls being disproportionately represented due to higher rates of involvement in the criminal justice system or whether they are more likely to be exploited or be in the sex trade (see Banks & Kyckelhahn, 2011; Dank et al., 2015; Fedina, Williamson, & Perdue, 2016). It should be noted that the girls identified as trafficked by the Safe Harbor docket do not reflect the demographics of women identified as trafficked in the adult correlate of this court in Cuyahoga County who are disproportionally white women with substance dependency issues, namely, opiate dependence (Margaret Baughman, personal communication).

During the researchers' time evaluating the Safe Harbor Project, no boys or young men were on the docket. Although several were assessed and a few even positively identified, none of them chose to participate. Advisory board members discussed how boys were even more reluctant to admit victimization. Based on our observations and upon information provided by the advisory board and court staff, the lack of boys and transgender youth on the docket likely stemmed from the fact that boys and transgender youth are overlooked by law enforcement when engaged in the sex trade, which would automatically make them eligible. Furthermore, the docket's outreach and education focus was on the girl's pod of the detention center and girls, in general, and has thus been seen as a "girls' court." Yet, research suggests that boys, particularly runaways, are a significant part of this population (Curtis, Terry, Dank, Dombrowski, & Khan, 2008). At the same time, the researchers did not observe any discussion of transgender youth who might be trafficked. According to the literature, transgender youth are at an even greater risk of being exploited in the sex trade than their cisgender counterparts (Curtis et al., 2008). That being said, because it is only cisgender girls participating in the Safe Harbor Project, the staff and advisory board were observed to be particularly sensitive to the needs of girls and promoted gender-specific therapies rather than a cookie-cutter approach that ignored gender differences.

Lastly, class also played a largely unexamined role, as the overwhelming majority of youth lived in poverty and the court's expectations of the youth relied on traditional middle-class ethos. The judge, who hails from a solidly middle-class background, admitted that she came from a home where "you went to work, and you did what you were supposed to do, and you listened to your parents, or there would be consequences," possibly producing a divide between her and the youth she saw.

Engagement: keeping youth in compliance

Going AWOL

Even though as a condition of remaining on the docket youth had to remain engaged with the court, throughout the evaluation, almost all of the participants went AWOL at some point, with most disappearing multiple times for various lengths of time. During these disappearances, the advisory board and/or court staff acknowledged that the youth were or were likely reengaging in the sex trade. Although other studies, including one conducted on the CATCH Court for human trafficking victims in Franklin County, Ohio, suggest that completers of diversion programs are less likely to re-engage in the targeted behavior (Miner-Romanoff, 2017), as previously stated, at least one of the four Safe Harbor graduates had returned to the sex trade after completing the program.

Although the court expected girls to go AWOL, it struggled with the appropriate consequences for this. Sometimes going AWOL was accepted, and sometimes it was grounds for dismissal from the program. In general, the court staff expected the youth to go AWOL at least a couple of times and would make allowances when possible to keep the youth on the docket for as long as reasonably possible. In some ways, the court's emphasis on remaining uncertified by the Ohio Supreme Court as an official specialized docket added to this confusion because the docket was not guided by structured metrics and strict participation guidelines, which allowed for flexibility but also inconsistency in how they worked with the youth.

The intervention

The advisory board and court staff frequently discussed having a lack of guidance on what exactly the "interventions" should be and where and for how long to keep youth in placement. This lack of clarity is particularly acute when compared to other specialized dockets, such as drug court, with its myriad of evidence-based practices for court-involved individuals with substance dependency (Henggeler, McCart, Cunningham, & Chapman, 2012).

Placement for the youth was of particular concern for the court. The judge's opinions on the efficacy of certain treatment strategies differed from the advisory board, particularly when it came to removing or leaving a youth in the community. Often the judge would be guided by the advisory boards' recommendations, but her preference was to remove the youth from the environment, which raised issues when residential treatment beds were not available. Others felt that removing the youth did not work to address the core issue – a neglectful and/or an abusive household. In the final stages of the study, funding had been secured to provide crisis housing (up to 21 days) for youth identified as trafficked. Up until that point, youth were sometimes sent to homeless shelters or left in the detention center if there were no residential treatment spaces available and the youth could not return home.

Residential treatment was further restricted by the fact that most programs would not accept girls with violent offenses or pregnant youth. Advisory board members consistently expressed concern about the role of "bottoms" or recruiters – girls who entice other girls to engage in the sex trade. The detention center and residential treatment centers were seen as difficult spaces to manage, as trafficking victims could be influenced by recruiters or actually act to recruit other girls while confined. Even if a youth was not acting as a recruiter, there was disagreement about whether youth who have been trafficked should be housed together. On the one hand, their experiences were considered so unique that it would difficult for other youth to relate to what they experienced and being around others with similar experiences can let them know they are not alone. On the other hand, in reality, youth often encouraged one another to return to the sex trade and defeat the purpose of being on the docket.

As mentioned previously, youth would be involved with the docket for a maximum of 270 days unless they received another trafficking-related complaint after exiting the program (either successfully or unsuccessfully). This time limit was viewed as a double-edged sword by the advisory board. On the one hand, some service providers advocated strongly for the court playing as small a role as possible in the lives of youth. They felt it would be too easy for the court to replace the exploiter in directing everything in the youth's life. They also believed the longer the youth and her family were involved in the court system, the worse their chances were for not continuing that relationship beyond juvenile court. Conversely, a maximum of 270 days is not much time to help a youth recover from the extensive trauma many had experienced. Even those who wanted more time recognized that compelling youth through punitive threats to participate in the docket would never be as effective as waiting until youth asked for intervention on their own.

Although the court regularly trained on victim-centered responses, the role of the youth is unclear. Youth often outright rejected the label of "victim" and resisted engaging in services, one of the ways they could be removed from the docket. There was a sense that even if the youth could not be blamed for their victimization, they were still potential delinquents who could go off the rails at any point. The process required that the youth accept that others played a role in their trafficking-related crimes but also accept accountability for their criminal behavior.

Discharge/graduation: quitting the sex trade

Youth were frequently discharged from the docket for going AWOL or otherwise failing to comply with the conditions of the court; however, the court also allowed the youth to come back to the docket at a later point. The court even allowed youth who were already adjudicated of their criminal complaints and on probation in another jurist's court to move to the Safe Harbor docket if they had been identified as victims of human trafficking. This indicates that, in general, the court attempted to be as flexible as possible in making the "carrot" of the program available to all youth who might qualify.

The court acknowledged from the beginning that they expected to have a small percentage of participants graduate; hence, the reason for their reaching out to the authors for an evaluation. In fact, when the youth did graduate, the court expended a great deal of effort to celebrate the accomplishment. They held separate "graduation parties" for each youth at their final court appearance (as compared to waiting and having a group graduation at designated time points, e.g., every three months), which including buying a cake of their choice.

We observed that the youth who made it successfully through the program often encountered a turning point in their lives outside of becoming or remaining system-involved. This supports the idea articulated by several advisory board members that it was important youth knew about services when that point turning point arrived, even if it was not at the current time. One person explained,

> "I think one of the major things that we do with this program that we do well is that whether or not they enter the program, they know where to go whenever they're ready and even if they're eighteen and they're ready, we've been lucky and blessed to have agencies that do cross over work from youth and adult level, so they know that they can turn to any of these agencies at any time. It's just like any other addiction or disease, whenever you're ready to

> stop, we [...] let them know you have six different agencies that you can call whenever you're ready. You have seventeen different people's business cards you've held at one time or another, whom you can call if you're in trouble or if you just want somebody to talk to or if you need somebody to come get you."

Goals of the docket and conflicting frameworks

Beyond issues specific to the phases in the process, ultimately, the court struggled with issues related to specifically stating the goals of the docket as well as overcoming the conflicting victim-delinquent framework. In interviews and focus groups, when asked by the evaluation team what the "value-added" of docket was, most viewed Safe Harbor as similar to traditional probation but with staff who were specifically trained to respond to and better meet the needs of victims of human trafficking, the services available to youth, and the possibility of an expedited expungement. Given that the youth were already in juvenile court, these "value-added" were seen an improvement for these youth; however, some advisory board members recognized that the system itself was punitive rather reformative.

However, when asked about the goals of the docket, the people working on the Safe Harbor docket gave conflicting definitions. Those discussed goals including creating a safe space for victims of trauma, changing a youth's outlook on the role of the court from a place of punishment to a place to get help, breaking a cycle of family violence, making sure youth are connected to services past their involvement with Safe Harbor, shifting the culture of law enforcement when dealing with vulnerable youth, and highlighting prevention. The only time desistance was discussed, it was framed as an unreasonable goal. The person said,

> "We have to change our mindset about what is success. I think that how we defined it for so long is unrealistic when it comes to this population of young ladies. We want to believe that the moment they end with our services they are not experiencing any more trauma, they are empowered, they are reunified with family and successful, they're not vulnerable anymore, they're not being trafficked, they're not going back and looking at that as an option, versus saying what the goal is that you have some skills, you have some supports, the hope is that even if at the point in time when we're letting you go, you are going back and forth, that you're still moving toward the process and getting out of that lifestyle and recognizing that there's something better for you, and that's very difficult, because when we look at treatment plans and objectives and goals, our goal is you're not going to be trafficked anymore and you're not going to be in that lifestyle anymore, and that unfortunately is not the reality of what we're dealing with."

Here the tension between the rhetoric of trafficking and the reality that these young women have agency is displayed in the frustration that the goal was simultaneously "you're not going to be trafficked" and "you're not going to be in that lifestyle anymore." This ambiguity led to practical considerations: court processes often shifted precipitously, making it difficult to identify which of the many interventions offered actually affected any particular youth's outcome. Throughout the study, qualifying criminal complaints for expungement changed from a broad definition of most things that occurred during the time period identified as when the youth was trafficked to very specific criminal complaints related directly to exploitation and then the pendulum seemed to be swinging back towards a more inclusive definition. This directly impacted the proceedings of the court, as did the shift from including only youth who positively identified as being victims, to youth who others identified as victims, to youth who were at-risk of victimization.

Beyond the conceptual messiness of what the aims of the court were, there were practical limitations on why the Safe Harbor Project was not meeting its own definition of success. Most of these limitations involved resource scarcity, but some also reflected the larger ambivalence about whether the youth on the docket were victims or delinquents. The court openly discussed their struggle with the fundamental framework of juvenile court. How does one work with a person who was both a victim and a delinquent? On the one hand, a trafficking model invoked "rescuing" a girl ("victim") from bad actor(s). On the other hand, all of the girls had criminal complaints ("alleged delinquents") and agreed to abide by the conditions of the court as well as abstain from activities that contributed to their complaint. However, practical experience had proven that youth repeatedly returned to the situations which had drawn the court's attention in the first place, namely engaging in the sex trade (sometimes with more or less agency). Compromises between these two worldviews – the youth as an exploited victim and the youth as a delinquent – involved obfuscating the purpose of the court.

Defining success

In some ways, the Safe Harbor Project had positive impacts on young women who were looking to change their lives. The intervention point that seems to clearest was if a girl was pregnant. Two of the four clients who successfully completed the program entered while pregnant or shortly after giving birth. In the one interview, the authors performed with a successful graduate, she expressed how grateful she was for the support she received, particularly regarding her baby's wellbeing. She emphasized how important it was for her to feel heard and respected and not treated like a child. She felt that she was held accountable for her actions but also that the team of people working with her were accountable for theirs as well. What she found valuable were the ways people respected her agency and worked with her, rather than dictating what she had to do.

Another key success identified in the evaluation was the court's changed approach to children identified as trafficked and the advisory board's extensive outreach to and training of community, which were offered frequently provided. Advisory board members often sought out and shared other training opportunities. As the Safe Harbor Project became more incorporated into the larger juvenile court system, advisory board members expanded training opportunities to other court staff, including probation officers, detention staff, and law enforcement. This training both raised awareness of human trafficking and, ideally, gave personnel more tools to deal with any youth impacted by trauma. Advisory board members have noted to the researchers a shift in how law enforcement treats youth engaged in the sex trade in first encounters – less as prostitutes and more as victims, which has the potential to improve trust with the youth.

Additionally, researchers observed that the Safe Harbor Project consistently used a trauma-informed approach throughout its process. Although some situations made it difficult to practice this approach, particularly assessment and placement, advisory board members and staff members, by and large, discussed their interactions and carried out their interactions with the youth in a way that acknowledged their trauma and supported them in their healing. On multiple occasions, the researchers witnessed staff and advisory board members discussing best practices to reduce retraumatization. This included reducing the number of times a youth had to recount their victimization and recognizing that some behaviors are reactions to trauma and not a general disregard for authority.

Incremental progress

One of the deliverables of this evaluation to the court staff was the development of outcome framework that would more accurately capture success as incremental progress, based very heavily upon the framework provided by Center for Court Innovations (2015) for them to begin the process of data collection. We recommended to the court that they diversify their key outcomes by capturing incremental progress via milestones of success instead of "result" outcomes, such as graduation rates. In other words, the outcomes should be able to capture "any positive change." We also recommended that the court elucidate its goals and how best to achieve them. Relatedly, in dialogue with youth and caregivers, the researchers recommended that the court create and share a definition of success that also meets the needs of the youth and family to ensure that the services provided matched with the services needed.

Discussion

The Safe Harbor docket struggled with significant "growing pains" that contributed to significant attrition in all phases of the process, resulting in a very small number of youth being able to meet the strictest definition of success – quitting the sex trade. We find that the fundamental dissonance that led to many of the struggles of the Safe Harbor Project was the conflicting "victim-delinquent" framework. A victim of trafficking framework demands a clear, sympathetic victim, exploited by identifiable persons who cause the victim to commit crimes against her will, particularly in a political context. A delinquent framework, following a neoclassical approach to the criminal justice system based on accountability and individualizations of punishment and deterrence, suggests that this same person must be held accountable for her actions. In reality, the youth on the docket were, in some ways, exploited and traumatized but were also actors in their own lives. They were both victim and delinquent. They came with reasons why engaging in the sex trade is an understandable, if regrettable, choice on their part. Often, no one specific person forced the victim to commit a crime. Their stories were like so many of the children at juvenile court; stories that involve trauma, poverty, abuse, etc. However, the youth on the docket were offered diversion and a little extra support because, in this political moment, there is an increased awareness and interest in helping ("saving") girls from the evils of sex trafficking.

The dissonance between the rhetoric of trafficking and the lived reality of these youth, highlights this conflict. Politically, people want sympathetic, clear-cut victims. In practice, these youth's exploitation is enmeshed with the failures of our social safety nets. Moralizing actors and actions into good and evil, which is what attracts the funds to pay for things like short-term housing, intensive therapy, and mentoring programs, leaves little room for incremental progress strategies. Funders want to see success. Court staff and advisory board members accept that some youth just do not want to change (even though it is assumed that no minor can choose the sex trade freely), and the most they can do is point youth in the direction of helpful people if they want to change in the future. This tension can be seen in the following statement by an advisory member on the desired outcome, "The goal of our program is when we define success we're looking for a reduction in high-risk behaviors and a reduction in trafficking behaviors and ultimately to cease trafficking behaviors." – where the child's own actions in trading sex for goods or money, as the purported victim of trafficking, are cast as "trafficking behaviors." Trafficking is something that is, by definition, something that has been done to them, not something they are actively doing themselves. Forcing all of the discussion into the black-and-white narrative of trafficking leads to a flattened discussion where youth are defined as "self-trafficked" or "engaging in trafficking behaviors," which only serves to obfuscate the real reasons the youth engage in the sex trade – sometimes coerced, sometimes on their own, and almost ways for a multiplicity of reasons.

The first and second author, who work closely together on a number of projects, have arrived at different conclusions for the implications of this work. Rather than eliding these differences, we present both in the hopes that by recognizing that our own perspectives shape the frameworks we use.

For [Second Author], if the ultimate goal of the program is for youth to desist engaging in the sex trade, it should be explicitly made a goal of the Safe Harbor Project and evidence-based strategies deployed and assessed to support youth in that endeavor. To date, there are no evidence-based models to inform practice. Ultimately, given the "delinquent" framework, the court's time constraints, and inflexibility of a criminal justice system, the court might not be the best entity to serve the majority of trafficking youth. For example, youth without a current or pending complaint were not eligible for the services offered under Safe Harbor, meaning that a large number of youth who could have been defined as trafficked in the community did not receive services that may have helped them. Instead, the court should likely be seen as more of a safety net for those already in the criminal justice system and not a panacea. There are many gaps a court is not able to fill. A more holistic, community approach would like better serve the youth – one that can be long-term, flexible in its approach and framework, and available to all.

For [First Author], the conflict that is created by the differences between the framework of human trafficking, the legal outlook needed to administer a court, and the lived experiences of youth is irreconcilable. All youth entering the juvenile justice system with trauma, regardless of whether it is perpetrated by family members or gang members or economic circumstances, deserve access to a system that is restorative and rehabilitative rather than punitive. Singling out a subsection of girls for special treatment because trafficking is a hot topic makes an experiment of their lives while offering few clear benefits. A harm-reduction model with willing participants has been shown to have a higher likelihood of helping people quit the sex trade (Cimino, 2017) but the court, as it was configured at the time of this evaluation, did not have the conceptual space for a model that acknowledged the agency of youth, particularly when making choices disdained by the majority of society. Court-based diversion, regardless of motivation, has been criticized for being an expansion of "penal welfare" (Gruber, Cohen, & Mogulescu, 2016), or a system of social services that are accessible through and administered by the courts which ensures a long-term entanglement with the criminal justice system.

Both authors agree that further work should be done on how social safety nets might be enhanced so that services are available without having to go through the court. Both authors also recognize the dangers of such a critique of a docket like this. Although there were numerous issues with the conceptualization and implementation of the docket, some individuals were able to benefit from participation, even without successfully graduating. However, prosecutors were not always on board with offering youth any leeway, and we know of at least one instance where our work was used as an argument against offering participation to a youth. Based on these findings, we do not recommend that the "baby be thrown out with the bathwater," to lose whatever trauma-focused strides the court has made.

Limitations

The research presented here is a case study of one jurisdiction's "growing pains" in implementing a docket for minor victims of human trafficking and therefore, is not generalizable. Additionally, due to the lack of consistently collected quantitative measures, we have relied primarily upon the qualitative data we collected, which also limits our ability to quantitatively test our observations regarding the factors that predicted attrition and, again, generalizability. Lastly, our difficulty in recruiting youth and their guardians in evaluation has limited the youths' and their families' voices in the study – a recommendation we provided the court and had difficulty fulfilling ourselves.

Future research

Given the research demonstrating that participants in human trafficking dockets are more critical of court intervention and the difficulty we had in interviewing victims and their guardians, in future research, the authors plan on focusing more extensively on capturing the experiences of youth and guardians. However, because of the issues we have in recruiting for this study, we will likely not recruit participants from the court but instead from social services agencies and/or service providers. We also hope to be able to analyze quantitative data collected by the court and services providers on the "incremental progress" outcomes to provide a quantitative examination of the program, as well as speak to the efficacy and dosage of services provided (or could be provided) to the youth (e.g., treatment models, mentoring, and placements with this population). Additionally, as an extension of this study, we would like to make a cross-site comparison of different dockets specific to the human trafficking of minors to aid in establishing best practices. Moreover, differences in the demographics between the adult court and juvenile court need further research to determine whether the girls in the Safe Harbor project are not identified by the criminal justice system further down the line because they are no longer in the sex trade (whether voluntarily or involuntarily) or if they are being charged with prostitution and/or similar charges and not being given access to adult trafficking courts because they are less likely to have substance dependency issues. The role of structural racism must also be examined in this difference.

Conclusions

We provide a case study that details the process and outcomes for the Safe Harbor Project – a specialized docket for minor victims of human trafficking in Cuyahoga County, Ohio. The purpose of the Safe Harbor docket is to divert youth from the juvenile justice system by substituting treatment and other interventions in lieu of incarceration. Overall, the findings of the docket indicate significant attrition in the process – a sizable number of girls have been identified as victims or possible victims of human, a large number of these identified youth who do not participate in the docket, and a very small number successfully graduate from the docket. Additionally, the evaluation finds that the docket has yet to be successful in getting the girls to quit the sex trade – only going AWOL and getting back into the life or coming back to the court with new complaints related to sex work. Our findings indicate that the docket experienced conceptual conflicts and other struggles that lead to attrition at key phases in the process – identification, intake, engagement, and discharge/graduation. In this paper, we detailed the main reasons for attrition at each phase. We also find that the court's conflicting victim-delinquent framework greatly complicates the docket's process and outcomes. We argue that the court would be better served by defining success via incremental progress and incorporating the voices of the youth served by the docket to ensure that the services provide match with the services needed.

Notes

1. For a discussion of the genesis of the ideology surrounding human trafficking, see Weitzer (2007), Blanchette and Silva (2012), and Bernstein (2012).
2. Here we speak about the process in past tense because major shifts occurred right around the time we presented our findings, partially in response to our work and partially in response to other shifts within the court. It should also be noted that the judge who ran the court was not re-elected and there is a good chance that if the program survives the transition, it may look radically different.
3. All juvenile records, except charges of aggravated murder, murder, or rape, can be sealed at eighteen at the discretion of a judge. Records are automatically expunged five years after sealing or at the age of 23. There are a few cases in which this process is automatic, including alcohol diversion programs, and if the only charge is unruly.

Acknowledgments

We want to thank the Safe Harbor youth and their guardians who agreed to speak with us and/or allowed us to observe their hearings. Thank you for sharing your experiences with us. We also want to thank the Safe Harbor Project staff, members of the advisory board, and others working in the community to improve the lives of vulnerable youth. Thanks for inviting us to sit at your table. Without your support, this project would not have happened. Lastly, thanks to the Jack, Joseph and Morton Mandel School of Applied Social Sciences at Case Western Reserve University for funding this research via a Research Training and Development Grant.

Disclosure statement

No potential conflict of interest was reported by the authors.

Funding

This work was supported by the Jack, Joseph and Morton Mandel School of Applied Social Sciences at Case Western Reserve University under a Research Training and Development Grant.

ORCID

Misty Luminais http://orcid.org/0000-0002-4190-2495
Rachel Lovell http://orcid.org/0000-0002-8998-6173

References

Banks, D., & Kyckelhahn, T. (2011). *Characteristics of suspected human trafficking incidents—2008–2010* (Special Report NCJ 233732). Retrieved from Washington, D.C.: https://www.bjs.gov/content/pub/pdf/cshti0810.pdf

Barber-Rioja, V., Rotter, M., Schombs, F., & Barber-Rioja, V. (2017). Diversion evaluations: A specialized forensic examination. *Behavioral Sciences & the Law*, *35*(5/6), 418–430. doi:10.1002/bsl.2309

Bergquist, K. J. S. (2015). Criminal, victim, or ally? Examining the role of sex workers in addressing minor sex trafficking. *Affilia*, *30*(3), 314–327. doi:10.1177/0886109915572844

Bernstein, E. (2012). Carceral politics as gender justice? The "traffic in women" and neoliberal circuits of crime, sex, and right. *Theory and Society*, *41*(3), 233–259. doi:10.1007/S11186-012-9165-9

Blanchette, T. G., & Silva, A. P. (2012). On bullshit and the trafficking of women: Moral entrepreneurs and the invention of trafficking of persons in Brazi. *Dialectical Anthropology*, *36*(1–2), 107–125. doi:10.1007/S10624-012-9268-8

Center for Court Innovation. (2015). *Responding to sex trafficking in your jurisdiction: A planning toolkit*. Retrieved from New York: http://www.courtinnovation.org/sites/default/files/documents/RespondingtoSexTrafficking.pdf_0.pdf

Center for the Human Rights for Children, Loyola University Chicago, & International Organization for Adolescents. (2011). *Building child welfare response to child trafficking handbook*. Retrieved from Chicago, IL.: https://www.luc.edu/media/lucedu/chrc/pdfs/BCWRHandbook2011.pdf

Cimino, A. N. (2017). Sex work and adult prostitution: From entry to exit. In V. B. Van Hasselt & M. L. Bourke (Eds.), *Handbook of behavioral criminology* (pp. 239–255). Cham, Switzerland: Springer International Publishing.

Collins, S. E., Lonczak, H. S., & Clifasefi, S. L. (2017, October). Seattle's Law Enforcement Assisted Diversion (LEAD): Program effects on recidivism outcomes. *Evaluation and Program Planning*, *64*, 49–56. doi:10.1016/j.evalprogplan.2017.05.008

Curtis, R., Terry, K., Dank, M., Dombrowski, K., & Khan, B. (2008). *Commercial sexual exploitation of children in New York City, volume one: The CSEC population in New York City: Size, characteristics, and needs*. New York, NY: Center for Court Innovation.

Dank, M., Yahner, J., & Yu, L. (2017). *Consequences of policing prostitution: An analysis of individuals arrested and prosecuted for commercial sex in New York City*. Retrieved from Washington, DC: https://www.urban.org/research/publication/consequences-policing-prostitution

Dank, M., Yu, L., Yahner, J., Pelletier, E., Mora, M., & Conner, B. (2015). *Locked in: Interactions with the criminal justice and child welfare systems for LGBTQ youth, YMSM, and YWSW who engage in survival sex*. Retrieved from Washington, DC: https://www.urban.org/research/publication/locked-interactions-criminal-justice-and-child-welfare-systems-lgbtq-youth-ymsm-and-ywsw-who-engage-survival-sex

Deruy, E. (2016, February 8). Kids are renewable resources: Authorities in Reno are finding it increasingly difficult to identify victims and perpetrators of sex trafficking. *The Atlantic*.

Retrieved from http://www.theatlantic.com/national/archive/2016/02/in-sex-trafficking-kids-are-renewable-resources/460485/
Fedina, L., Williamson, C., & Perdue, T. (2016). Risk factors for domestic child sex trafficking in the United States. *Journal of Interpersonal Violence*, *34*(13), 0886260516662306.
Flahive, P. (2015, April 10). *County helping sex trafficking victims become survivors*. Texas Public Radio. Retrieved from http://tpr.org/post/county-helping-sex-trafficking-victims-become-survivors//stream/0
Gibbs, D. A., Hardison Walters, J. L., Lutnick, A., Miller, S., & Kluckman, M. (2015). Services to domestic minor victims of sex trafficking: Opportunities for engagement and support. *Children and Youth Services Review*, *54*, 1–7. doi:10.1016/j.childyouth.2015.04.003
Golke, M. (2011). The age of consent: How Minnesota's safe harbor for sexually exploited youth act of 2011 falls short of fully addressing domestic child sex trafficking. *Hamline Journal of Public Law & Policy*, *33*(1), 201–234.
Gruber, A., Cohen, A. J., & Mogulescu, K. (2016). Penal welfare and the new human trafficking intervention courts. *Florida Law Review*, *68*(5), 73.
Henggeler, S. W., McCart, M. R., Cunningham, P. B., & Chapman, J. E. (2012). Enhancing the effectiveness of juvenile drug courts by integrating evidence-based practices. *Journal of Consulting & Clinical Psychology*, *80*(2), 264–275. doi:10.1037/a0027147
Huck, J. L., & Morris, C. S. (2017). Jail diversion and recidivism: A case study of a municipal court diversion program. *Criminal Justice Policy Review*, *28*(9), 866–878. doi:10.1177/0887403415619986
Kretschmar, J. M., Butcher, F., Flannery, D. J., & Singer, M. I. (2014). Diverting juvenile justice-involved youth with behavioral health issues from detention: Preliminary findings from Ohio's Behavioral Health Juvenile Justice (BHJJ) initiative. *Criminal Justice Policy Review*, *27*(3), 302–325. doi:10.1177/0887403414560885
Kretschmar, J. M., Tossone, K., Butcher, F., & Marsh, B. (2018). Examining the impact of a juvenile justice diversion program for youth with behavioral health concerns on early adulthood recidivism. *Children and Youth Services Review*, *91*, 168–176. doi:10.1016/j.childyouth.2018.06.010
Lippmann, J. (2013). Announcement of New York's human trafficking intervention initiative. *Center for Court Innovation*. Retrieved from http://www.courtinnovation.org/research/announcement-new-yorks-human-trafficking-intervention-initiative
Lutnick, A. (2016). *Domestic minor sex trafficking: Beyond victims and villains*. New York, NY: Columbus Press.
Malangone, D., Mazur, R., & Goodman, M. (2015, June). Responding to sex trafficking in your jurisdiction: A planning toolkit. *Center for Court Innovation*. Retrieved from http://www.courtinnovation.org/sites/default/files/documents/RespondingtoSexTrafficking.pdf_0.pdf
Mears, D. P., Kuch, J. J., Lindsey, A. M., Siennick, S. E., Pesta, G. B., Greenwald, M. A., & Blomberg, T. G. (2016). Juvenile court and contemporary diversion. *Criminology & Public Policy*, *15*(3), 953–981. doi:10.1111/1745-9133.12223
Miner-Romanoff, K. (2017). CATCH court: Changing actions to change habits—A preliminary evaluation study. *Journal of Human Trafficking*, *3*(2), 136–162. doi:10.1080/23322705.2016.1194039
Pope-Sussman, R. (2015). Responding to homelessness: 11 ideas for the justice system. *Center for Court Innovation*. Retrieved from https://www.courtinnovation.org/sites/default/files/documents/FINALResponsestoHomelessnessforWeb.pdf
Preble, K. M., Praetorius, R. T., & Cimino, A. (2015). Supportive exits: A best practices report for a sex worker intervention. *Journal of Human Behvior in the Social Environment*, *2*, 162–178.
Ray, A., & Caterino, E. (2014). Criminal, victim, or worker? The effect of New York human trafficking intervention court on adults charged with prostitution-related offenses. *Red Umbrella Project*. Retrieved from http://redumbrellaproject.org/wp-content/uploads/2014/09/RedUP-NYHTIC-FINALweb.pdf

Sevigny, E. L., Fuleihan, B. K., & Ferdik, F. V. (2013). Do drug courts reduce the use of incarceration?: A meta-analysis. *Journal of Criminal Justice, 41*(6), 416–425. doi:10.1016/j.jcrimjus.2013.06.005

Shcauben, L., Atella, J., Imberston, K., Turner, L., & Highum, K. (2017). *Safe harbor evaluation report.* Saint Paul, MN: Wilder Research. Retrieved from https://www.wilder.org/sites/default/files/imports/SafeHarbor_EvaluationReport_10-17.pdf

Shields, R. T., & Letourneau, E. J. (2015). Commercial sexual exploitation of children and the emergence of safe harbor legislation: Implications for policy and practice. *Current Psychiatry Reports, 17*(3), 1–7. doi:10.1007/s11920-014-0542-0

Supreme Court of Ohio. (2016). *Frequently asked questions: Specialized docket certification.* Retrieved from https://www.supremecourt.ohio.gov/JCS/specDockets/certification/FAQ.pdf

Weitzer, R. (2007). The social construction of sex trafficking: Ideology and institutionalization of a moral crusade. *Politics & Society, 35*(3), 447–475. doi:10.1177/0032329207304319

Weitzer, R. (2015). Human trafficking and contemporary slavery. *Annual Review of Sociology, 41*(1), 223–242. doi:10.1146/annurev-soc-073014-112506

White, E., Swaner, R., Genetta, E., Hynynen Lambson, S., Johnson Dash, J., Sederbaum, I., & Wolf, A. (2017). *Navigating force and choice: Experiences in the New York City sex trade and the criminal justice system's response.* Retrieved from New York: https://www.courtinnovation.org/publications/NYC-sex-trade

Yale Global Health Justice Partnership. (2018a). *Diversion from justice: A rights-based analysis of local "prostitution diversion programs" and their impacts on people in the sex sector in the United States.* Retrieved from New Haven, CT: https://law.yale.edu/yls-today/news/ghjp-releases-reports-prostitution-diversion-programs

Yale Global Health Justice Partnership. (2018b). *Un-meetable promises: Rhetoric and reality in New York City's human trafficking intervention courts.* Retrieved from New Haven, CT: https://law.yale.edu/yls-today/news/ghjp-releases-reports-prostitution-diversion-programs

Yerramsetti, A. P., Simons, D. D., Coonan, L., & Stolar, A. (2017). Veteran treatment courts: A promising solution. *Behavioral Sciences & the Law, 35*(5/6), 512–522. doi:10.1002/bsl.2308

Harlem Pimps' Reflections on Quitting: External and Internal Reasons

Amber Horning, Lyndsay Thompson, and Christopher Thomas

ABSTRACT

Pimps quit their illicit work in sex markets for many reasons, such as job dissatisfaction, having a child, going to prison, and feeling guilty. In this study, we used a mixed methods approach to explore pimps' interdiscursive reasons for quitting. Our analytic sample focuses on 43 self-identified former pimps, who were interviewed in situ in housing projects in Harlem, New York. Based on existing desistance research, we hypothesize that pimps would express external or internal themes of quitting. External reasons involve changes due to the environment, (e.g., job dangerousness), events (e.g., going to prison) or opportunities (e.g., getting a legitimate job). Internal reasons center on change from within, such as in their morality. First, we qualitatively identify these themes and how they are connected within the accounts. Many accounts are interdiscursive, i.e., with multiple themes or some themes occurring across categories, such as having children and moral reasons. Second, we use non-metric, Multi-Dimensional Scaling (MDS) to triangulate and systematically assess our qualitative findings. We find adequate support for this External to Internal typology, with 67.5% of the cases being classified as dominantly within one theme. Using non-metric MDS is a novel method to triangulate this type of qualitative data.

Introduction

Desisting from crime requires a conscious effort to permanently quit (Maruna, 2001). Desistance scholars have typically focused on and debate the length of time an offender must be "crime-free" to be a desister. At the extreme, purists like Farrington and Hawkins (1991) posited that "desisters" have to be crime-free for eleven years, and Bottoms, Shapland, Costello, Holmes, and Muir (2004) called for complete "abstaining." Maruna (2001) only required that desisters be crime free for one year, and "persisters" had to admit that they would continue crime. Alternatively, Matza (1964) argued that offenders drift in and out of "deviant" activities so quitting should never equal desistance. Recent critiques of Matza focused on his analysis not accounting for life-course-persistent offenders or those who do not drift; however, most studies have shown that typical offenders do drift (Blomberg, Cullen, Carlsson, & Jonson, 2017). Maruna interpreted those drifters as "in-betweeners" and included them as one type of desister. Although Maruna and some

---

Color versions of one or more of the figures in the article can be found online at www.tandfonline.com/uvao.

other desistance scholars, such as Massoglia and Uggen (2007) included slowing down or drifting in and out as types of desistance, throughout the rest of this paper we use the term "desistance" to indicate complete desistance. This study explores pimps' accounts of quitting that includes desistance as well as other circumstances that make these offenders stop or slow down.

In this study, we defined a pimp a someone who has facilitated or managed commercial sex transactions. We discuss this study's inclusion and exclusion criteria in the methods section below. We acknowledge that "pimp" is a highly contested, racialized term, but this term is more recognizable than alternatives like "third party" to readers as well as participants in this study.

Based on the literature about quitting crime, we expect pimps to describe both *external* and *internal* reasons for stopping (see Table 1). There are external factors involved in the decision to quit, such as incarceration, poor job performance, job danger, and fear of arrest (Campbell & Hansen, 2012; Davis, 2017). Many of these external reasons are related to the perils of this type of illicit activity. Post- incarceration, pimps may find it difficult to return to work in the illicit market because they have lost touch with workers and they are not familiar with changes to the market. This temporary incapacitation can make it difficult for them to return (Davis, 2017). Davis (2017) researched why pimps quit, and she also found that pimps describe the job as tiring or they were not good at it. Just like any job, there will be those who burn out or fail and move on to other things. A few studies about pimps in the United States found that they expressed fear about the danger of the job, including fear of being hurt or being arrested (Dank et al., 2014; Davis, 2017) and both are plausible reasons for quitting.

Much of the life-course literature discussed life changes, such as going to school, having a new relationship or marriage, having a child, joining the military or aging out (Giordano, Cernkovich, & Rudolph, 2002; Laub & Sampson, 1993; Paternoster & Bushway, 2009; Sampson & Laub, 1993; Teachman & Tedrow, 2016; Theobald & Farrington, 2009). These researchers conceptualized these life events as potential "turning points", which may include change in routine behavior (i.e., routine activities) or internal change.

Many desistance researchers have focused on internal reasons that involve changes in self-perception or to their sense of morality. In Maruna's (2001) Liverpool Desistance Study (LDS), he found that his participants relied on portrayals of "good" me in accounts or selves

Table 1. The internal/external quitting framework: Prior desistance studies.

Focus	Study	Crime Type	Research approach
External factors/Turning points	Campbell and Hansen (2012)	Drug Trafficking	Qualitative
External factors/Internal change	Davis (2017)	Pimping	Qualitative
Turning points/Internal change	Giordano et al. (2002)	Serious juvenile offenses	Mixed methods
Turning points/Bonds	Laub et al. (1998)	General	Quantitative
Turning points	Laub and Sampson (1993)	Not specified	Theoretical
Turning points	Sampson and Laub (1993)	Not specified	Theoretical
Turning points	Teachman and Tedrow (2016)	General	Quantitative
Turning points	Theobald and Farrington (2009)	General	Quantitative
Internal change/Turning points	Maruna (2001)	General (many drug offenses)	Qualitative
Internal change/Turning points	Maruna and Roy (2007)	None specified	Theoretical
Internal change/Turning points	Paternoster and Bushway (2009)	None specified	Theoretical
Internal change	Presser (2004)	Violent	Qualitative

*This table outlines key literature used in this paper and it is not a comprehensive representation of the desistance literature.

who changed in positive and more internal ways. His sample of generalists consisted of 30 desisters and 20 persisters who had varied criminal histories often with convictions for drug use, drug sales, burglary, or car theft. He found that many "desisters" interpreted their "real me" as being hidden or muted, since even when they were "at their worst," desisters maintained "deep down" they were "good" people. Presser (2004) also produced analyses of criminal narratives that relied upon portrayals of "good me" with a focus on locating "moral" selves. She surmised that the violent offenders (participants convicted of assault, rape and homicide) in her sample, constructed "moral" selves as a response to being evaluated by her. The ways and reasons that offenders search for the "good" or "moral" self may be contingent upon the type of offenders and the context of the interview.

Much of the research on desistance is based on samples of generalists, or those who commit many types of crimes, most of which is not status enhancing, such as drug use or those who specialize in low status crime, such as violent crime. As a result, there is little research that explores those who worked in the illicit economy and who may consider themselves to be higher status due to their success in the illicit market. Pimping is distinct from many other illicit activities because it involves the important Mertonian cultural goal of money-making, and pimps have a long history of being portrayed as relatively high status. Pimping has been depicted in some parts of the media, as well as by some pimps themselves, not only as an alternative for disenfranchised entrepreneurs, but as an aspirational lifestyle (Malcolm, 2015; Messerschmidt, 1997; Milner & Milner, 1973; Slim, 2009). For these reasons, we do not expect internal explanations to predominate in this sample, but we do expect that some will focus on these reasons.

We qualitatively explored pimps' external and internal themes of quitting and how interdiscursive accounts emerge in single accounts. Then, we used a quantitative technique, Multi-Dimensional Scaling, that is useful for identifying and confirming themes in narrative data.

Literature review

Quitting: internal and external reasons

There is extensive literature on "desistance" or veering off the "bad" path, with different theoretical frameworks explaining why people quit crime (see Giordano et al., 2002; Laub & Sampson, 1993, 1993; Maruna, 2001; Paternoster & Bushway, 2009). Maruna (2001) called the narratives of desisters, "redemption scripts," and interpreted them as "willful, cognitive distortions." Many of his participants spent time in correctional facilities. Their "cognitive distortions" may have been due to participation in treatment programs, such as 12 step programs where finding the "good me" is a central part of the recovery narrative. Further, Maruna (2001) found that persisters in crime employed "condemnation scripts" through which offenders opined that they had little control over their destinies and, as a result, they were fated to a life of crime, deemed as bad.

Giordano et al.'s (2002) qualitative analysis about the meaning of desistance was derived using an innovative approach. They linked their theory to symbolic interactionism because of Mead's idea that "cognitions serve as an organizing process, so identity provides a higher level of organization and coherence to one's cognitions (2002, p. 1001). They used unstructured life history narratives to formulate cognitive and identity shifts that they felt were essential to the desistance process. The process involved 1) a shift in the persons' openness to change 2) exposure to "hooks" or prosocial opportunities 3) crafting a conventional "replacement self" that "can suppliant the marginal one that must be left behind (2002, p. 1001)." Others researchers, such as Maruna critique this concept as a new self does not need be crafted, but offenders must search for this "good" self who was hidden or muted during the period of illicit activities.

Many contemporary desistance researchers resist the idea of "desistance by default," that is, the notion that prosocial events change selves. Instead, they focus on events changing behavioral patterns (see Giordano et al., 2002; Laub & Sampson, 1993; Paternoster & Bushway, 2009; Sampson & Laub, 1993). Typically, researchers in this tradition conceptualize agency from the perspective of rational choice theory where actors use a cost-benefit analysis to decide whether to act. Rational choice is often linked to social bonds where the value and investment to convention such as prosocial others, school or work, often outweigh non-conventional benefits in the calculation.

Many seminal works on desistance have used life course theory to explain patterns of offending over time, and this theory emphasizes these developmental and life events to make sense of continuity/discontinuity in offending (see Laub, Nagin, & Sampson, 1998; Laub & Sampson, 1993; Sampson & Laub, 1993). In these works, the theoretical underpinnings to explain periods of quitting crime are overly speculative. The trajectories of offending are thought to be shaped by investments in "social capital" or how an individual derives benefits through social networks, in this case conventional networks. People are thought to be inhibited from persisting in crime because of potential losses derived through being "bad." In these studies, researchers typically infer that these human calculations happen when their findings show decreases in recidivism in conjunction with increases in social capital. These changes toward prosocial behavioral patterns are called "turning points" (see Sampson & Laub, 1993). The data used in many of these studies were not based on first-hand interviews, rather on secondary longitudinal data sources. While this was the best-case scenario to obtain data, they were unable to ask respondents questions specifically pertaining to their theoretical framework.

Subsequently, Giordano et al. (2002) conducted a mixed methods study (qualitative and quantitative) to test the idea that structural factors are "turning points." Based on their research they created a theory of cognitive change to understand why and how individuals come to desist from crime. Unlike prior studies, Giordano et al. (2002) found that conventional lifestyles such as getting married or getting a job were not factors associated with desistance. They attributed the novelty of their findings to their sample, who were predominantly minorities; however, it is unclear if minority status, age or both influenced their findings. They discussed that there are "structural" constraints on opportunities that may in turn limit one's ability to get good jobs and have stable marriages and these factors could explain their unexpected findings.

Campbell and Hansen (2012) found from life history interviews with thirty ex-traffickers that the principal factors related to leaving drug trafficking were punishment, self-image and identity, social ties, life course changes, and drug abuse. Though all informants had complex and multi-layered motivations for exiting drug trafficking, it is important to note that the disease of addiction, an internal motivation, played a role in keeping traffickers from the game and pursuing financial gain to support their drug consumption, a powerful factor that we expect to be less salient in the current study with pimps. Furthermore, the respondents were all mid-level players in the marketplace and responsible to suppliers and cartels, and the threat of violence from the upper levels of the market, an external motivation, was an ever-present factor in their lives, with more immediate and serious threats motivating hasty and desperate departures. While fear of going to prison was a strong motivating factor that we expect to also be present in the current sample, this fear of punishment for drug traffickers is intrinsically linked to fear that they will be "x'd out" (i.e., murdered) by the cartel before or while in prison to prevent them from ratting out the cartel. Since most of the pimps in our study were not part of a larger enterprise, we cannot expect that pressures from and fear of other players will be influential, but street crime is inherently dangerous so we expect some of them to more generally fear being injured or hurt on the job.

Davis's (2017) qualitative study of ex-pimps' exit from "the game" using a narrative methodology is the most directly comparable study to the current study. Pimps in this study revealed a variety of reasons for desistance, with cumulative traumatic events over a long-term career causing emotional stress and hardships that facilitated their eventual exit. Notably, events that caused violence toward sex workers caused guilt in the respondents for placing her in the situation. To avoid feelings of guilt, respondents employed neutralization techniques that included denying the victim and placing the blame itself on "The Game" itself and not the players. Davis notes that emotions are taboo in "The Game", and thus coping mechanisms must be employed, including these neutralizations to persist. Davis' study shows accounts can be interdiscursive with both external and internal factors present. Furthermore, while fear of prison in the Campbell & Hansen study facilitated hasty exits from drug trafficking, the role of punishment in the Davis' study was unrelated to emotional fear and served as a "push" factor out of The Game; the longer and more frequent prison sentences become, the more likely that a pimp's workers will be "poached" by other pimps, and the return to the streets to restart a pimp's career becomes increasingly difficult the longer he is away from it. Thus, unlike the linking of traumatic events to emotional stress, punishment in these cases served as an external event detached from internal reasons.

Paternoster and Bushway (2009) theorized that the impetus to quit crime is initially rooted in a "crystallization of discontent," which includes a cost/benefit analysis of whether crime is worth it. These external factors, such as fear of arrest, of being alone, or of getting killed, culminate in what they termed the "feared self." They looked at the cumulative influence of mainly external factors indicating that they may have some thematic similarities and that they may work in tandem to facilitate the decision to quit.

In the quantitative studies involving life course changes, the individual's reasons for quitting are often inferred by the researchers who lack first-hand interviews. In the qualitative studies, many of the participants were self-proclaimed desisters who may have had ample opportunities to rehearse their quitting story. In both scenarios, the findings about why offenders quit were often reductive. In a qualitative study of quitters who were not expressly desisters, we expect the data to be noisier because without these imposed simplifications, offenders do not have a streamlined script, and they may be sifting through their multiple reasons for quitting.

Method

Sample and data collection

In order to investigate why pimps stop doing this illicit work and how their accounts of quitting are connected to these reasons, 43 males identifying as former pimps were recruited from housing projects in Harlem for qualitative interviews.

We used the term "pimp" during recruitment because other academic terms, like "third-party," are unfamiliar to this population. To qualify for this study, participants had to have played at least an ancillary role in commercial sex, such as connecting sex workers and clients and/or facilitating sex work through providing resources or other aid (Overs, 2002); however, all of these participants were directly involved in managing sex workers. These inclusion and exclusion criteria were expressed in clear language to make sure that participants had actually procured, facilitated, managed, or otherwise contributed to commercial sex.

The majority of the interviews took place in open courtyards in a three housing projects in East Harlem, New York, with people from these communities. East Harlem has one of the largest concentrations of low-income housing in the country and has more than 16 public housing developments with over 16,000 residents (NYC Public Housing Authority, 2011).

The first and primary location was Taino Towers in East Harlem. The complex spans one city block and has over 3,000 residents. Other research sites for this study included the George Washington Carver House. People living in these housing projects are at high risk for family poverty, under-employment, and high rates of juvenile delinquency (Harlem Community Justice Center, 2011). East Harlem is one of the nation's poorest communities. According to census data from the Office of Juvenile Justice and Delinquency Prevention, Harlem is rated 10 out of 10 on the community disadvantage index, which means that it is poorer than 99% of communities nationally (as cited in Harlem Community Justice Center. East Harlem Juvenile Gage Task Force, 2011).

Harlem residents fit Wacquant's categorization of those experiencing new kinds of exclusion at the margins, or *advanced marginalization*. Wacquant identified distinctive properties of the rise of marginality, including de-socialization of wage labor; mass joblessness; concentrated advanced marginalization in bounded territories, such as housing projects; and the alienation and deteriorating sense of community in these spaces (Wacquant, 2008). The levels of deprivation experienced by those relegated to American ghettos influences how they connect to licit sectors and how they operate in the overall commercial sex market. The residents of public housing in the United States in urban areas are predominately poorer ethnic and racial minorities and this is similar in Europe, except they are more often immigrants (Carter, Schill, & Wachter, 1998). There is growing spatial stratification in urban America based on these differences in intersectionality (Carter et al., 1998). The participants in this study operated in the ground-floor tier of the market, and historically this work is street-based.

Our sample was not representative, which is typical of most studies conducted on this hidden population. Snowball sampling was the intended strategy because it typically is used in non-probability fieldwork studies, particularly when participants are active offenders (Flick, 2009). In this sampling technique, initial research participants (or gatekeepers) refer similar participants in a chain of referrals. One limitation of snowball sampling is selection bias, because the pool of participants is derived through a few initial contacts or seeds. With this hard-to-reach population, the initial gatekeepers remained the primary sources of referral.

The study shifted to a convenience sample and an *agora* sample, or a sample obtained from public open space (Horning & Sriken, 2017). Interviews took place in housing project courtyards that are akin to a town square. Residents and their friends and acquaintances socialize in these spaces. Participants witnessed the on-site interviews and asked about the study. Those participants who were actively offending may have feel more comfortable because they could see that other participants safely completed interviews without being arrested.

Access to these communities was facilitated by two gatekeepers. They both lived in these housing projects and formerly worked as pimps within families who sold sex. The gatekeepers escorted the team through security at different housing projects (since only residents or those with permission were allowed entrance). During the winter months, we moved indoors to two nonprofit organizations in Harlem.

In studies with hidden and lower SES populations, there can be a problem where participants "fake" their way into the study. Scott (2008) did a study of Injection Drug Users (IDU's) where "fakers" made up stories to make some money. We had gatekeepers vouching for most of our participants. Towards the end of our study, our gatekeeper was arrested, and we decided to continue interviews on our own for two more days. We discovered a group of boys who put on different outfits and tried to be interviewed twice. We did not use any of their interviews in the final sample. We believe that our gatekeepers weeded out most of the "fakers." Another technique we used was to have participants draw the area in the city where they pimped. Interviews where participants fumbled through the drawings and gave general answers were excluded from the final sample. These occurrences were not common. In total seven interviews were eliminated.

Interviews and ethics

The interviews were semi-structured and lasted from 30 to 90 minutes. Pimps were paid $30 for participation. Pimps were asked about how they conduct work on a daily basis and about their relationships with sex workers and clients. Interviews were confidential and tape-recorded, and verbal consent was given for participation. We received Institutional Review Board (IRB) approval for participants in the study to waive written documentation of their informed consent, because the main threat to these participants would be the existence of written documentation of their participation in the study. There are no identifiers, and participants gave pseudonyms. Participants were warned about the potential risks and benefits of participation. Participants were given the option to do interviews inside or in public space.

Analytic approach

First, we qualitatively explored the accounts using the Grounded Theory (GT) approach (Glaser & Strauss, 2017). We did not use the purist GT approach, because our analysis was guided using the sensitizing concepts (see Blumer, 1954) of *external* and *internal* reasons. These reasons for quitting were identified by the existing literature on quitting, including desisting. We expected some of the social processes involved in pimping to differ from these other samples of desisters. We expected narratives to be partially in response to being involved in a status enhancing act. We explored how multiple reasons are used within single narratives. Due to interdiscursive accounts, we sought to verify dominant themes of quitting and we use a novel way to triangulate our findings.

Second, we used a technique called non-metric, Multi-Dimensional Scaling to confirm the utility of the External/Internal dichotomy in pimps' decisions to quit. We determined that this was the best method because it is a good way to test for different themes using categorical data. The technique has been used to understand complex behavioral patterns (Canter & Fritzon, 1998). Also, it has been successfully used to derive themes within narrative data (e.g., Friedman & Mann, 1993; Lyons, Higgins, & Duxbury, 2010; Schwartz & Bilsky, 1987). This is one of the best techniques for noisy data. Every participant had more than one reason for quitting, with some having many reasons. The procedure involves computing the association coefficients between all variables by estimating their multi-dimensional Euclidean distance from each other. The coefficients are then used to form a three-dimensional spatial representation of items, with points in a geometric space representing variables (Horning, Salfati, & LaBuschagne, 2015). The more often the variables co-occur, the closer the points will be located on the three-dimensional plot (Salfati & Canter, 1999). Those points that are furthest away are the least likely to co-occur. Next, each case was classified as Internal, External or Turning Point. This procedure will be elaborated on in the Results section.

The first and second authors of this paper coded the 43 accounts. Based on the existing literature on quitting and desisting, we were guided by "sensitizing concepts" or a list of preliminary themes (Blumer, 1954). This list consisted of many of themes that are present in this study, however we found some additional themes, such as having a child. We read through the accounts twice to be sure that we captured all of the relevant themes. Themes reached saturation (Glaser & Strauss, 2017) with some themes such as bad ass me reaching saturation more quickly. 43 participants an adequate sample to reach saturation (Onwuegbuzie & Leech, 2007).

Next, we coded the cases quantitatively. In order to establish the inter-rater reliability for the present study, the two coders independently coded four cases. The overall agreement was 86%, and errors were extensively reviewed and discussed. All of the subsequent questions raised during coding the rest of the cases were discussed as part of the coding process.

In all, 85 pimps were interviewed for this study. Of the 85 pimps interviewed, 43 were no longer pimping. Most of the participants are racial minorities: African-American, (n = 29, 67.4%); Latino (n = 10, 23,3); Other (n = 4, 9.3%). The prevalence of African-American participants is higher and the percent of Latinos is lower as compared to the local population. All participants are male. The average number of sex workers a pimp manages is five (1–15 workers). The average time spent pimping is 6.6 years (2–35 years). Most pimps started this labor when they were young, with the average starting at age 17 (9–30 years old). The mean average current age is 31 years old (range 18– 67 years old; median = 25).

Limitations

Some of the limitations of this study involve potential issues with validity. One concern involves the validity of the pimps' self-descriptions. We assumed that pimps would prettify their accounts, but many openly discussed their failures as pimps, ranging from the inability to manage sex workers to earning meager amounts (Horning, Thomas, Marcus, & Sriken, 2018). Further, unexpected common themes and parallel facts emerged in strangers' accounts (see Glaser and Strauss (2017) on grounded theory and saturated themes). Further, we triangulated our qualitative findings through a quantitative technique that is known to be effective with "noisy" data.

The external validity of this study is limited because it is not a probability sample. The findings may differ in other communities in New York City or elsewhere, and they may differ in other echelons of the sex trade, such as among more experienced pimps. The study is only claiming to reflect or be generalizable to the experiences of these particular 43 pimps in Harlem during the period in which they were interviewed. There are very few studies about pimps or pimps who quit especially with such a large sample size. We hope the findings about this hidden population might apply more broadly, of course, and we hope we have provided enough thick description for readers to draw their own conclusions about other contexts in which the findings might be applicable.

Last, while we did not explicitly analyze interviews where the interview site is conceptualized as a meaning-making process like Presser (2004), we expect that this process occurred. Those pimps who quit were interviewed by one cis-gendered female and one who identifies as non-binary. In some accounts, particularly with the cis-gendered female, some accounts focused on changes in morality related to quitting misogynist masculinities. The respondent and the interviewer are inherently engaged in a meaning-making process in interviews (Holdstein & Gubrium, 1997). We note that some interviews with the cis-gendered interviewer were very focused on this type of morality change. These biases are integral to the interviewing process, but they should still be noted.

Results

External reasons for quitting

There were different types of external factors that pimps described as pushing them to quit, such as working conditions, fear of punishment and prison (see Table 2). These reasons did not necessarily involve changes in moral values or even emotional attitudes about pimping. These external changes were heavily influenced by historical changes within the criminal justice system, to the law and to policing strategies. These factors influenced pimps' perceptions of risks and their decision-making. History is an important factor because some pimps in this sample started this work as early as the 1970s. Further,

Table 2. Reasons for quitting by theme.

External	Internal	Turning Points
(prison)	(moral)	(lifecourse)
(punish)		*relationship, child, job, education, ageing out
(yoyo)		
(hassle)		
(badatjob)		

External
yoyo (Someone who may move back and forth between illicit and licit worlds. There is discussion of returning to pimping)
badatjob (The participant discusses how they were inept at their jobs)
hassle (The participant talks about how pimping is too difficult or tiring)
punishment (The participant discusses how they quit because of a fear of being hurt or arrested)
Internal
moral (Participant discusses how bad pimping is with a focus on morality)
Turning points
lifecourse (Participant talks about how they quit due to a major change, such as getting a licit job, starting a new relationship, having a child or ageing out)

many pimped through major changes to open air illicit markets, such as the crack era (1984–1990) (Curtis & Wendel, 2007; Maher, 1997). In New York City, there were also major changes in how street crime was policed that was largely inspired by Broken Windows theory. Former Mayor Giuliani militarized the NYPD and instructed them to sanitize Manhattan through increased police presence and arresting people for low-level crimes, including prostitution (Thompson, 2015). Many major strolls or outdoor areas where sex was sold were pushed out of Manhattan, i.e., Times Square and 42nd street and into the outer boroughs (Dank, 2011). Last, there have been legal changes, such as the Trafficking Victims Protection Act of 2000, 22 U.S.C. §7105(b)(1)(E)(u) (2000), where many who were typically arrested for pandering are now charged with sex trafficking. Changes in sentencing occurred during different historical eras, such as mandatory minimums (1986-current), the crack-cocaine disparity (1990–2010), the war on drugs and its various iterations (1971-current) (Alexander, 2012), and lengthy prison sentences for sex trafficking (15 years or more) (2000-current). These changes were not always the sole reasons why pimps quit, but they are factors that respondents in this sample discussed in their accounts.

The crack epidemic played a role in the desistance decisions of pimps of that era. These former pimps in this sample discussed the toll that crack cocaine had taken on their workers, in particular with their unreliability as workers and cheaper prices they would charge clients. Pimping became "a hassle" and "not worth it" for some respondents. Pimps quickly became aware that they were losing profits to drug dealers. A former pimp named Jay, who was involved in pimping in the 1980s, said "It was around the time [the crack era]. That's another reason why I quit too man. Once them girls they started. Forget all your money man. You know I really had to stay on top of it. And all the money is going to the crack man. The crack man the crack man was the pimp then. Hah. Everybody was giving him the money. I said 'no' [it was] time for me to get out." However, some saw this as a chance to transition to drug sales, which was perceived as easier money to make and an easier product to manage. For a lot of former pimps, particularly pimps who operated in the 1980s and 1990s, it was not pimping but their involvement with drug selling that triggered long prison sentences due to the harsher mandatory sentencing policies of the war on drugs and led to their eventually desisting from a criminal lifestyle altogether.

The majority of pimps who cited avoiding incarceration as a motivating factor for quitting had already experienced time in a correctional facility and were aware of the losses that they could accrue with repeated stints. Within their individual accounts were different motivations for avoiding incarceration ranging from an awareness of stiff sentences to being more seasoned and realizing that many conventional opportunities would be lost. They did not wish to return only to have to re-accrue those assets once they return to their old lives. Frederick feared the place that he would have to do time as a young person. Frederick also knew that, had he been a few years older, given the crack-cocaine sentencing disparity still in place, he could have been given a much longer sentence for selling crack cocaine as an adult. Being sent to a facility with a reputation for housing the most hardened, violent young offenders his age caused him to take into account the losses he would accrue should he continue his criminal career. He said:

> I'm dead scared … I've been to jail before. Riker's Island facility. That shit crazy. I went in … it was close to pimping. I stopped pimping before I hit 16 cause I was 15 years and 4 months.

> Feel me? So when I was 16, that was the first time I was sent to Riker's Island cause when you're 16, you get sent there. And it was for crack cocaine. I done stopped pimping and I didn't touch the crack money. But I weighed out the difference, I thought about it, I was 16 and I was like, "Should I put my foot back in there? Am I ready for this yet?" I was like "Nah.

An awareness of stiff sentences did make a difference for some of the younger pimps who were aware that the focus on human trafficking and changes to federal law would have an impact on their pimping activities and cause them to get much longer sentences than pandering charges that pimps of the '70s and 80s had faced. A pimp named Arro discussed his awareness of the impact of the change of public views of pimps. Arro said "There's a lot of things that you might not have done but just off the fact that you being a pimp they can slay you. They can give you a whole lot of time in jail. You be gone." He referred to the additional federal charges, such as kidnapping and transporting a minor and RICO and conspiracy charges for pimps who are aligned with others in the criminal world. A former pimp named Kelvin expressed a similar awareness of the impact of the new laws. He said "And if I got busted, I'd gotten life cause it's called white slavery. I can't afford to get busted. The older you get, that shit start coming up in your mind. Life. Life. Life." Many pimps were unaware that they could be charged with sex trafficking, but others were acutely aware, which contributed to their decision to quit.

A former pimp and drug dealer named Tony had recently returned from a six-year prison sentence for drug selling, accompanied by a substance abuse problem. He pimped through the crack era and in part he pimped to support his own crack habit. He was motivated to change his life and stay away from the street crime lifestyle that would inevitably cost him more time with the accumulation of charges. He expressed an awareness of how being identified as a habitual career criminal could potentially bring a life sentence. Tony said:

> Bring incarcerated really woke me up (–). Now they test you for drugs see if you messing with drugs. That can cost you to lose your day, your day means they can take, maybe you're going home next month, they can take all that time and hold you a little longer from having your freedom. I been upstate four times. You see that's the whole thing. They tell me one more time they're gonna throw the keys away.

Some ex-pimps said that it caused them to take into account the losses that prison time would cost them, both in years and in accomplishments and relationships made. A former pimp named Jamaica said a stint in prison cost him everything he acquired during his many years of staying "straight." Jamaica left pimping for a legal job, he got married, and started a family after his first prison sentence. We know from a plethora of desistance research that some offenders do not completely desist but may go back and forth between the criminal and mainstream world for a while before making a final decision to leave completely. Jamaica also attributed his second trip to jail to his best friend's son, while seeing his own actions in an altruistic light wherein it was "doing a favor" for his best friend's son that cost him. One last task in the criminal world ultimately caused him to lose the investments in social capital he made through living an otherwise pro-social life and caused him to permanently leave the criminal world this time:

> It cost me to go to jail. And came outta jail and said I would never touch that shit again. And I was on my job for 15 years and did a favor for my best friend's son and he wound up was dealing with a confidential informant for like ATF. So I would up doing 18 months. Just came

> home. June 24th. And um it destroyed everything. I was I had like four more five more years to do on my job and I woulda had my 20 years in. I was on the same job for 15 years. Wife, kids, everything. Now I'm gonna have to start all over.

When pimps spent time in prison, they often lost their businesses, or they reflected on how the job was not worth it. A pimp named Darnell told us that when pimps are arrested and incarcerated, their sex workers often leave them and seek out other pimps. Thus, pimps risked losing their entire business by being incarcerated. He said "I used to do it hard until 2009. I went to jail and you know the chicks just they just gonna find somebody else. They need to be under somebody wing." Time in prison not only meant that they lost their businesses, but many also lost the advantages of being young, including their ability to attract sex workers. Padro, who was just released from prison, reflected on this: "I wouldn't call myself a pimp today, anymore. (–) When I was younger, I was like fifteen years old, and I figured out the power I had over women. That I'm a good-looking man, the way I speak to them, and how they respond to me physically." The ability to charm and seduce women is particularly relevant to pimps who use "loverboy" techniques to recruit sex workers.

The criminal lifestyle pimps were involved in also brought its own dangers and everyday violence that they described seeking to avoid. An ex-pimp named Tenacious who had seen a fellow pimp killed by police, saw this fate and possible paths his life could take before his eyes and said "A lot of guys man that I came up with they didn't make it you know. They got caught up in the mix, they got killed. One guy got killed by the police. One you know different things happen to different people man." Tenacious went to prison during the 1980's when educational opportunities were readily available to inmates. Most of these programs are no longer available (Phelps, 2011) making the transition from prison to turning points less tenable. He used this opportunity and received his college degree and he was able to get a legitimate job. While these turning points are pivotal to his quitting pimping, the underlying reason is an awareness that his lifestyle would cost him his life. In this account, Tenacious described a combination of external factors and turning points, and the cumulative effect of these reasons prompted Tenacious to quit. A number of respondents discussed turning points and a fear of punishment, i.e., the dangers of street life or incarceration in single narratives.

An ex-pimp named Mont, however, feared that being unable to find a good job is causing him to be pulled back into criminal activity, lured by the easy money of pimping and drugs. He said, "I'm trying to be good. But it's getting harder. It's getting harder. There are no jobs. Ain't like that. You know you can't just walk out get a job like that. I been looking for a while now. I'm really thinking about going back to doing what I was doing. I was making good money." For some like Mont, this lure of easy money was too great of a reward to resist at times. Respondents weighed risks and rewards in their accounts. The ease with which a lot of money could be made in criminal activities was a topic brought up in many interviews. The money made through criminal enterprises and the respect that they felt it give them on the streets was often not within their reach in the legitimate world, given the lack of education and employment history most had.

In contrast to the scenario where quitters knife off their old selves in order to make a cognitive change, some respondents vacillated back and forth between their old selves and new selves in their accounts. This group expressed that if they are able to yo-yo, that is return to pimping, they would. Often, they described external reasons for stopping, such as being incarcerated or getting old and retiring, but they ultimately expressed a desire to return to the pimp lifestyle.

The respondents in this study who used yo-yo discourse, also often reflected on their life pimping as high status, exciting and as their best years. We call this type of discourse the "bad ass me." The "bad ass me" takes many shapes and usually pivots around different masculine selves ranging from an oppositional masculinity where street credibility and the thrill of surviving dangerous work are present to a more conventional masculinity where success in the U.S. marketplace is their source of pride. We asked Mega, who was recently released from prison on an unrelated charge if he planned on returning to pimping. He discussed how he lost touch with his workers, but he reflected on how the lure of pimping was rooted in his desire to make fast money. "I'm not gonna say I'm not [going to return]. You know when you like money'll make you a slave at the end of the day. That's what I always learned. Money'll make you a slave, love will make you a fool. You feel me?" Even those who did not want to return, reflected on both the positive feeling of pimping and the feelings of power derived from making easy money, being financially successful and living the "high-life" replete with not only cash, but all the perks that come with making money through pimping. Many discussed missing the sensation of pimping, that is the excitement of the pimp lifestyle. Kelvin was nostalgic for the sensations of pimping.

> At night, the city just changes. It's not like it is in the daytime anymore. It becomes a big ass party, really. That's what it really is. I like the feeling of that. I like the fucking clothes I was wearing, I like the money, I like the car that I was driving. And especially, I like the girls that was working for me.

Some respondents reflected on the "bad ass me" as the pinnacle of their masculinity, but they did not necessarily want to return. While Sampson identified as a "pimp for life," he vacillated about whether he would return to it. He discussed pimping as his "golden years" or the years that he is most proud of.

> It was at that time and that era in the 80s, early 80s it was it was about this it was about it was about living in Harlem and getting money. That's what it was about. You shine, I shine and I wanted to shine you know what I'm saying and I wanted the money, the cars, the jewelry, I wanted the pussy. I wanted it all. You know what I'm saying. And I got it.

The "bad ass me" interfered with knifing-off and a commitment to stopping more permanently especially with the respondents who used the yo-yo discourse. However, many others were able to incorporate their badass identity into their new desisted self. They could quit without having to knife off the "bad."

Turning points and links to external and internal change

Several of the pimps described encountering life-course turning points, which offered them reasons to quit, including finding a licit job, going back to school, finding a stable romantic relationship, becoming a parent, and aging out. Sometimes one conventional change led to another, with pimps describing having multiple life course reasons for quitting.

A former pimp named Alex, who had last pimped in New Jersey in the 1970s and had been out of the lifestyle for more than three decades, said that he realized the value of earning a living in a new job versus the lifestyle of easy money that he had been accustomed to:

> I do ceramic tiles you know. I do custodial maintenance. You know what I'm saying downtown. It's like pretty much I'm alright. You know what I'm saying like from being in that position where it was like I didn't have job you know I was just running around. I didn't give a fuck. I had my girls. They was selling they ass. They was bringing me the money. I said I can care less on how it was coming to me. I didn't give a fuck if the person that called me was giving they last dime as long as I was getting paid. That was the only thing that mattered to me, but now I look at it like ... I work hard. I'm earning this money. So, I understand what people was going through.

A former pimp named Kev, who had a relatively short year-long pimping career in Harlem, said that his recently deceased father's wishes to have his children complete their schooling motivated his desistance:

> That was his like his dream to have one of his kids go to college. But none of us ever went. He had eight kids and we all failed to like succeed at his goal. So, I just like and then he passed away last year. I just wanted to at least finish school. At least get my GED. He just wanted someone to go to college. None of my brothers and sisters went to college. So, I will try to finish that.

These turning points, importantly, not only gave respondents a new role to "hook" onto, but a new role within traditionally acceptable gender norms with which to reframe what being a man means and be able to perform their new masculinity within gender role constraints. One example of this hook within acceptable gender roles is fatherhood, which many of our respondents "hooked" onto in order to make the transition out of a "badass" criminal role and into one that still allows them to perform their masculinity but in a non-criminal way.

Those respondents who had children described being concerned about staying out of prison so they could be present in their children's lives, for their children's physical safety and they also emphasized moral reasons, especially when they had a female child. These turning points link to both external and internal reasons for quitting.

Orlando, who previously spoke of wanting to maintain his pimping as a source of income while in school, also realized that in doing so, he was taking a big risk that he might not be around for his children. His primary concern was if he was incarcerated, he would miss his daughter's early years. "Now because I got a child I don't wanna be locked up while my child grow up. And my child five years old like where daddy? Oh he locked up. He'll be home in a few years." Jeremiah, who had worked in the late 2000s, discussed not wanting to raise his children in a criminal environment. He was concerned about the safety of his children because of his criminal lifestyle that included violence. Jeremiah said "I did it before [pimping] you know up until a little while ago. I had my children so I kinda started to relax. I don't want to bring them into that same type of atmosphere. It [pimping] involves gangs and other things are intertwined with it." These former pimps connect their life course reasons with more external reason for quitting. They experienced parenthood and the internal changes related to that, but their reasons were not rooted in shifts in morality, but rather in improving their children's environment through increased safety and security.

We found that pimps who were able to hook onto new turning points with moral implications such as having a child were less likely to have bad ass identities that interfered with quitting. Instead, they often held onto both identities, but they emphasized how they cannot lead both lives. Respondents had different underlying reasons for doing so.

We found that becoming a father to a daughter as opposed to a son had a particular effect on respondents, causing them to reflect on their treatment of women as moral reasons for quitting. Flow talked about realizing that he would not want to see his daughter treated the way he had treated women. He emphasized how it was really having a daughter as opposed to as son that made the difference. Flow said, "I don't wanna see nobody else doing that to one of mines even though I didn't have no problem doing that to anyone else's. So, maybe if I had a son or something I'd still be in the game. But my daughter changed me (–)." A former pimp named Chuck-a-Nut, who'd had a lengthy pimping career that spanned the 1970s to the 1990s, reflected on how the birth of his first daughter made him rethink his treatment of women. He was concerned not only with how they would view him, but that they would also work in the sex trade. He was so concerned that he made sure his daughters were not so naïve.

> That's when I had my first child, so and she was a girl so I kinda like you know I don't want my daughter to be around this and I don't want my daughter knowing that I'm doing this to other women. So, I just kinda after my first one and then I had another child, which was a girl, because I have three girls now. So I'm like hold up. That's when it really kinda started affecting me. Cause hey I said hey I'm doing this. Suppose somebody do that to my daughter, how would I feel? And basically, I you know kinda brought my daughters up to not be so naive.

Though he discussed being tempted back into pimping, Flow felt that, as a father, he would not be able to integrate his former identity into a new self:

> And then from there on I just turned around and I had a daughter somewhere down the line. I look at her differently. Like I try to look at my daughter like I would never ever let you be taken advantage of like I would never put you in that position. Understand what I'm saying. I did a lot of foul things you know. That I would never want her to go through. So that's one of the main reasons why I really left it alone. Cause like I could a went back several times. I could a went back at any given day like right now I could probably call him right now and tell him yo listen I wanna be on right now.

Specifically, however, Flow was concerned with how his daughter would see him as a man. He was worried that she would see him as a criminal as opposed to a conventional father who works hard through legitimate means to provide for his family. As she grew up and become more aware, he was worried about her impending judgment of him. Flow said "my daughter's getting older. She's five years old now. So she's getting old enough to understand. And I don't want her to know me as a drug dealer. I'd rather, you know, hard workin' father."

The presence of a daughter or even the thought of having a daughter made several pimps question what they were doing, and for some it was a reason for stopping. The realization that they may be degrading or harming women was highly integrated with moral reasons for stopping. For instance, Miguel did not have a daughter, but he started to spend a lot of time with his niece. He said "I kinda got attached to the kid. I don't think I'll feel right knowing that she was doing that shit later. I don't think I could do it anymore. That's the real reason I pretty much stopped. Why I'm not trying to anymore." Benny did not have a child, but he formulated his quitting around the immorality of "degrading females." He imagined himself having a female child and he said that "I don't want anybody doing that to her." This hook was powerful within some narratives, -whether it was real or imagined.

Internal reasons for quitting

Many respondents discussed moral reasons for quitting. The majority of these reasons involved distancing themselves from misogynist or violent masculinities that are associated with pimping. Some of those who used moral reasons have to knife off in order to firmly distance themselves from that "bad" masculine self. Rip said "if I could turn the hands of time I would go, I would go back and change my life. It's not me; I'm not the type of person to go and hurt women like that." He not only distanced himself from this identity, but he said that he wished that he never did it. Rip admitted to treating his sex workers very poorly. He discussed how he targeted promiscuous women and got them addicted to crack. He also admitted to hitting them and threatening to kill them if they misbehaved. It was unclear if Rip was truly remorseful, but he was ashamed of this former self. He may have been expressing this deep regret because he was interviewed by a cis gendered female, and this interaction could have biased his response.

There were several respondents who interpreted their work as contributing to the degradation or mistreatment of women. Rip was an extreme example, but other former pimps who were not physically violent, eventually viewed sex work as bad for women, which is why they said they stopped. Kid, who pimped in high school, felt that he was "doing bad" because of how he was treating women.

Tony, who was formerly a sex worker turned pimp, viewed his former job as a way of protecting women. He did have a deeper understanding of the dangers formerly having worked in strip clubs and as a sex worker. He conceptualized his work as "good" because of his intensive role in their safety and security, but he also came to view sex work and his life on the street as "bad." Tony was hoping for permanent, conventional hooks to come his way. He said, "I wanna change my life totally. Right now I'm looking for a good girl to settle down and live a good life you know what I'm saying. Settle down, get me a nice little job where she can work we do our part, you know what I'm saying?" Tony and some of his workers also had substance abuse issues and he went to prison four times. He was sick and tired of life on the "streets" and all of the street life activities.

A few former pimps discussed how they were unable to successfully perform this job because they were unable to be violent due to their respect for women. Spanky described himself as "the worst pimp in the world." He was raised in a family of pimps and he was fired due to his inability to control sex workers. Spanky attributed this to his being "too soft" and his disdain for getting physically violent with women. Frederick also worked for his cousin briefly. He discussed becoming close with sex workers and how upset he was when one of them got hit by a pimp. His cousin fired him. He attributed his inability to perform the job on his dislike for harm against women. Subsequently, Frederick became a Muslim. He viewed his brief stint in pimping as somewhat negative, but he also remembered feeling on top. Once he started pimping, the other kids in high school quit teasing him. He felt powerful and independent. Frederick said

> I'm telling you when you're younger, somebody laugh at you, you can't control your feelings. You know you get emotional. So, my mentality used to be "They laugh at me, they won't be laughing at me once I get this money and flashing it." I used to go school flashing money sometimes. "Boy, you ain't got this in your pocket. What you talkin' about? Look at you bought shit ... " You know how kids is, anyway.

Those who expressed moral changes did not necessarily knife off the "bad ass me" rhetoric as it seemed to be deeply embedded in positive emotions associated with pimping. Those who pimped in the 70's and 80's often stayed because of the power of hustler identities, including pimping that originated from resistance to white culture and subverting existing power structures (Cleaver, 1968; X & Haley, 1965). In this single narrative, the new moral self and the "bad ass me" co-existed.

Some of the retired pimps reflected on how they missed opportunities for conventional lives. Debonir, who was older and pimped for several decades, discussed his childhood friends who were "good" and held conventional law-abiding lives. He talked about his former sex worker who went straight doing legitimate work driving a bus. He reflected a lot about his lack of contribution to the betterment of the planet. His believed that conventional work equals contributing to the planet and that everything that he did was "crazy" or "bad." He seemed to crave an autobiography where he made a contribution. Debonir said "You know a law-abiding citizen doesn't live his life like that. You know. It's all about working. You know doing something for the planet. Making something work for the planet before you die and leave the planet. You know leave your mark somehow besides pimping and hoing."

Those who quit pimping because they aged out often have interdiscursive narratives where pimping is described as a "high point," but they also regretted missing out on turning points and a conventional life. In these single narratives, pimping was "bad" and "bad ass." Jay, who was trained by his brother to be a somewhat brutal pimp, also reflected on pimping as "bad," but mostly because his mother rejected his money and discredited his material gains as coming from "filthy" criminal enterprises. His morality was in response to his mother's opinion of him. He also viewed his pimping as simultaneously "bad" and "bad ass."

Many accounts were interdiscursive, as pimps had multiple reasons for quitting in single accounts. Overall, 76.7% (n = 33) of respondents had at least two reasons for quitting. In order to triangulate external and internal themes found in the qualitative portion and to look at the overall patterns of co-occurring themes, we used non-metric Multi-Dimensional Scaling (MDS).

Triangulating qualitative findings through non-metric MDS

The first stage of non-metric, MDS involves determining the frequencies of variables in the data. We conducted a frequency analysis of the pimps' explanations of quitting, which is summarized in Table 3. The Valid % represents the frequency of the variable out of the total sample.

Table 3. Frequency of reasons for quitting.

Variable	Total (N)	Percent Total (%)
Prison	20	46.5
Moral	18	41.9
Life course	17	39.5
Punishment	12	27.9
Yoyo	9	20.9
Hassle	7	16.3
Bad at job	6	14.0

High frequency variables

High frequency reasons, i.e., those found in more than 50% of cases, showed typical reasons for quitting in this sample. High-frequency variables are not useful for differentiating between cases and therefore should be excluded from the analysis (Horning et al., 2015; Salfati & Canter, 1999). The only high frequency variable in this sample was the "bad ass me" (67.8%, n = 27). This did not reflect an internal or external reason for quitting but rather is when pimps reflect on pimping as part of their "best years" or "golden years." Campbell and Hansen (2012) noted that this was prevalent in accounts of drug traffickers. We recognized this variable when we were looking at pimps who yo-yo'd or discussed returning to pimping, and it could have been a distinguishing aspect of internal or external accounts. However, it was too high frequency to include.

Variables within the 30-50%

The reasons within the 30–50% range included three variables highlighted in the quitting and desistance literature (Table 3).

Prison. Offenders may quit crime due to being incarcerated. In 46.5% of the cases, offenders discussed prison as a reason for quitting. When offenders are incarcerated they experience a disruption in their criminal careers. Another process that can occur is a conscious effort to rehabilitate that Maruna called "making good" (Maruna, 2001). In many scenarios, being incarcerated did seem to disrupt their involvement in their pimping businesses. Offenders in this sample were rarely convicted of charges related to pimping or sex trafficking, but rather they primarily were convicted of drug possession or intent to sell/distribution charges.

Moral reasons. There is a lot of literature that discusses the search for the "good self" as a necessary rhetorical and cognitive process to stay straight. There is a search for the "good" and "moral" self, and by seeing the crime as "bad" and the self as now "good", offenders may desist more permanently. In this sample 41.9% of offenders discussed moral reasons for quitting pimping.

Life-course reasons. Those who study desistance, particularly quantitative desistance researchers, look for turning points, or major life changes to explain quitting. Some of these reasons are getting a licit job, finding a new romantic partner, having a child or ageing out (Laub & Sampson, 1993; Sampson & Laub, 1993). In this sample, 39.5% discussed life-course reasons for quitting.

Several of the pimps encountered life course turning points, which offered them reasons to quit, including finding a licit job (14%, n = 6), going back to school (11.6%, n = 5), finding a stable romantic relationship (7%, n = 3), becoming a parent (14%, n = 6), and aging out (4.7%, n = 2). Sometimes one conventional change led to another, with 11.6% (n = 5) of these pimps having multiple life course reasons for quitting.

Variables within the 19-29%

This range of frequencies include fear of *punishment* and *yo-yo*. Fear of punishment is an external reason such as fear of being hurt on the job or fear of arrest. In 27.9% of the cases, offenders included fear of punishment as a reason. In 20.0% of the cases, offenders discussed the possibility of returning to pimping. Maruna referred to these offenders as "inbetweeners" as they are neither desisters or persisters. They are not committed to quitting and they may have quit for superficial reasons.

Variables within the 1%-18%

This range of more low frequency variables include discussing being *bad at the job* or viewing it as a *hassle*. These variables were mutually exclusive because some discussed being very bad at controlling workers or running the job, whereas those who described it as a hassle were often tired of managing sex workers. In this sample, 16.3% described the job as a hassle and 14% admitted to being terrible at pimping.

Non-metric multi-dimensional scaling

We aimed to explore whether the External/Internal dichotomy could be used to differentiate pimp' reasons for quitting. In order to test if this dichotomy exists, seven variables were assessed. Many of these variables were selected based on prior studies (Campbell & Hansen, 2012; Davis, 2017; Giordano et al., 2002; Laub & Sampson, 1993; Maruna, 2001; Paternoster & Bushway, 2009; Presser, 2004).

To test the External/Internal dichotomy, non-metric, Multi-Dimensional Scaling was used. This is a procedure based on the idea that interdiscursivity in narratives could be more readily understood if the relationship between each and every other variable is evaluated simultaneously. The non-metric procedure entails computing the association coefficients between all variables. These coefficients are used to form a spatial representation of items with points in a geometric space representing variables. The more often the variables co-occur, the closer the points will be in the plot. The points that are furthest away are least likely to occur in a single narrative.

There were a few reasons for using non-metric, Multi-Dimensional Scaling. First, it is effective as reliably analyzing "noisy" data (Horning et al., 2015). Narrative data can be very noisy, especially when participants show indiscursivity or complex narrative structures. In this sample, 55.8% of had at least two reasons for quitting and 20.9% had more than two. Overall, 76.7% of the sample, has at least two reasons for quitting pimping. Multi-Dimensional Scaling, through calculations of all relationships, determines which reasons covary and are thematically similar. Second, we wanted to assess if Multi-Dimensional Scaling could be useful to confirm qualitative themes already identified.

This could be a very useful tool to triangulate qualitative data analysis, such as Grounded Theory (GT) approaches.

The closer the rank orders of the original matrix and the MDS solutions, the better the fit of the solution (Santtila, Häkkänen, Canter, & Elfgren, 2003). The MDS is calculated by estimating the Euclidean distance configurations that minimize a measure called *stress* (defined as the normalized residual variance), and an influential goodness-of-fit rule of thumb developed by Kruskal (1964, p. 3) is that stress estimates under 5% indicate good, monotonic relationships between the model's distances and the actual similarities. In this MDS, the stress measure was 4.68% in 10 iterations, indicating a very good fit for the data.

Based on our examination of the associations among variables shown in the plot in Figure 1, there were three clearly defined regions. There were External reasons (prison, hassle, bad at job, yo-yo, and punishment), as well as Internal reasons (moral). Life course reasons were not closely associated with either External or Internal reasons. It appeared to be its own category and separate from the External/Internal dichotomy. Alternatively, it may sit between external and internal themes because, as demonstrated in the qualitative

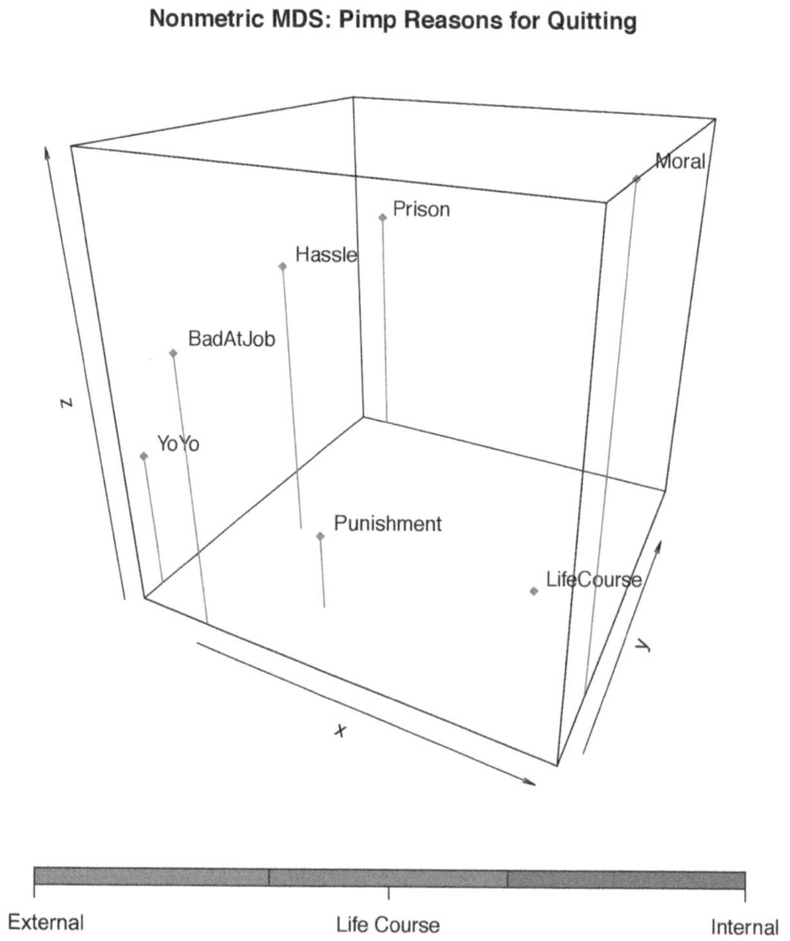

Figure 1. Nonmetric multidimensional scaling of pimps' external, life course, and internal reasons for quitting.

analysis, these life course reasons can be connected to both external change or changes in morality.

Our second aim was to thematically classify offences. To test this threefold framework of reasons that pimps quit their jobs, each of the 43 cases were examined to determine if they could be assigned to a dominant theme based upon variables that co-occurred in accounts. Every case was given a score indicating the number of External/Turning Point/Internal variables occurred in the account. Using at least a 2:1 requirement, a total of 67.4% (29/43) could be classified as belonging to the External/Internal or Turning Point themes. This indicates that the themes shown in in Figure 1 are an adequate representation of thematic reasons for quitting pimping. Of the total sample, 48.8% (21/43) of the cases were classified at External, 11.6% (5/43) were Internal, 7% (3/43) were Turning Points and 32.5% (14/43) of cases were mixed. The External theme was very prevalent within this sample of pimps in New York City

This classification is adequately useful to classify the thematic reasons of pimps in New York City who quit. The model is an excellent tool to assess those who dominantly discuss External reasons for quitting. However, the Internal reasons, which can be more subjective and perhaps connected to more complex interdiscursivity were not easily classified using this model. The internal and life course reasons occurred at high frequencies, but offenders often discussed these reasons in combination with external reasons. It may be that major changes in life or moral perspectives generally happen in conjunction with external reasons or that that are more connected to multiple reasons for quitting.

Discussion

In this sample, pimps' accounts of their reasons for quitting fit into the dichotomy of *external* and *internal* reasons that was found in the existing literature on desistance; however, the fit was "noisy," and many accounts were interdiscursive. Their reasons were rarely singular with many events contributing to their impetus to quit. This supports Paternoster and Bushway's (2009) finding that cumulative, intersecting reasons are generally necessary. In these accounts, those who discussed external reasons rarely discussed the search for a "good" me or a change in morality that is emphasized in some of the desistance literature (Maruna, 2001; Presser, 2004). Their experiences in prison did not generally lead to these types of changes. This may be due to them no longer being in a correctional facility where biases such as the halo effect can influence responding. Alternatively, it may be due the fact that incarceration has moved away from being rehabilitative (Tonry, 2011). Those who discussed external reasons did also discuss some life course changes, such as getting a job or having a new romantic relationship. It was unclear whether being incarcerated and removed from their criminal lifestyles allowed them to experience new opportunities upon release or whether they spent unusually long periods of time in prison due to criminal justice policies in place at the time of their convictions (i.e., mandatory minimums, the crack-cocaine disparity, and the war on drugs) and that they simply wanted different things based on maturation.

The historical moments when they pimped and when they were incarcerated seem to influence decision making. For instance, many of those who pimped during the crack era quit because the open air illicit markets were dangerous, they feared contact with the police or with other pimps and many of their workers became difficult to manage.

Research exploring those quitting illicit markets should account for the context, including history, laws and criminal justice policies. Campbell and Hansen (2012) illustrate this when they discuss drug traffickers working on the American-Mexican border who feared quitting and subsequently getting arrested and facing violence from gangs with cartel affiliations in correctional facilities. In this sample, especially the younger pimps were aware of the changes to sex trafficking laws in the U.S. and how sentences could be from 15 years to life. This new law may be more pertinent to those who are younger because they risk losing their entire youth to a life in the prison industrial complex.

We hypothesized that life course reasons would be more connected to external reasons with the concept of "desistance by default" being a possibility. The life course reasons were most complicated because they involved external and internal reasons for quitting in these accounts. Some pimps wanted to hold onto their newfound conventional activities, so while they wanted to return to pimping, they feared punishment. The closeness of these two variables on the MDS plot illustrated the strength of this relationship. This fits in with the original conception of life course reasons set forth by Laub and Sampson (1993) and Sampson and Laub (1993) where turning points facilitate social bonds that pimps want to maintain, and therefore the last thing they want is to lose that. However, some of the life course changes were deeply connected to moral changes. This was particularly acute with those who had children or even imagined having children, particularly female children. Through the child they were able to empathize, and most of their moral changes centered around pimping changing how they viewed women.

It should be noted that the majority of our sample consisted of racial minorities who had grown up during a time of great urban economic disparity, during a time when the decline of urban manufacturing created widespread unemployment amongst black men in urban areas, which William Julius Wilson (1990) argues facilitated their entry into drug and other illegal markets. While we did not explicitly analyze the roles that race and class played in our participants' desistance from pimping and other criminal activity, there is an opportunity for future research into how the masculinities explored intersect with both race and class in the desistance literature.

The MDS plot showed that life course reasons are in a separate category, which may be due to its close associations with both external and internal reasons. However, few cases could be classified as being dominantly life course. The connections of life course reasons with external and internal reasons should be explored in more qualitative depth and with larger samples.

We did find that some respondents wanted to return to pimping, or yo-yo. This confirms how offenders drift in an out of crime (Matza, 1964). Purists who study desistance would not classify these offenders as desisters. We emphasized that they are merely quitters. Those who yo-yo often express a "bad ass me" identity and reflect on their lives pimping as a highlight or the "golden years". Campbell and Hansen (2012) had a similar finding in their study of drug traffickers. Overall, two-thirds of the sample expressed "bad ass me" rhetoric, indicating that many quitters view that period of their lives positively, and that the Mertonian goal of money-making is powerful. Interestingly, many of these respondents did not have to knife off the "bad" me in order to quit, as discussed in Maruna (2001) and Maruna and Roy (2007). They were simultaneously able to reflect on the "bad ass me" and quit. Some of them even discussed the "good" or "moral" me and simultaneously held on to the "bad ass me." In future research, the "bad ass me" should be explored in more depth and in conjunction with neutralization techniques known to internally absolve respondents of guilt or blame through excusing or justifying crime.

The moral reasons for quitting, or the search for the "good" me, was present in many accounts. However, it was not closely associated with external reasons or even life course reasons on the MDS plot. With a larger sample, it may be connected to those who have children, but this would have to be tested. The cumulative reasons for a moral change should be explored in more depth.

We were able to classify 67.5% of the cases as dominantly within an external, turning point or internal theme. However, very few of the cases were classified as life course, suggesting that it could be connected to both the external and internal themes. This makes sense, as some people change "by default' or perhaps based on changes in routine (Laub & Sampson, 1993), whereas others may experience turning points in more internal ways (Maruna, 2001). The external/internal dichotomy should be tested on other samples of pimps who quit and on other types of offenders who quit or desist to confirm their presence across samples.

The non-Metric MDS technique was an excellent way to triangulate our qualitative findings and provide a visual representation of the themes in accounts. This technique could be used before embarking on qualitative analyses, or it could be used after themes are fully explored in the data. We chose to use this technique after the qualitative analysis because the data showed interdiscursive patterns, and we wanted to confirm our findings. While purist qualitative researchers may object to introducing a quantitative technique to triangulate qualitative analysis, we found that it was a very useful way to both visualize and triangulate our data.

Acknowledgments

We give a special thanks to our two gatekeepers (who will remain unnamed) for allowing us access to their communities and to all of the participants who agreed to share their stories. We also thank Sara V. Jordenö and Antonio Pontón-Núñez for their fieldwork and other assistance. This work was funded by The Graduate Center, CUNY (Grants DSRG #6, #8) and the CUNY Graduate Dissertation Fellowship.

Disclosure statement

No potential conflict of interest was reported by the authors.

References

Alexander, M. (2012). *The new Jim Crow: Mass incarceration in the age of colorblindness*. New York, NY: The New Press.

Blomberg, T. G., Cullen, F. T., Carlsson, C., & Jonson, C. L. (Eds.). (2017). *Delinquency and drift revisited, Volume 21: The criminology of david matza and beyond*. New York, NY: Routledge.

Blumer, H. (1954). What is wrong with social theory?. *Journal of American Sociological Society, 19* (1), 3–10.

Bottoms, A., Shapland, J., Costello, A., Holmes, D., & Muir, G. (2004). Towards desistance: Theoretical underpinnings for an empirical study. *Howard Journal of Criminal Justice, 43*, 368–389. doi:10.1111/j.1468-2311.2004.00336.x

Campbell, H., & Hansen, T. (2012). Getting out of the game: Desistance from drug trafficking. *International Journal of Drug Policy, 23*(6), 481–487. doi:10.1016/j.drugpo.2012.04.002

Canter, D., & Fritzon, K. (1998). Differentiating arsonists: A model of firesetting actions and characteristics. *Legal and Criminological Psychology, 3*(1), 73–96. doi:10.1111/lcrp.1998.3.issue-1

Carter, W. H., Schill, M. H., & Wachter, S. M. (1998). Polarisation, public housing and racial minorities in US cities. *Urban Studies, 35*(10), 1889–1911. doi:10.1080/0042098984204

Cleaver, E. (1968). *Soul on ice.* London, UK: Panther Modern Society.

Curtis, R., & Wendel, T. (2007). "You're always training the dog": Strategic interventions to reconfigure drug markets. *Journal of Drug Issues, 37*(4), 867–891. doi:10.1177/002204260703700407

Dank, M. (2011). *The commercial sexual exploitation of children.* El Paso, TX: LFB Scholarly Publishing LLC.

Dank, M. L., Khan, B., Downey, P. M., Kotonias, C., Mayer, D., Owens, C., & Yu, L. (2014). *Estimating the size and structure of the underground commercial sex economy in eight major US cities* (pp. 348). Washington, DC: Urban Institute.

Davis, H. (2017). Exit from the game: Ex-pimps and desistance in the USA. In Horning, Amber, Marcus, Anthony (Eds.),*Third party sex work and pimps in the age of anti-trafficking* (pp. 111–129). New York, NY: Springer.

Farrington, D. P., & Hawkins, J. D. (1991). Predicting participation, early onset and later persistence in officially recorded offending. *Criminal Behaviour and Mental Health, 1*(1), 1–33. doi:10.1002/cbm.1991.1.issue-1

Flick, U. (2009). *An introduction to qualitative research* (4th ed.). Thousand Oaks, CA: Sage Publications.

Friedman, I. A., & Mann, L. (1993). Coping patterns in adolescent decision making: An Israeli Australian comparison. *Journal of Adolescence, 16*(2), 187. doi:10.1006/jado.1993.1016

Giordano, P. C., Cernkovich, S. A., & Rudolph, J. L. (2002). Gender, crime, and desistance: Toward a theory of cognitive transformation. *American Journal of s=Sociology, 107*(4), 990–1064. doi:10.1086/343191

Glaser, B. G., & Strauss, A. L. (2017). *Discovery of grounded theory: Strategies for qualitative research.* Chicago: Routledge.

Harlem Community Justice Center. East Harlem Juvenile Gage Task Force. (2011). *2011 Needs assessment.* New York, NY. Retrieved from http://www.courtinnovation.org/sites/default/files/documents/Juvenile_Gangs_Strategic_Plan.pdf

Holdstein, J. A., & Gubrium, J. F. (1997). Active interviewing. In Silverman, D. (Ed.),*Qualitative research-theory, method and practice* (pp. 113–129). Thousand Oaks, CA: Sage Publications.

Horning, A., & Sriken, J. (2017). Pimps, bottoms, and the nexus of caring and cash in a harlem sex market. In *Third party sex work and pimps in the age of anti-trafficking* (pp. 71–88). New York, NY: Springer.

Horning, A., Thomas, C., Marcus, A., & Sriken, J. (2018). Risky business: Harlem pimps' work decisions and economic returns. *Deviant Behavior*, 1–26. doi:10.1080/01639625.2018.1556863

Horning, A. M., Salfati, C. G., & LaBuschagne, G. N. (2015). South African serial homicide: A victim-focused behavioural typology. *Journal of Investigative Psychology and Offender Profiling, 12*, 44–68. doi:10.1002/jip.v12.1

Kruskal, J. B. (1964). Multidimensional scaling by optimizing goodness of fit to a nonmetric hypothesis. *Psychometrika, 29*(1), 1–27. doi:10.1007/BF02289565

Laub, J. H., Nagin, D. S., & Sampson, R. J. (1998). Trajectories of change in criminal offending: Good marriages and the desistance process. *American Sociological Review*, 225–238. doi:10.2307/2657324

Laub, J. H., & Sampson, R. J. (1993). Turning points in the life course: Why change matters to the study of crime. *Criminology, 31*(3), 301–325. doi:10.1111/crim.1993.31.issue-3

Lyons, S. T., Higgins, C. A., & Duxbury, L. (2010). Work values: Development of a new three-dimensional structure based on confirmatory smallest space analysis. *Journal of Organizational Behavior, 31*(7), 969–1002.

Maher, L. (1997). *Sexed work: Gender, race, and resistance in a Brooklyn drug market.* Oxford: Oxford University Press.

Malcolm, X. (2015). *The Autobiography of Malcolm X.* New York, NY: Ballantine Books.

Maruna, S. (2001). *Making good: How ex-convicts reform and rebuild their lives.* Washington, D.C: American Psychological Association.

Maruna, S., & Roy, K. (2007). Amputation or reconstruction? Notes on the concept of "knifing off" and desistance from crime. *Journal of Contemporary Criminal Justice, 23*(1), 104–124. doi:10.1177/1043986206298951

Massoglia, M., & Uggen, C. (2007). Subjective desistance and the transition to adulthood. *Journal of Contemporary Criminal Justice, 23*, 90–103. doi:10.1177/1043986206298950

Matza, D. (1964). *Delinquency and Drift.* New York, NY: John Wiley and Sons, Inc.

Messerschmidt, J. (1997). *Crime as structured action: Gender, race, class, and crime in the making.* Thousand Oaks, CA: Sage.

Milner, C., & Milner, R. (1973). *Black players: The secret world of black pimps.* New York, NY: Michael Joseph.

New York City Public Housing Authority. (2011, February). *New York city housing authority safety and security task force report resident survey based on a representative sample of 1100 NYCHA residents in May 2010.* Retrieved from http:www.nyc.gov/html/nycha/downloads/pdf/safety_and_security_task_force_2_17.11webfinal. pdf

Onwuegbuzie, A. J., & Leech, N. L. (2007). A call for qualitative power analyses. *Quality & Quantity, 41*(1), 105–121. doi:10.1007/s11135-005-1098-1

Overs, C. (2002). *Sex workers: Part of the solution.* An analysis of HIV prevention programming to prevent HIV transmission during commercial sex in developing countries. Geneva, Switzerland: World Health Organization (WHO).

Paternoster, R., & Bushway, S. (2009). Desistance and the" feared self": Toward an identity theory of criminal desistance. *The Journal of Criminal Law and Criminology, 99*(1)1103–1156.

Phelps, M. S. (2011). Rehabilitation in the punitive era: The gap between rhetoric and reality in US prison programs. *Law & Society Review, 45*(1), 33–68. doi:10.1111/j.1540-5893.2011.00427.x

Presser, L. (2004). Violent offenders, moral selves: Constructing identities and accounts in the research interview. *Social Problems, 51*, 82–101. doi:10.1525/sp.2004.51.1.82

Salfati, C. G., & Canter, D. V. (1999). Differentiating stranger murders: Profiling offender characteristics from behavioral styles. *Behavioral Sciences & the Law, 17*(3), 391–406. doi:10.1002/(SICI)1099-0798(199907/09)17:3<391::AID-BSL352>3.0.CO;2-Z

Sampson, R. J., & Laub, J. H. (1993). Structural variations in juvenile court processing: Inequality, the underclass, and social control. *Law and Society Review*, 285–311. doi:10.2307/3053938

Santtila, P., Häkkänen, H., Canter, D., & Elfgren, T. (2003). Classifying homicide offenders and predicting their characteristics from crime scene behavior. *Scandinavian Journal of Psychology, 44* (2), 107–118.

Schwartz, S. H., & Bilsky, W. (1987). Toward a universal psychological structure of human values. *Journal of Personality and Social Psychology, 53*(3), 550. doi:10.1037/0022-3514.53.3.550

Scott, G. (2008). "They got their program, and I got mine": A cautionary tale concerning the ethical implications of using respondent-driven sampling to study injection drug users. *International Journal of Drug Policy, 19*(1), 42–51. doi:10.1016/j.drugpo.2007.11.014

Slim, I. (2011). *Pimp.* Simon & Schuster.

Teachman, J., & Tedrow, L. (2016). Altering the life course: Military service and contact with the criminal justice system. *Social Science Research, 60*, 74–87. doi:10.1016/j.ssresearch.2016.04.003

Theobald, D., & Farrington, D. P. (2009). Effects of getting married on offending: Results from a prospective longitudinal survey of males. *European Journal of Criminology, 6*(6), 496–516. doi:10.1177/1477370809341226

Thompson, J. P. (2015, May). Broken policing: The origins of the "Broken Windows" policy. In *New Labor Forum, 24* (2): 42–47. Sage CA: Los Angeles, CA: SAGE Publications.

Tonry, M. (Ed.). (2011). *The Oxford handbook of crime and criminal justice.* Oxford, UK: Oxford University Press.

Wacquant, L. (2008). *Urban outcasts: A comparative sociology of advanced marginality.* Massachusetts, USA: Polity Press.

Wilson, W. J. (1990). *The truly disadvantaged: The inner city, the underclass, and public policy.* Illinois, USA: University of Chicago Press.

X, M., & Haley, A. (1965). *The autobiography of Malcolm X.* New York, NY: Random House Publishing.

The Recursive Relationship between Substance Abuse, Prostitution, and Incarceration: Voices from a Long-Term Cohort of Women

Ronet Bachman, Samantha Rodriguez, Erin M. Kerrison, and Chrysanthi Leon

ABSTRACT

Relying on interview data from a cohort of drug-involved women originally released from prison in the 1990s and interviewed between 2010 and 2011, this paper examines the role that prostitution played in their lives. These women were arrested an average of 16 times in their lives, and their criminal records prevented them from obtaining legitimate employment, which resulted in nearly half of the sample engaging in "survival prostitution." Consistent with the Identity Theory of Desistance, narratives from those who successfully exited prostitution reveal the cognitive transformations that began when they envisioned their "feared self" (e.g. dying on the street). This research illuminates the complexities inherent in the desistance process for a contemporary sample of drug-involved adult women entrenched within the criminal justice system.

Introduction

At the end of 2016, there were nearly 112,000 adult women in state or federal correctional facilities and thousands more in jails or on parole or probation (Bureau of Justice Statistics, 2018). Across racial and ethnic groups, a large percentage of this population were also drug users (Bronson, Stroop, Zinner, & Berzofsky, 2017).[1] Unfortunately, many of these women cycle in and out of prison for illicit substance possession charges, violations of the conditions of their parole or probation, or for committing other low-level offenses, including prostitution (Bachman, Kerrison, O'Connell, & Paternoster, 2013). Society and criminal justice policy makers alike have only recently begun to investigate the factors that impact the desistance process for women, and these findings remain equivocal at best.

One of the problems that limits consensus on the factors related to desistance for women stems from differences in observed samples and in the operationalization desistance. For example, some research has relied on community samples of female adolescents who were not embedded in an adult correctional system (Giordano, Seffrin, Manning, & Longmore, 2011; Kreager, Matsueda, & Erosheva, 2010), while others studies have been based on samples of women who have all been detained in adult correctional facilities, sometimes on multiple occasions (Bachman, Kerrison, Paternoster, O'Connell, & Smith,

Color versions of one or more of the figures in the article can be found online at www.tandfonline.com/uvao.

2015; Brown & Bloom, 2009; Robbins, Martin, & Surratt, 2009). This sample variability is also true for research examining the factors related to leaving prostitution. Studies that have examined desistance from prostitution have relied on several divergent samples including, adolescents (Reid & Piquero, 2014), individuals seeking services from "prostitute service organizations," (Oselin, 2014, p. 3), or participants from specialized prostitution courts or other specialized court programs (Sallmann, 2010; Shdaimah & Leon, 2015).

Defining desistance is also a precarious business, especially when most official and self-reported offending data indicate that many individuals intermittently engage in criminal behavior (Carlsson, 2013; Piquero, 2004), especially for those battling addictions (Bachman et al., 2013). This makes operationalizing desistance extremely problematic as someone may not be counted as crime- and substance-free for the past year, but would be counted as desisting if the threshold of observation had been six months.

The results from the extant literature on desistance from prostitution are as varied as the samples and definitions of desistance. Moreover, virtually no research has examined the road to desistance over a long time period for women generally, or for a diverse sample of women leaving prostitution specifically.[2] Our study of persistence in and desistance from self-reported prostitution relies on in-depth interviews with a cohort of drug-involved women who were surveyed when they were originally released from a state prison in the early 1990s, and then interviewed again between 2010 and 2011. Thus, our study offers insight into the long-term patterns of entry into and desistance from this form of sex work. Results indicate the inherent complexities in this cyclical process when battling addiction, along with the barriers to desistance placed in front of those re-entering society with a criminal record and a history of stigmatized sexual conduct.

Literature review

While many terms have been used to describe prostitution, the vast majority of contemporary research uses the terms *prostitution, survival prostitution*, or *sex work*, although most studies rely on the term, *sex work*. In fact, scholarly definitions of each term are relatively similar. For example, the National Institute of Justice defines prostitution as, "the offering of something of value in exchange for sexual activity. By definition, prostitution is a form of commodification" (Moses, 2006, note 6). Sex work has been defined as "encompassing an exchange of a wide variety of sexual services for money or in-kind goods or services such as shelter, drugs, or clothing … . 'sex work' also indicates that sex work is a form of employment, thus acknowledging its legitimacy as a choice by which people earn a living and sustain themselves with dignity" (Hail-Jares, Shdaimah, & Leon, 2017, p. 9). However, others contend that the term sex work implies an occupational choice, which many involved in street-level prostitution did not make (Shdaimah & Leon, 2015). In the effort to present an authentic account of the stories shared by the voices from our sample, we will defer to their authority and use the terms *sex work, prostitution*, and *survival prostitution* interchangeably, as they did.

In the United States, prostitution is only legal in parts of Nevada. After the U.S. Congress passed the Trafficking Victims Protection Reauthorization Act in 2008 to combat human trafficking, more pressure was placed on local jurisdictions to criminalize "pimping, pandering, prostitution, and commercial sex" (U.S. Department of Justice, 2014). As a result, sex work is largely relegated to underground economies and remains hidden from mainstream exposure, except when individuals are arrested for either soliciting, pimping, or prostituting. Due to the hidden nature of this work, it is extremely difficult to validly estimate the prevalence of individuals who make a living from sex work. In fact, prior to increased global attention given to human trafficking, there was little research investigating either the prevalence or the etiology of sex work. In the past decade, however, the increased demand for research on human trafficking specifically, has provided the research community with substantially more knowledge about sex work more generally (Finn, Muftić, & Marsh, 2015; Kempadoo, Sanghera, & Pattanaik, 2015).

Sex work encompasses a broad array of activities including high-end escort services, erotic massage parlors, commercial stripping, and street and internet solicitations (Dank et al., 2014). Street-based sex work is at the low end of the earnings market, and is occupied by high percentage of drug-addicted workers who also face a greater risk of victimization than what workers are exposed to in other forms of sex work (Dalla, Xia, & Kennedy, 2003; Muftić & Finn, 2013). The use of the internet and other social media platforms have allowed many sex workers to move off the streets, increasing their invisibility and making prevalence estimates more elusive. To estimate the magnitude of the underground commercial sex economy (UCSE), Dank et al. (2014) utilized a very complicated econometric analysis to extrapolate its net worth in eight U.S. cities. Except for Atlanta, results indicated that the UCSE significantly decreased between 2003 and 2007. In 2007, estimates of the UCSE ranged from a high of $290 million in Atlanta to a low of almost $40 million in Denver (Dank et al., 2014, p. 281). Although the number of workers involved in this economy remains hidden, the monetary value of the UCSE indicates that it is a significant industry in many urban areas today.

The desistance process

Theoretical speculation about the factors related to desistance began to emerge with the research by the Gluecks (Glueck & Glueck, 1950), but remained virtually dormant until Gottfredson and Hirschi (1990) and Sampson and Laub (1993) catalyzed interest in the topic in the early 1990s. Sampson and Laub's (1993) age-graded theory of informal social control, and its subsequent revision (Laub & Sampson, 2003), was based on the original Glueck Boys data, which they extended by conducting life-history narratives with a small group of the original sample. The backbone of their theory of desistance asserts that individuals quit crime when they establish strong conventional bonds through marriage, military service, and stable employment. The slightly revised theory developed in 2003 featured a broader set of contributing factors, including "the interplay of human agency and choice, situational influences, routine activities, local culture, and historical context" (Laub & Sampson, 2003, p. 9). Essentially, this life course perspective of desistance hypothesized that exogenously generated turning points such as finding the right partner, landing a stable and satisfying job, or serving a successful stint in the military could each produce a prosocial deflection in an individual's previous criminal offending trajectory because it strengthened a weak social bond and gave them what Toby (1957) long ago called a greater stake in conformity.

Recent research relying on more contemporary samples indicate that Sampson and Laub's age-graded informal social control theory (Laub & Sampson, 2003; Sampson & Laub, 1993) may be deficient when predicting desistance in the current cultural and economic climate (Bachman et al., 2015; Giordano, Cernkovich, & Rudolph, 2002;

Giordano, Schroeder, & Cernkovich, 2007; Maruna, 2001, 2004; Maruna & Roy, 2007). The sample of men upon which much of Sampson and Laub's theory was based featured a cohort of young White males who came of age in the 1950s when well-paying industrial jobs were available and who, as a result, appear to have been amenable to changing their criminal behavior via prosocial routes such as employment and good marriages. The applicability of a theory that explains desistance for an exclusively White male sample whose prosocial journeys were scaffolded by heteronormative marriage dynamics and the security of a booming industrial labor market has since come under scrutiny. Furthermore, recent theorizing about desistance has added to this structural background the psychological manifestations that appear to affect the success of the desistance process for actively criminally-involved individuals today.

Paternoster and Bushway (2009); Bushway & Paternoster, 2011, Bushway & Paternoster (2013)) offer one of the most recent theoretical formulations explaining desistance, called the identity theory of desistance (ITD). Individuals, Paternoster and Bushway (2009) contend, will retain an "offender" working identity as long as they perceive they are netting more benefits than costs from their behavior. While many may confront failure (e.g. getting arrested, going to jail), as long as they attribute these failures to "bad luck" or "the costs of doing business," rather than their own behavior, they will most likely continue to commit crimes. The process of changing an offender identity is gradual and begins to occur when they begin to question that illusion. Specifically, Paternoster and Bushway contend that the process of change begins, "when perceived failures and dissatisfactions within different domains of life become connected, and when current failures become linked with anticipated future failures" (2009, p. 1105). Baumeister (1991) referred to the linking of previously isolated dissatisfactions and senses of failure in life as the crystallization of discontent; the ITD proposes this discontent as part of a subjective process of self-interpretation or self-knowledge. Initial moves toward desistance may come about upon identifying a *feared self*, or an image of what a person does not want to be or fears becoming.

The feared self often provides the first steps toward desistance, but to maintain these initial steps, the criminally-involved individual must craft a new, more positive image of what they want to become – the possible law-abiding self. This newly emerging prosocial identity triggers a diminished preference for things like quick and easy money, and motivates a move to make one's social network more prosocial as well. It is this internal change in identity and the recognition of the kind of person that one wants to be that both motivates behavior consistent with a prosocial identity (change in preferences, desire for legitimate work, and conventional friends) and sends a signal to others (like potential prosocial intimates and employers) that the person is making positive changes in their life.

According to IDT, it is this agentic change in identity that both explains the movement into conventional roles, and explains why those who had previously been involved in crime would be receptive to prosocial influences. In sum, IDT contends that identity change is *essential* for desistance in a way that satisfying intimate relationships and stable employment are not.

Recent research investigating contemporary samples of criminal justice-involved people, including both males and females, has found support for the need for identity change prior to desistance (Aresti, Eatough, & Brooks-Gordon, 2010; Bachman et al., 2015; Bachman, Kerrison, Paternoster, Smith, & O'Connell, 2016; Healy, 2013, 2014; Opsal,

2012). Importantly for this paper, research examining the process of exiting sex work has also noted the importance of identity transformation. For example, results from a large-scale study of 4 "prostitute-serving organizations" (PSOs) within the United States led Oselin (2014) to conclude that having the motivation to exit sex work was "a necessary but not sufficient condition to this transition" (2014, p. 46). Unlike IDT, Oselin describes the phases of the prostitution career as "entrance, experience during, and then the process of role exiting … … [which] unfolds in three stages: initial exit, role distancing, and new role embracement and identity change" (2014, p. 18). However, when reading the narratives provided to illustrate the reasons sex workers gave for attempting to exit sex work, they clearly illuminate concepts from IDT, including notions of an undesired feared self. For example, when describing one respondent's thought processes regarding exiting sex work, Oselin (2014) states:

> Aretha, who engaged in prostitution for 28 years, also expressed that returning to prison was her biggest fear and caused her substantial worry. She espoused: "I had been to the penitentiary twice, one more arrest and I would have gone away for a long, long time. I became so scared of getting in a car with an undercover cop … that was a big fear for me. Because when you go to prison, you don't really know if you'll get out alive" (pp. 39-40).

Importantly, only a few women in Oselin's sample had permanently exited sex work as the author reported, "most of the women in this sample are in the midst of role exiting" (2014, p. 19). Thus, it is not clear what the temporal order of identity change and desistance would be for those women in her sample who had maintained their exit for an extended period of time.

One of the issues that complicates our understanding of exiting sex work is that a large percentage of the population engaged in sex work, at least those working on the street, is also navigating a substance use disorder (Baker, Dalla, & Williamson, 2010; Sarteschi & Vaughn, 2010). While scholars lack agreement on the directionality of substance abuse and sex work, virtually all studies have found a strong association between the two (Inciardi & Surratt, 2001; Smith, 2017). Unfortunately, research investigating desistance from sex work has generally relied on the recall accounts of individuals from cross-sectional samples, with very few employing a longitudinal methodology that could validly measure the onset of either sex work or substance use (Potterat, Rothenberg, Muth, Darrow, & Phillips-Plummer, 1998; Young, Boyd, & Hubbell, 2000). For example, ethnographic and interview data collected from over 800 chronicled these deleterious effects, citing that crack, "was a great equalizer on the street, in that it forced most crack-dependent women – regardless of age, race/ethnicity, occupation, religion, or family background – into sex trading or commercial sex work in order to support their drug-taking" (Inciardi & Surratt, 2001, p. 384). Moreover, conducting research that investigated this issue in the late 1980s and early 1990s – at the height of the crack cocaine epidemic – is also problematic because of the highly addictive nature of crack and its effects on its users and their subsequent attrition from research participation (Claus, Kindleberger, & Dugan, 2002; Scott, 2004).

One recent study has been able to examine the temporal order of sex work and substance dependency using the Pathways to Desistance study of delinquent youth who were followed over a 7-year period (Reid & Piquero, 2014). This research found that substance use occurred several years prior to prostitution for the majority of the youth studied and that, "substance use may function as a 'launch' mechanism, starting youth off on a long-term course of problem behaviors" (Reid & Piquero, 2014, p. 255). It is important to note that the Pathways sample used for this research is relatively young, with a mean baseline age of 16 years. As a result, the temporal order with substance use and sex work may not be generalizable to older sex workers or to those who have been engaged in sex work for longer periods of time. However, after exploring the narratives of a sample of women working towards desistance from substance abuse and prostitution, Kerrison, Bachman, and Paternoster (2016) cited that for some of the women they interviewed, the repeated discontents associated with trading sex for drug use, coupled with the knowledge that sexually transmitted infection, unplanned pregnancy, and persistent victimization were likely inevitable fates, prompted a reprioritization of their desires and potential to secure enhanced wellbeing. Still, despite confronting this reality it was often years before they could disentangle themselves from both harmful behaviors.

Regardless of the temporal order, it is clear that substance dependency is inextricably related to sex work, at least for those involved in low-echelon work on the streets. Moreover, there is likely a recursive relationship between drug use and sex work. As Young et al. (2000) explain, "[I]t is likely that prostitution and drug use is a self-perpetuating cycle in which the engagement in one leads to an increase in the other. Although women may start working as prostitutes in order to finance their drug habits, there are a number of aspects of prostitution that often cause psychological distress and trauma, which in turn may lead to increased drug use as a means of coping" (*p*. 795).

What is important to deduce from this literature is that exiting sex work is complicated by the nexus of sex work with substance addiction and conquering an addiction may be the first step in exiting sex work for many. For example, Oselin (2014) noted that all the women in her sample, except one, "admitted they were addicted to drugs while working in prostitution" and that they were not able to focus on desistance from the sex trade until they were sober (*p*. 49). Consistent with other research, this demonstrates that research examining the process of exiting sex work must also consider the role of substance abuse in that process (Baker et al., 2010; Dalla, 2006).

In sum, the extant literature has provided a great deal of insight into the complexities inherent in exiting sex work, particularly for those who are also contending with drug abuse. Although identity has been implicated in the process of this desistance, most of the work to date has not opened the black box of agentic identity change nor have results been placed within the broader theoretical discourse of desistance. To help fill this gap, this paper relies on a sample of 118 women who were surveyed upon release from prison at the height of the drug war in the early 1990s, rearrested on several occasions thereafter, and interviewed in 2010 and 2011. The goal of this paper is to examine the long-term patterns of entry into and desistance from sex work, identify how these patterns are shaped by drug addiction, and consider how the obstacles associated with a criminal record has on this process.

Methods

Sample

The data for this study come from a longitudinal analysis of serious drug-involved men and women who were originally surveyed upon release from the state of Delaware correctional system between the years 1990 and 1996, with a subsample re-interviewed between 2010 and 2011. The baseline study was designed to examine the effectiveness of a drug therapeutic community (TC), and consisted of 1,250 incarcerated men and women who were randomly assigned to enroll in the TC treatment condition (Inciardi, Martin, & Butzin, 2004). Subjects in the study were first interviewed while still incarcerated, approximately nine months prior to release (referred to throughout this paper as the baseline incarceration), and were re-interviewed after that baseline release at 6, 18, 42, and 60 months.

To determine patterns of desistance within this cohort, arrest histories for each individual that covered the years 1990 to 2008 were obtained from the Delaware Statistical Analysis Center, which records all arrests and imprisonments in the state of Delaware. These data were augmented by arrest data from the National Criminal Information Center in order to capture arrests that occurred outside the state of Delaware. With these data we amassed a count of the number of arrests for each person per year. Incarceration data were also collected for each individual since 1990 and included the entrance and exit data from prison for each sentence. This information was used to compute the number of days free per year, to control for the time the individuals were in a correctional setting. To illuminate the various paths of desistance for the original cohort, our analysis strategy began with the estimation of a group-based trajectory model for this arrest history data (Nagin, 2005). A graph of the offending trajectories for the five-group model (all quadratic) that best fit the data is shown in Figure 1 (for a full discussion of the procedures used for this trajectory analysis, see Bachman et al., 2013). We present this model only because it was used as the sampling frame for the qualitative component of our study, which constitutes the primary data used for this paper.

Respondents from the original cohort were randomly selected from within each of the five trajectory groups depicted in Figure 1, which resulted in n = 304 who participated in intensive face-to-face interviews. The focus of this paper is exclusively on narratives provided by the 118 female respondents from this sample.[3] The average age of this sample of females was 45 years and the mean number of arrests they had experienced at the time of their interview was 16.2. The purpose of these qualitative interviews was to illuminate

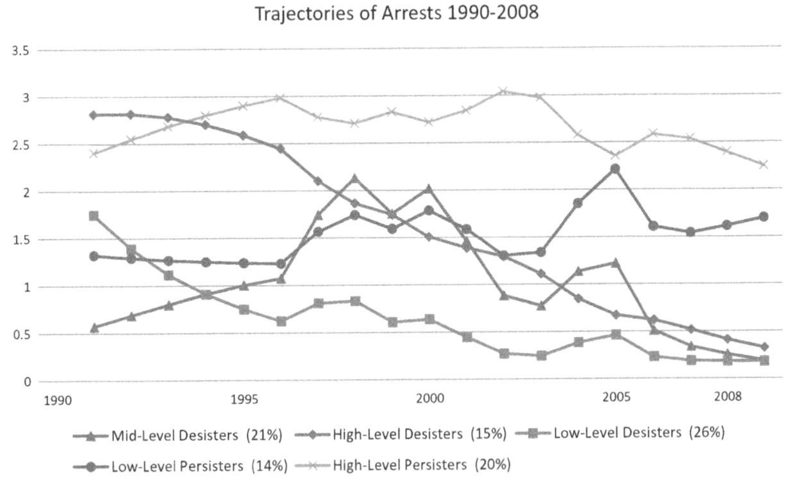

Figure 1. Trajectory model of arrest histories for original sample of 1,243 that was used as sampling frame for intensive interviews.

the mechanisms for change in offending over time and allow the respondents to speak directly for themselves about what changes they felt they had undergone over the years since their baseline incarceration.

Interview methods

Respondents selected for interviews were first contacted by mail requesting that they call a research office phone number at a local university if they were willing to participate in the interview. Follow-up was needed in many cases, and was done first by mailing another letter, then by making phone calls, and finally by personal visits in a few cases. All interviews lasted from 1 to 3 hours and were digitally recorded. Respondents were compensated $100 for their time and travel expenses. Not surprisingly, sample attrition was a significant problem when attempting to contact this cohort almost 20 years after their baseline incarceration release. Approximately 11 percent of the original sample was deceased, 13 percent were still incarcerated, 3 percent were living out of state, and 7 percent were unreachable by any means.

While we originally did not want to conduct interviews with those still in prison because the Department of Corrections did not allow the admittance of tape recorders on-site, three women who were in the "Persister" offending trajectories were interviewed while in custody in an effort to increase the sample size of respondents representing these persisting trajectory groups. Interviewer field notes were used to analyze the three interviews conducted in correctional settings as well as two digitally recorded interviews whose files were corrupted.

Because of the relatively small number of women from other race/ethnic groups in the original cohort, only Black and White women were selected for the sample. The response rate for those who were successfully contacted and living in Delaware was approximately 96 percent. The majority of the women were Black (73%), and had a mean age of 44 years at the time of the interview. In their baseline interview for the original study, 43% of this sample self-reported engaging in prostitution prior to being incarcerated. Prior to the interviews conducted in 2010 and 2011, over half of the women (54%) self-reported using drugs or alcohol and about 1 in 4 self-reported engaging in other criminal activity. Only a few were still actively engaging in prostitution, although a few others reported that they were being taken care of by "former Johns," or were living with other men they "manipulated" to take care of them.

The goal of the interviews was to uncover what Agnew (2006) refers to as "storylines" in understanding criminal offending. A storyline is a "temporally limited, interrelated set of events and conditions that increase the likelihood that individuals will engage in crime" (2006, p. 121) or for our purposes, desist from it. The interview guide resembled an Event History Calendar (EHC) (partially displayed in Figure 2), which proved to be an extremely useful tool for collecting retrospective data on life events within different domains such as subjects' relationship changes, medical history, and offending (Belli, Stafford, & Alwin, 2009). Another important tool we used in our interview guide to facilitate respondents' recall was the placement of arrest and incarceration dates obtained from official data within the calendars, as well as key life events such as birthdays to be used as heuristic cues to aid recall. These cues were also useful for helping respondents recall both their offending histories as well as other salient life events. Despite the utility of the EHC-

INSERT BIRTHDAY/HOLIDAYS/KNOWN CRIMINAL JUSTICE EVENTS												
XYEAR												
First, where were you living in XYEAR?	January	February *Birthday 2/18*	March	April	May	June	July	August	September *Arrest 9/3*	October	November	December
A. RESIDENCE												
A1. Did you live in Delaware? If no, where did you live?												
Specifically, where did you live in XYEAR? A2. Lived Alone a. rented b. owned												
A3. Lived With Partner/Spouse a. rented b. owned												
A4. Lived with Own Children a. rented b. owned												
A5. Lived with Partner/Spouse and Children a. rented b. owned												
A6. Lived with other family members												
A7. Lived with friends												
A8. Was in correctional setting e.g. prison, work release												
A9. Was homeless												
A10. Other												

Figure 2. A component of the event history calendar used as a heuristic device to enhance recall.

inspired interview guide, however, the interviews were primarily open-ended and resembled conversations rather than an exchange of formal survey questions and answers.

For each criminal and drug relapse event self-reported or obtained from official records, respondents were asked to recreate the event both perceptually and structurally, and interviewers probed for respondents' cognitive decision making processes surrounding those events. All interviews were transcribed verbatim and imported into NVivo for coding (for a more detailed discussion of the interview and coding processes, see Bachman et al., 2014).

Although the interview guide did not specifically probe for performing sexual acts in exchange for money, drugs, or other services, self-reports of prostitution were often given when respondents were asked about criminal activity or arrests. However, the absence of a specific probe for this behavior is an obvious limitation of this paper. Importantly, the purpose of this paper is not to estimate the prevalence of prostitution for this sample, but to explore the effects it had on recidivism and desistance from substance abuse and other crime generally, and to explore the desistance of prostitution specifically.

Results

Getting into the business

Like previous research using drug-involved individuals entrenched in the criminal justice system, the majority of women in this long-term sample began to prostitute because they required money for drugs. Similar to the results found by Rosen and Venkatesh (2008), this choice was made with "bounded rationality," or having to choose between undesirable options with little information and time to think critically. The women interviewed describe bleak contexts marked by having a criminal record, little education, and low job skills, which made employment elsewhere difficult at best. Hannah[4] explained her road to the business:

> *"I started using cocaine casually, like 1 day a week, to 3 days, and then to 7 days … and it just took over. For 10 years I found myself not caring about anything but getting high … I started getting charges and then being on probation and then prostituting … I did everything I could to get money to get the drug."*

These women were typically introduced to sex work by friends who also made their living in the sex trade. For example, Chris, who became addicted to cocaine in her early 20s, worked as a flagger after her first release from prison. When she was laid off from that job, she could not live on her unemployment so she "hooked up with a crowd" who taught her "the ropes of how to find men who would pay." Since then, she reported being "out there on the street since I was 25. Off and on being in and out of jail and prison." For virtually all of those who self-reported engaging in sex work, the primary reason was for getting money for their drug habits, although several women reported that the money was spent both on drugs and caring for their children.

Several of the women in the sample had childhoods riddled by physical and sexual abuse, and as a result, self-medicated with drugs and/or alcohol, which in turn led to addiction and then the need for money for drugs. For these abused women, recalling anything about their childhoods was difficult except the onset of the abuse, and the chaos that followed for the majority of their adult lives. Donna recalled, "it was something that shouldn't have been going on with a child. My mom's boyfriend was molesting me and that's why we don't get along because I swear to God she knew, I really do … I was only 5." Donna was molested for several years by her mother's boyfriend and alleviated this trauma by drinking and using drugs. She was addicted to cocaine by the age of 13. While she was sent to various extended relatives after a juvenile arrest, her learned way of survival always led back to the streets to sex work, selling drugs, and substance abuse. The good times she recalls in her adult life were when she stopped using cocaine and her only addiction was heroin. With only a heroin addiction, she didn't have to "hustle" so much and could almost make a living and secure her own drugs by selling them. At the time of her interview, she was still addicted to substances and trying to survive. She was currently awaiting adjudication for a shoplifting charge.

Similarly evidencing the role of childhood chaos and mistreatment, Dominique was put into foster care when she was 6 months old because her birth mother was an alcoholic. When she was 6 years old, her birth mother regained custody of Dominique and her older sister, despite still being addicted to alcohol. They lived in Section 8 housing and there were times when Dominique's mother didn't come home for weeks. Dominique started drinking alcohol, dating a man who was 15 years older than she – whom she called, "her child molester" – and was eventually placed in a juvenile detention center. She married an abusive man, had 2 children, and maintained an addiction to alcohol, which was her drug of choice. When the substance abuse led to her hospitalization, she called her aunt to take her children so she could be sure they were safe when she ended her marriage. This is when a "frenemy," as she described them, introduced her to cocaine. Dominique described how her world changed thereafter:

> *"I cut ties with my kids and my husband and went directly into the drug world. I cut everybody off. That's when I started picking up charges for possession, prostitution, stealing … .I was just self-destructing."*

Dominique was in and out of prison, in and out of treatment programs, in and out of halfway houses, and on and off the streets for the next 20 years.

While a few of the women worked for a pimp, the majority of the women in this sample did not. For example, Manhattan was introduced to crack by an older man at a party, who eventually got her a hotel room where she would bring back tricks for money. After he started taking all the money, she and another woman "wised up and started doing it for ourselves." When she needed more money, she would rob her "Johns." After stabbing one man when he tried to get his money back, he called the police and told them he was just giving her a ride and she attacked him. "They'd [the police] look at me and they'd look at him, and my word didn't stand for nothing." For this, she was sentenced to 5 years in prison. She still used cocaine but the streets have changed and the quality of the available drugs can no longer be trusted, she warned, "It's not the same. You don't want it. It's nasty. There's so much stuff you don't even know. It's terrible." Although she still occasionally had sex for money, she did not do it regularly and therefore perceived that "it is [not] the same prostitution that I've done." Manhattan had episodes of being clean, sometimes as long as a year, but would eventually relapse again. Her most recent relapse was 4 months before her interview, and she was since prescribed medication for anxiety and ADHD, which she believed was helping to alleviate her symptoms.

Only a few of the women reported that prostitution came before drug addiction. For example, Brandy who self-reported a good childhood, fell in love with a man and they had two children together. When he left her for another woman, she started sex work to provide for her family. Substance use soon followed as she explains, "when you start taking your clothes off with dirty, ugly, nasty men that think you're trash, you do drugs to forget. I had everything. Then I had nothing – just abuse." Brandy grew up in a middle-class home but soon found herself responsible for two kids and engaging in behavior that was previously out of her realm of possibility. She explained, "If they said I would become a prostitute, I would have said, 'you're out of your fucking head." Brandy had been surviving on the streets all of her adult life and was now in her late 40s. She still used drugs to self-medicate and was still self-sustaining day-to-day. When asked about her present life, she reported, "I still have morals. You may say, yes, but you take drugs, and sell your ass, but I still have morals." When she is under correctional supervision, she reported using prescription drugs to avoid a parole violation, "When I'm on probation, I can't use some drugs, but I can take Xanax or Percocet [which] will take my pain away [and won't be detected]. I'm not Mother Theresa – I don't know what is going to happen tomorrow. Today I feel good … .this money [from doing the interview] is going to get me groceries. I have a free ride waiting out there – it is a good day." This narrative reflects the nuanced picture of "moral and rational choice-making" depicted by Shdaimah and Leon (2015) to describe the decision-making process of the sex workers in their sample. Brandy had few options, but made rational choices based on her circumstances and survival needs.

Despite operating with the instinct to survive reflected in narratives like Brandy's, virtually all of the women who self-reported engaging in prostitution perceived a sense of shame about this behavior. In fact, a few did not disclose engaging in prostitution when probed about criminal activity, but eventually disclosed these histories at a later stage in the interview. For example, when asked about the biggest incentive for getting treatment for her addiction, Cherise stated:

Cherise : I didn't want to go to prison and I didn't want to prostitute or none of that stuff no more.
Interviewer : So you had done that? You didn't tell me about that.
Cherise : Oh, I did say that.
Interviewer : Did you?
Cherise : Yeah. I didn't say it like "prostitution," but I probably used a term like "degrading my body" or tried to cover it up, make it sound good.

In sum, the primary reason for engaging in sex work for this sample of drug-involved and criminal justice immersed sample of women was economic necessity. While this need was most often related to satisfying their addictions, a nontrivial number of women also engaged in sex work for basic survival needs like food and shelter.

Although over half of the women we interviewed had used drugs and alcohol during the 12 months prior to our interview, only about 10% were still actively engaged in prostitution. As noted above, however, several others were living with "former Johns," or with other men who "took care of them and their needs." The majority of the women who were still using drugs had developed significant health issues, which required them to "slow down their use." Several of these women were able to get off the streets when they were able to obtain medication-assisted treatment from Methadone and Suboxone clinics. Others used drugs "only when I can afford to," and were able to maintain their needs via their disability insurance income. However, the vast majority of the women we interviewed who had actively engaged in prostitution had successfully exited the sex work trade.

Exiting sex work

I'm going to die out here if I don't quit

The majority of the women in this sample continued to engage in sex work as long as they were substance addicted. For many of these women, their stated survival needs included maintaining their addiction, eating occasionally, and hopefully finding a place to sleep. Janice was addicted to heroin by the time she was 19 at a time when "they didn't even know what an addiction was." Her boyfriend was the first person to give her a shot of heroin and, "it was the best feeling in the world. That was it … I asked him what it was and he said, 'it's called heroin … ' everybody had heroin." Within a month Janice was addicted and woke up feeling sick and her boyfriend told her she was "heroin sick" and gave her another shot and she "was in the clouds in heaven." In that moment she recalled thinking to herself, "Oh my God, I'm stuck."

After her boyfriend left her, Janice "ended up on the streets prostituting for years after that … and the first time I went to jail for prostitution I was like 23 … then my life was just crap. I shot drugs, prostituted, and was in and out of jail." She used cocaine to get herself up to work, and then heroine so she could sleep. Years of this "hard living" eventually had severe health consequences for Janice. She ended up in the hospital with endocarditis of the heart from all of her drug use and heard the doctor say, "call her family. She's not going to live 48 hours." Janice was still alive six weeks later and the doctors "believed it was a miracle." It was this incident that led to her crystallization of discontent, where she realized "I was going to die if I didn't do something different." Although Janice recalled that she had been "sick and tired of being sick and tired," prior to this near death experience in the hospital, it was only after this incident that her feared-self emerged: "dying an addict." Following this life event, Janice began the process of identity transformation by making decisions to change her life. After she was released from the hospital, she admitted herself to an in-patient treatment facility and had remained clean for almost two years.

While several of the women's identity transformation was triggered by a traumatic event similar to Janice's, the transformation for most of the other women was a slow and nonlinear decline into an abyss where they knew they would die if they didn't change. Finding legitimate employment with a long criminal record was extremely difficult for many of these women, and finding a job that paid a living wage was virtually impossible. Sex work was one of the only methods for making money. For over two decades, many of these women maintained their addictions in survival mode, while their bodies and minds suffered the deleterious consequences.

Because of their age, these women were very conscious of their declining market value on the street despite their attempts to remain attractive. The declining benefits obtained from sex work also served to increase the costs associated with their drug use, which facilitated the connection between past failures becoming future failures. These cognitive connections were described by many women, including Elizabeth, who was 54 at the time of our interview. Elizabeth described the illumination of her feared-self very graphically:

> *When I was getting older, I started seeing young girls prostituting in their 20s. I was in my middle 40s – come on now. Cars started passing me to go to the young ones. I still had my regulars but it was time to do something different ... when I became 50, I knew I couldn't prostitute forever ... I had to accept scary rides that often didn't end well ... I knew I had to change or I would die out there.*

At the time of her interview, Elizabeth had been in and out prison and in and out of treatment her entire life. It was not one incident that precipitated her desistance, but instead, she described the process of realizing that nothing was going to change unless she changed herself. She called her mother and promised her that if her mother helped her get into a treatment program, this time she would make it work. Elizabeth had been clean for almost three years but knew she had to remain vigilant about not aligning herself too closely with "those women" who are still "on the stroll" or she would end up back on the street. She noted:

> *If I pass the working girls now, I might wave if I know them but I don't affiliate myself in that circle anymore ... .sometimes if they call me from the streets [and I might let them] come over and take a shower ... but this is not a hotel. That's where I stand and I have to. If I don't I could find myself right back on the streets.*

Finding a savior among tricks

In addition to the few women who were actively engaged in sex work, a few other women were currently living with "former tricks," and several others had moved in with clients at other times in their lives. For example, after over 20 years on the street, Tonya moved in with one of her "tricks" She said, "Brian made me his woman, but to me he was a trick. Once a trick, always a trick. I don't feel anything for him ... But I never want for anything."

The other women who were currently living with former clients had similar stories. It is clear from the women's narratives that the men in these accounts were truly benevolent actors, not simply doing it for sexual favors. For two of the women in this group, their families of origin had severed all ties with them because of their continued failed attempts at recovery. These women understood their abandonment as justified because they had "stolen from their family to buy drugs," and "let them down so many times that they couldn't take it anymore." The older men who had taken them in clearly represented a surrogate parent. They provided them with food and shelter and although they wanted and encouraged them to get clean, they didn't kick the women out when that was not possible. While providing much needed support and safety, respondents admitted that these men often did not provide the long-term platform for change needed for meaningful desistance from crime and substance abuse.

Conclusion

The interview narratives presented here offer several new insights into the pathways into and out of prostitution for women who are drug-involved and justice-impacted. Results indicate that substance addiction was the underlying factor that compelled the majority of the women in this sample to engage in street level prostitution. Moreover, when these women were arrested and incarcerated for drug possession or other offenses, the vast scope of collateral consequences attached to their offender status exacerbated reintegration hurdles and further distanced these women from pro-social ties and gainful, steady, and legitimate employment.

These women's stories and arrest histories – captured both through self-report and official records – provide further evidence that drug addiction is a chronic lifetime disease characterized by relapses and behavior (e.g. survival prostitution) that appears undeterred by the threat of formal sanctions. This supports the contention that criminal justice sanctions are an inefficient intervention for deterring vulnerable individuals from prolonged substance abuse or the survival prostitution that is associated with it. As noted by Hail-Jares, Shdaimah, and Leon (2015, p. 299), "[we must question] why criminal justice tools are the ones we most often use to address sex work, particularly the types that are most socially marginalized." The many periods of incarceration experienced by this sample neither steered these women away from prostitution nor addressed the underlying motivations animating their decision to engage this world. Instead, the criminal justice apparatus only exacerbated their chances at healthy (re)integration and left them more vulnerable and reliant upon one of the only economies accessible to poor drug-involved women burdened with criminal records.

Importantly, our research also supports previous work that has placed female criminality within a larger context of a violent childhood and cycle of violent relationships (Chesney-Lind & Pasko, 2013; Inciardi & Surratt, 2001). Many of the women interviewed here acknowledged the use of drugs and alcohol as a salve or escape from these traumas, which included the trauma related to survival prostitution. Helping women heal from primary traumas would seem to go a long way to reducing recidivism, net of drug treatment programs. As Harrison noted over ten years ago, "Drug abuse is often regarded as a symptom of underlying problems, and those underlying problems must be treated for the individual to stop abusing drugs." (Harrison, 2001, p. 474). Programs that fail to consider the auxiliary trauma endured by many females will inevitably fall short.

Another finding from this diverse sample of women is that several offered accounts of exiting prostitution work with the help of a partner who had committed to providing for them. However, the availability of the sort of savior identified in these scenarios is not a given for all women navigating this world, as even clients regard women engaged in sex work with varying levels of dignity and empathy, and against a hierarchical rubric of respectability (Grant, 2014; Hoang, 2015). Intersectional analyses suggest, too, that many racist and classist taxonomies of sympathetic sex works cast more privileged women as unwilling victims, and more marginalized women as undeserving law-breakers. In reality, many women come to occupy both constructions (Phillips, 2015; Wesely & Miller, 2018).

And finally, a novel finding in this research is the suggestion that women's very identities as trapped and confined to this reality, are inextricably linked to their persistent offending patterns. Women who can neither imagine nor support an identity that challenges the more dangerous fates known to many engaged in street-level sex work, regrettably continue to engage in the very practices that seal those fates. These data lend support for the Identity Theory of Desistance in that those who identified a feared self and then constructed a possible self who need no longer rely on more dangerous forms of street level prostitution, were the ones who were more likely to desist from committing those offenses and make moves towards substance abuse recovery. One therapeutic intervention that may accelerate this self-discovery process is cognitive-behavioral therapy (CBT). CBT is premised upon several principles including helping clients improve cognitive skills such as the skills necessary to identify problems, consider alternative courses of action to solve those problems, evaluate possible solutions before adopting a course of action, engage in critical reasoning and rational deliberation skills, focus on long-term planning, and the importance of taking the position of other people within one's social environment (Latessa, Listwan, & Koetzle, 2013). Although the CBT model is not theoretically based on the identity theory of desistance, the practices of this therapy appear to provide individuals with exactly those cognitive and rational skills that would enable them to more easily connect past and future events and realize that the life of an "offender" and "drug-abuser" will likely result in becoming their "feared self" (e.g. dying an addict). Such self-awareness would be instrumental in getting individuals ready to change, ready to adopt a new identity, and beginning the process of movement toward a non-offender identity. While CBT has been shown to be one of the more effective prison-based therapy programs in reducing recidivism (Latessa et al., 2013; Lipsey, Landenberger, & Wilson, 2007), study findings suggest that more can still be done to ensure that its merits can be enjoyed by a more diverse population of participants, the largest gulf of which exists for Black women in these treatment settings (Jemal, Gunn, & Inyang, 2019; Kerrison, 2018). As such, these programs would be most effective when combined with the trauma-informed therapies noted above and an earnest incorporation of effective acceptability structures for a diverse array of gender, racial, and cultural representations among treatment participants.

While the extant research, including findings presented here, have advanced our understanding of factors related to drug and criminal justice-involved individuals' use of sex work as a means for survival, further research is needed to document the persistence and desistance experiences of marginalized groups of sex workers. These groups include foster and homeless youth, those from the LGBTQ community, undocumented individuals, and those ensnared in sex trafficking. In the interim, these data suggest that drug-involved women's entry to and exit from the sex work economy is only exacerbated by criminal justice intervention, and that more targeted service-providing and trauma-informed approaches are needed to ensure their safety and increase the likelihood of permanent recovery and desistance.

Notes

1. Importantly for the sample used in this paper, the percentage of the correctional population serving sentences related to drug law violations increased dramatically after 1980. For example, drug law violators made up 22% of the federal prison population in 1980, but increased to 48% in 1990 (Bureau of Justice Statistics, 1991).
2. While both males and females engage in sex work, the present study will focus exclusively on females because there were too few males in this sample who self-reported engaging in sex work.
3. This research was approved the University of Delaware's Institutional Review Board.
4. Names provided are pseudonyms and used to protect confidentiality.

Acknowledgements

We would like to thank the anonymous reviewers for their comments and suggestions for improvement to earlier drafts of this paper. Our deepest gratitude goes to the women who gave us their time, energy, and trust to share their stories.

Disclosure statement

No potential conflict of interest was reported by the authors.

Funding

The corresponding author for this paper is Ronet Bachman. This project was supported by grant number 2008-IJ-CX-0017 awarded by the National Institute of Justice, Office of Justice Programs, U.S. Department of Justice. Points of view are those of the authors and do not necessarily represent the official position or policies of the U.S. Department of Justice.

ORCID

Erin M. Kerrison http://orcid.org/0000-0003-1300-3983

References

Agnew, R. (2006). Storylines as a neglected cause of crime. *Journal of Research in Crime and Delinquency*, *43*(2), 119–147. doi:10.1177/0022427805280052

Aresti, A., Eatough, V., & Brooks-Gordon, B. (2010). Doing time after time: An interpretative phenomenological analysis of reformed ex-prisoners' experiences of self-change, identity and career opportunities. *Psychology, Crime & Law*, *16*(3), 169–190. doi:10.1080/10683160802516273

Bachman, R., Kerrison, E., O'Connell, D., & Paternoster, R. (2013). *Roads diverge: Long-term patterns of relapse, recidivism and desistance for a cohort of drug- involved offenders (Grant Number 2008-IJ-CX-1107)*. Washington, DC: National Institute of Justice, United States Department of Justice..

Bachman, R., Kerrison, E., Paternoster, R., O'Connell, D., & Smith, L. (2015). Desistance for a long-term drug-involved sample of adult offenders: The importance of identity transformation. *Criminal Justice and Behavior*, 1–25.

Bachman, R., Kerrison, E., Paternoster, R., Smith, L., & O'Connell, D. (2016). The complex relationship between motherhood and desistance. *Women & Criminal Justice*, 1–20.

Baker, L. M., Dalla, R. L., & Williamson, C. (2010). Exiting prostitution: An integrated model. *Violence Against Women*, *16*(5), 579–600. doi:10.1177/1077801210367643

Baumeister, R. F. (1991). *Meanings of life*. New York, NY: Guilford Press.

Belli, R. F., Stafford, F. P., & Alwin, D. F. (2009). The application of calendar and time diary methods in the collection of life course data. In R. F. Belli, F. P. Stafford, & D. F. Alwin (Eds.), *Calendar and time diary: Methods in life course research* (pp. 1–4). Thousand Oaks, CA: Sage Publishers.

Bronson, J., Stroop, J., Zinner, S., & Berzofsky, M. (2017). *Drug use, dependence, and abuse among state prisoners and jail inmates, 2007-2009* (NCJ 250546). Bureau of Justice Statistics. U.S. Department of Justice.

Brown, M., & Bloom, B. (2009). Reentry and renegotiating motherhood. *Crime & Delinquency*, *55* (2), 313–336. doi:10.1177/0011128708330627

Bureau of Justice Statistics. (1991). *Drugs and crime facts, 1990* (NCJ-128662). U.S Department of Justice.

Bureau of Justice Statistics. (2018). Corrections statistical analysis tool (CSAT) – Prisoners. U.S. Department of Justice. Retrieved from https://www.bjs.gov/index.cfm?ty=nps

Bushway, S. D., & Paternoster, R. (2011). Understanding desistance: Theory testing with formal empirical models. In J. MacDonald (Ed.), *Measuring crime and criminality: Advances in criminological theory* (Vol. 17, pp. 299–333). New Brunswick, NJ: Transaction Publishers.

Bushway, S. D., & Paternoster, R. (2013). Desistance from crime: A review and ideas for moving forward. In C. L. Gibson & M. D. Krohn (Eds.), *Handbook of Life-Course Criminology* (pp. 213–231). New York, NY: Springer.

Carlsson, C. (2013). Processes of intermittency in criminal careers: Notes from a Swedish study on life courses and crime. *International Journal of Offender Therapy and Comparative Criminology*, *57*(8), 913–938. doi:10.1177/0306624X12443656

Chesney-Lind, M., & Pasko, L. (2013). *Girls, women, and crime: Selected readings*. Thousand Oaks, CA: Sage Publications.

Claus, R. E., Kindleberger, L. R., & Dugan, M. C. (2002). Predictors of attrition in a longitudinal study of substance abusers. *Journal of Psychoactive Drugs*, *34*(1), 69–74. doi:10.1080/02791072.2002.10399938

Dalla, R. L., Xia, Y., & Kennedy, H. (2003). "You just give them what they want and pray they don't kill You": Street-level sex workers' reports of victimization, personal resources, and coping strategies. *Violence Against Women*, *9*(11), 1367–1394. doi:10.1177/1077801203255679

Dank, M., Khan, B., Downey, M. P., Kotonias, C., Mayer, D., Owens, C., … Yu, L. 2014. Estimating the size and structure of the underground sex economy in eight major US cities. Research Report. The Urban Institute.

Finn, M. A., Muftić, L. R., & Marsh, E. I. (2015). Exploring the overlap between victimization and offending among women in sex work. *Victims and Offenders*, *10*(1), 74–94. doi:10.1080/15564886.2014.918069

Giordano, P. C., Cernkovich, S. A., & Rudolph, J. L. (2002). Gender, crime, and desistance: Toward a theory of cognitive transformation. *The American Journal of Sociology*, *107*(4), 990–1064. doi:10.1086/343191

Giordano, P. C., Schroeder, R. D., & Cernkovich, S. A. (2007). Emotions and crime over the life course: A neo-meadian perspective on criminal continuity and change. *American Journal of Sociology*, *112*(6), 1603–1661. doi:10.1086/512710

Giordano, P. C., Seffrin, P. M., Manning, W. D., & Longmore, M. A. (2011). Parenthood and crime: The role of wantedness, relationships with partners, and SES. *Journal of Criminal Justice*, *39*(5), 405–416. doi:10.1016/j.jcrimjus.2011.05.006

Glueck, S., & Glueck, E. (1950). *Unraveling juvenile delinquency*. New York, NY: Commonwealth Fund.

Gottfredson, M. R., & Hirschi, T. (1990). *A general theory of crime*. Stanford, CA: Stanford University Press.

Grant, M. G. (2014). *Playing the whore: The work of sex work.* New York, NY: Verso.
Hail-Jares, K., Shdaimah, C. S., & Leon, C. (2017). *Challenging perspectives on street-based sex work.* Philadelphia: Temple University Press.
Harrison, L. D. (2001). The revolving prison door for drug-involved offenders: Challenges and opportunities. *Crime and Delinquency, 47*(3), 462–485. doi:10.1177/0011128701047003010
Healy, D. (2013). Changing fate? Agency and the desistance process. *Theoretical Criminology, 17*(4), 557–574. doi:10.1177/1362480613494991
Healy, D. (2014). Becoming a desister: Exploring the role of agency, coping and imagination in the construction of a new self. *British Journal of Criminology, 54*(5), 873–891. doi:10.1093/bjc/azu048
Hoang, K. K. (2015). *Dealing in desire: Asian ascendancy, western decline, and the hidden currencies of global sex work.* Berkeley: University of California Press.
Inciardi, J. A., Martin, S. S., & Butzin, C. A. (2004). Five-year outcomes of therapeutic community treatment of drug-involved offenders after release from prison. *Crime and Delinquency, 50*(1), 88–107. doi:10.1177/0011128703258874
Inciardi, J. A., & Surratt, H. L. (2001). Drug use, street crime, and sex-trading among cocaine-dependent women: Implications for public health and criminal justice policy. *Journal of Psychoactive Drugs, 33*(4), 379–389. doi:10.1080/02791072.2001.10399923
Jemal, A., Gunn, A., & Inyang, C. (2019). Transforming responses: Exploring the treatment of substance-using African American women. *Journal of Ethnicity in Substance Abuse.* doi:10.1080/15332640.2019.1579141
Kempadoo, K., Sanghera, J., & Pattanaik, B. (Eds.). (2015). *Trafficking and prostitution reconsidered: New perspectives on migration, sex work, and human rights* (2nd ed.) New York, NY: Routledge.
Kerrison, E. M. (2018). Exploring how prison-based drug rehabilitation programming shapes racial disparities in substance use disorder recovery. *Social Science & Medicine, 199,* 140–147. doi:10.1016/j.socscimed.2017.08.002
Kerrison, E. M., Bachman, R. D., & Paternoster, R. (2016). The effects of age at prison release on women's desistance trajectories: A mixed-methods analysis. *Journal of Developmental and Life-Course Criminology, 2,* 341–370. doi:10.1007/s40865-016-0039-0
Kreager, D. A., Matsueda, R. L., & Erosheva, E. A. (2010). Motherhood and criminal desistance in disadvantaged neighborhoods. *Criminology, 48*(1), 221–258. doi:10.1111/crim.2010.48.issue-1
Latessa, E. J., Listwan, S. L., & Koetzle, D. (2013). *What Works (and Doesn't) in Reducing Recidivism.* New York, NY: Routledge. doi:10.4324/9781315721224
Laub, J. H., & Sampson, R. J. (2003). *Shared beginnings, divergent lives: Delinquent Boys to Age 70.* Cambridge, MA: Harvard University Press.
Lipsey, M., Landenberger, N. A., & Wilson, S. J. (2007). Effects of cognitive-behavioral programs for criminal offenders: A systematic review. *Campbell Systematic Reviews, 6,* 1–27.
Maruna, S. (2001). *Making good: How ex-convicts reform and rebuild their lives.* Washington, DC: American Psychological Association.
Maruna, S., & Roy, K. (2007). Amputation or reconstruction? Notes on the concept of "knifing off" and desistance from crime. *Journal of Contemporary Criminal Justice, 23*(1), 104–124. doi:10.1177/1043986206298951
Moses, M. C. (2006). Understanding and applying research on prostitution. *NIJ Journal, 255.*
Muftić, L. R., & Finn, M. A. (2013). Health outcomes among women trafficked for sex in the United States: A closer look. *Journal of Interpersonal Violence, 28*(9), 1859–1885. doi:10.1177/0886260512469102
Nagin, D. S. (2005). *Group-based modeling of development.* Cambridge, MA: Harvard University Press.
Opsal, T. (2012). "Livin'" on the straights": Identity, desistance, and work among women post-incarceration. *Sociological Inquiry, 82*(3), 378–403. doi:10.1111/soin.2012.82.issue-3
Oselin, S. S. (2014). *Leaving prostitution: Getting out and staying out of sex work.* New York: New York University Press.
Paternoster, R., & Bushway, S. (2009). Desistance and the "feared self": Toward an identity theory of criminal desistance. *The Journal of Criminal Law and Criminology, 99*(4), 1103–1156.

Phillips, J. (2015). Black girls and the (im)possibilities of a victim trope: The intersectional failures of legal and advocacy interventions in the commercial sexual exploitation of minors in the United States. *UCLA Law Review, 62*(6), 1642–1675.

Piquero, A. R. (2004). Somewhere between persistence and desistance: The intermittency of criminal careers. In S. Maruna & R. Immarigeon (Eds.), *After crime and punishment: Pathways to offender reintegration* (pp. 101–120). Portland, OR: Willan Publishing.

Potterat, J. J., Rothenberg, R. B., Muth, S. Q., Darrow, W. W., & Phillips-Plummer, L. (1998). Pathways to prostitution: The chronology of sexual and drug abuse milestones. *The Journal of Sex Research, 35*(4), 333–340. doi:10.1080/00224499809551951

Reid, J. A., & Piquero, A. R. (2014). On the relationship between commercial sexual exploitation/ prostitution, substance dependency, and delinquency in youthful offenders.". *Child Maltreatment, 19*(3–4), 247–260. doi:10.1177/1077559514539752

Robbins, C. A., Martin, S. S., & Surratt, H. L. (2009). Substance abuse treatment, anticipated maternal roles, and reentry success of drug-involved women prisoners. *Crime & Delinquency, 55*(3), 388–411. doi:10.1177/0011128707306688

Rosen, E., & Venkatesh, S. A. (2008). A "perversion" of choice: Sex work offers just enough in Chicago's urban ghetto. *Journal of Contemporary Ethnography, 37*(4), 417–441. doi:10.1177/ 0891241607309879

Sallmann, J. (2010). Living with stigma: Women's experiences of prostitution and substance use. *Journal of Women and Social Work, 25*(2), 146–159. doi:10.1177/0886109910364362

Sampson, R., & Laub, J. (1993). *Crime in the making: Pathways and turning points through life.* Cambridge, MA: Harvard University Press.

Sarteschi, C. M., & Vaughn, M. G. (2010). Double jeopardy: A review of women offenders' mental health and substance abuse characteristics. *Victims and Offenders, 5*(2), 161–182. doi:10.1080/ 15564881003640728

Scott, C. K. (2004). A replicable model for achieving over 90% follow-up rates in longitudinal studies of substance abusers. *Drug and Alcohol Dependence, 74*(1), 21–36. doi:10.1016/j. drugalcdep.2003.12.007

Shdaimah, C. S., & Leon, C. (2015). First and foremost they're survivors: Selective manipulation, resilience, and assertion among prostitute women. *Feminist Criminology, 10*(4), 326–347. doi:10.1177/1557085114553832

Smith, V. C. (2017). Substance-abusing female offenders as victims: Chronological sequencing of pathways into the criminal justice system. *Victims and Offenders, 12*(1), 113–137. doi:10.1080/ 15564886.2015.1017131

U.S. Department of Justice. (2014). *Model state provisions on pimping, pandering, and prostitution.* Retrieved from https://www.justice.gov/olp/model-state-provisions-pimping-pandering-and-prostitution

Wesely, J. K., & Miller, J. M. (2018). Justice system bias perceptions of the dually marginalized: Observations from a sample of women ex-offenders. *Victims and Offenders, 13*(4), 451–470. doi:10.1080/15564886.2017.1362614

Young, A. M., Boyd, C., & Hubbell, A. (2000). Prostitution, drug use, and coping with psychological distress. *Journal of Drug Issues, 30*(4), 789–800. doi:10.1177/002204260003000407

Uncovering Intentions to Exit Prostitution: Findings from a Qualitative Study

Andrea N. Cimino

ABSTRACT

Exiting prostitution is a process for which we have little empirical understanding. This study provides evidence of a process-oriented theory of intentions to exit prostitution that operationalizes key aspects of exiting. Interviews from 16 persons formerly and actively selling sex helped define intentions to exit as a combination of glamorization and risk-recognition attitudes, stigma from significant others, one's own resilient self-efficacy beliefs, and agency. Findings contribute to our understanding of the cognitive changes that occur when a person decides to leave prostitution, which can be used to inform a readiness to exit assessment and interventions that increase intentions to exit.

Street prostitution[1] has garnered attention from scholars, law enforcement, and social service providers with the shared goal of helping women – should they choose – to exit. More so than other types of sex work (Cimino, 2018), street prostitution is associated with violence (Plumridge & Abel, 2001; Seib, Fischer, & Najman, 2009), health threats (Farley et al., 2003), trauma (Raphael & Shapiro, 2004; Surratt, Inciardi, Kurtz, & Kiley, 2004), and psychological effects including depression and suicide (Burnette et al., 2008). As a result, formal exiting interventions, law enforcement-led diversion initiatives, and harm-reduction approaches have been designed to help women to leave prostitution (Mueller, 2012; Preble, Aguirre, & Cimino, 2015). However, there are few theoretical models that explain the street prostitution-exiting process. This qualitative study applies an extension of the Integrative Model of Behavioral Prediction (IMBP) to develop and qualitatively test a theory of intentions to exit street-level prostitution.

Literature review

There is limited but growing literature on what it takes to exit prostitution (Baker, Dalla, & Williamson, 2010; Cimino, 2012; Hedin & Månsson, 2004; Matthews, Easton, Young, & Bindel, 2014; Oselin, 2010; Sanders, 2007). Most scholars agree that exiting street prostitution is more complex than ceasing to sell sex (Dalla, 2006; Saphira & Herbert, 2004; Williamson & Folaron, 2003). One study found that women made five or more attempts over two years to finally exit prostitution (Benoit & Millar, 2001). Barriers to exiting include poverty, mental health and addiction, lack of formal and informal supports,

Color versions of one or more of the figures in the article can be found online at www.tandfonline.com/UVAO.

unaffordable housing, bleak employment opportunities, legal barriers, and stigma (see Baker et al., 2010 for a review). Interventions that include a combination of counseling, housing, employment training, and education address many barriers (Arnold, Stewart, & McNeece, 2000; Mayhew & Mossman, 2007); however, reentry is routine. Less than a third of women successfully exit even with exiting interventions (see Dalla, 2006; Davis, 2000; Saphira & Herbert, 2004), suggesting that alleviating resource-related barriers are not enough. Even criminal sanctions appear ineffective. For example, of 293 women eligible for a comprehensive diversion program in Texas, only 53% (n = 157) chose to enroll, of which 33% (n = 52) completed the program (Felini et al., 2011). Half of the completers (n = 27) were re-arrested after three years, yielding a 16% success rate. These statistics demonstrate that despite prostitution-exiting interventions, some women may not be "ready" or motivated to exit.

Theorizing the street prostitution exiting process

Exiting is a process whereby the realization that selling sex is no longer beneficial and steps are taken to disengage from prostitution. Exiting theories describe women's experiences as they transition out of prostitution and into a conventional lifestyle. Månsson and Hedin (1999) base their breakaway model on role exit theory, whereby turning points introduce doubts about one's identity as a prostitute; these can include positive experiences that give her purpose (e.g., pregnancy) or traumatic events like violence (Oselin, 2010), incarceration (Sanders, 2007), burn out (Vanwesenbeeck, 2005), and/or declining economic viability (Dalla, 2006). Sanders (2007) identified four exiting pathways: (a) *reactionary transition, (b) gradual transition, (c) natural progression, (d) and "yo-yoing"*, and notes that a woman's willingness to change, cut off old ties and develop new ones, and the availability of affordable housing and employment are integral to exiting. In the final stage of Williamson and Folaron (2003) exit-to-entry model, *taking stock and getting out*, occurs as " … the sum total of daily hassles, acute traumas, and chronic conditions" take their toll (*p*. 283). Lastly, Baker et al. (2010) defined stages of exiting starting with visceral or conscious awareness about exiting, deliberate exiting attempts, and a final exit.

These theories acknowledge the complex interplay of structural (e.g., employment, welfare), relational (e.g., family, friends), and individual (e.g., drug and/or mental health treatment, belief in personal change) factors that coalesce to facilitate one's ability to leave prostitution (Cimino, 2012; Hedin & Månsson, 2004; Månsson & Hedin, 1999; Matthews et al., 2014; Williamson & Folaron, 2003). Success often hinges on access to supports and resources (Sanders, 2007). Moreover, women must possess a desire to change (Månsson & Hedin, 1999); in other words, they *must want or intend to leave* prostitution. However, cognitions accompanying this desire are ambiguously defined (e.g., visceral/conscious awareness, internal driving force). As a result, we do not fully understand why some women fail to exit despite making deliberate attempts, such as enrolling in a prostitution-exiting program.

Rationale and theoretical foundation for the current study

While psychosocial changes appear essential to understand the exiting process, research on this aspect is lacking. Moreover, the field lacks theoretical and process-orientated models that can be tested quantitatively (Gerassi, 2015). Without a theoretical and process-oriented model to define the exiting process, we have limited empirical understanding of the factors associated with a successful exit from prostitution and why some women fail to exit despite making deliberate attempts to do so (i.e., enrolling in a prostitution-exiting intervention). Moreover, we do not understand the degree to which structural, relational, or individual factors coalesce, or how to effectively harness supports and services for women who want to exit.

IMPB and its relationship to exiting prostitution

Intentions to Exit Prostitution (IEP) is a theoretical model that aims to explain and predict an actual exit from prostitution. This model synthesized prostitution-exiting literature with the *Integrative Model of Behavioral Prediction* (IMBP), a well-known behavioral prediction model based on the theory of reasoned action, theory of planned behavior, social cognitive theory, and the health belief model, all of which link intention to the actual performance of a behavior (described below). IEP is the only known adaption of IMBP to prostitution-exiting, but IMPB was adapted in over 600 studies (Ajzen, 2010; Francis et al., 2004) predicting related behaviors like leaving an abusive relationship (Byrne & Arias, 2004), perpetrating abuse (Betts, Hinsz, & Heimerdinger, 2011), ceasing violent behavior (Tolman, Edleson, & Fendrich, 1996), and seeking drug treatment (Webb, Sniehotta, & Michie, 2010). IMBP/IEP model and definitions are illustrated in Figure 1.

IMBP says the performance of a behavior requires (1) skills to perform the behavior, (2) a lack of environmental constraints prohibiting the behavior, and (3) the intention to perform the behavior (Fishbein, 2000; Fishbein & Ajzen, 1975; Fishbein et al., 2001). Intention is a key determinant predicting behavior that consists of one's (a) attitudes, (b) norms, and (c) efficacy beliefs about the behavior. If a person has favorable attitudes towards the behavior, experiences social pressure to perform the behavior, and feels efficacious in performing the behavior, they intend to perform the behavior, and will perform the behavior if they have the skills and lack environmental constraints to do so.

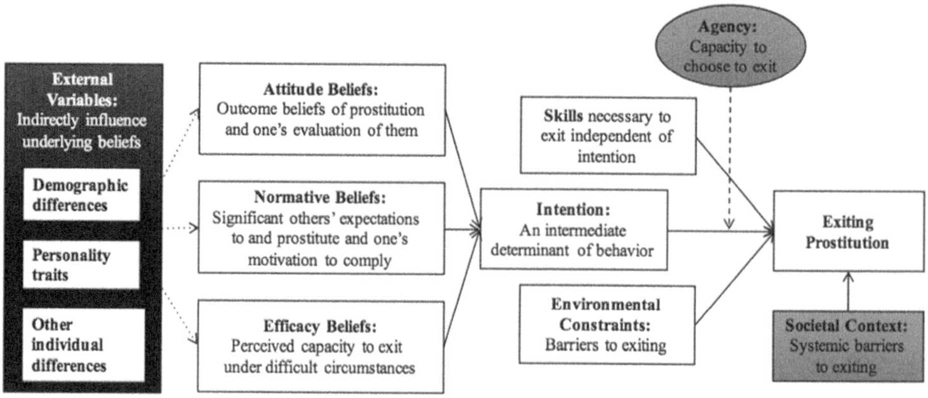

Figure 1. *Intentions to exit prostitution (*Cimino, 2012). Constructs in white are from IMBP (Fishbein, 2000) and those in gray were added to address prostitution-specific phenomenon.

Attitudes are the outcome beliefs of a behavior (i.e., what the behavior results in) and a person's evaluation of those outcomes (i.e., consequences of performing/not performing the behavior). *Norms* refer to significant others' (versus unimportant others) expectation beliefs regarding the behavior and one's motivation to comply with those expectations (akin to social pressure). *Efficacy* is a person's belief that he/she can perform the target behavior under specific barriers or obstacles. IMBP also accounts for demographic differences and personality traits, which may indirectly influence any underlying beliefs.

Intention and its core constructs are where IMBP helps define and measure psychosocial changes required to exit (Cimino, 2012). For instance, *attitude beliefs* are analogous to Baker et al.'s (2010) visceral and conscious awareness about exiting and disillusionment described by Williamson and Folaron (2003). *Normative beliefs* refer to the social/relational influences described by Hedin and Månsson (2004) and Oselin (2010). *Efficacy beliefs* parallel Månsson and Hedin (1999) desire for change. The *skills* and *environmental constraints* constructs represent the individual (e.g., job skills, education) and structural factors (e.g., affordable housing, welfare) that are requisites of exiting identified by Matthews et al. (2014) and Sanders (2007). Lastly, IEP includes the constructs *agency* and *societal context*, which address prostitution-specific experiences, such as a woman's inability to choose to exit (e.g., from severe addiction or pimp-control) and macro/structural conditions (e.g., the economy, criminalization) that affect one's actual ability to leave prostitution, unrelated to her intentions to exit (see gray areas in Figure 1). Intentions to exit (or a lack thereof) may explain high rates of recidivism and unsuccessful exiting attempts among these women (Cimino, 2012, p. 2013).

Purpose of the study

The purpose of the current study is to qualitatively elucidate IEP/IMBP theoretical constructs (i.e., attitude, norm, and efficacy beliefs, agency) related to the prostitution exiting process. The primary benefit of applying theory is to define and eventually measure relevant constructs that may explain and predict an exit from prostitution. Methods to quantify the constructs are described elsewhere (Ajzen & Fishbein, 1980; Fishbein et al., 2001), but the first step is to identify – through qualitative interviews – contextual evidence that the theory fits for prostitution. This study addresses a gap in understanding exiting by focusing on psychosocial shifts, rather than a resource- or skill-related barrier as typically described in the literature and intervention programs. Because skill, environmental, and societal facilitators and barriers are well described in the literature (Baker et al., 2010; Matthews et al., 2014; Oselin, 2010; Sanders, 2007), this study focuses on constructs that underlie or have a relationship with intention.

Methods

The current study reports the qualitative component of an exploratory sequential mixed-methods study (Creswell & Plano Clark, 2011), the purpose of which was to define, operationalize, and quantitatively test a theoretical model of intentions to exit prostitution (Cimino, 2013). The qualitative component sought to identify attitude, norm, and efficacy beliefs specific to exiting prostitution, yet be flexible enough to reveal new relationships and constructs that emerge during the interview process. It was guided by constructivist principles, a feminist methodology that encourages free interaction between researcher and subject, offering an opportunity to discuss and clarify participants' worldviews rather than superimposing dominant cultural assumptions (Reinharz, 1992). All protocols were approved by university Institutional Review Board.

Recruitment

Participants were recruited in 2013 via ads posted in high prostitution neighborhoods, at a support group for women exiting prostitution, and in the "Adult Jobs" section of Backpage.com, a website known to facilitate prostitution. The ads asked persons who "ever engaged in prostitution" to contact the researcher. At the point of contact, participants were told about the study (to understand how people enter and leave prostitution) and were asked what type of prostitution (e.g., on/off-street) they were involved in and for how long, then were invited to participate. Stratified purposeful sampling was used to select participants representing major variations of U.S.-based prostitution (on/off-street; pimp/non-pimp-controlled; see Table 1 for details) and the exiting process (time in/out of prostitution, active vs. exited; Patton, 1990). These differences helped compare and contrast findings ("negative cases"; Lincoln & Guba, 1985) as it is not yet known whether there are subgroup differences in exiting. The sampling method helped strengthen the study's transferability as a proportion of sex workers engage in multiple types of sex work throughout their career (Cronley, Cimino, Hohn, Davis, & Madden, 2016; Sanders, O'Neill, & Pitcher, 2009).

Procedure

Participants were interviewed face-to-face or, if requested, via phone. Interviews followed a narrative tradition to produce stories that flowed from events and actions over a person's life experiences (Polkinghorne, 2010). A semi-structured interview guide was developed

Table 1. Prostitution history of the sample (N = 16).

Name*	Type of sex work	Number of "pimps"	Age of entry	Years in prostitution	Years out of prostitution
Becky	Street	–	37	19	1
Sierra	Pimp-controlled street	3	17	12	0.25
Mara	Street	1 as a partner	15	13	5
Sandy	Street	–	19	24	0.5
Serenity	Street	3 as a partner	10	24	9
Fiona	Pimp-controlled street	5	15	4	0.04
Megan	Online, Street	2 as a partner	20	2	1
Stephon (male)	Street, Online, Street	–	16	10	13
Theresa	Online	–	26	0.25	–
Katy	Online	1 as a partner	23	4	0.25
Donald (male)	Online	–	17	3	2
Mila	Agency, Online	–	20	1	–
Erika	Escort	–	21	16	8
Roxanne	Escort, Online	–	46	3	1
Beth	Escort, Online	–	19	4	1
Brian (male)	"Gigolo"	–	22	6	3
Mean (*SD*)		2.5 (1.5)	21.4 (8.8)	9.1 (8)	3.2 (3.9)

*All names are pseudonyms. *Note*: Pimps are persons living off the earnings of a prostitute. Gigolo refers to a male prostitute.

focusing on the participants' entire prostitution experience (e.g., "how did you first become involved in prostitution?" "what made you decide to leave prostitution?") as well as probes to identify (1) *attitudes*: benefits/advantages and risks/disadvantages of prostitution; (2) *norms*: specific individuals who encouraged their decision to stay/leave prostitution; (3) *efficacy*: situations or circumstances where they might return to prostitution; (4) *agency*: feeling free to choose to exit prostitution. The guide was based on IMBP constructs (see Francis et al., 2004). The use of open-ended questions may have minimized reactivity and researcher biases (Denzin, 1989). Informed consent was provided orally. Compensation was a \$15 gift card. The audio-recorded interviews averaged 71 minutes (R = 45–109 minutes).

Participants

In-depth interviews were conducted with 14 former and 2 active prostitutes, the majority of whom where female (n = 13, 87.5%) and Caucasian (n = 10, 62.5%), followed by non-white Latinas (n = 4, 25%), and African Americans (12.5%). The average age of the sample was 33.8 years old (SD = 11.9; R = 19–57). Two of the three males self-identified as "gay." Half of the women had children (M = 2.4, SD = 1.4). See Table 1 for more information.

Analysis

Because a theory of behavior was already specified, grounded theory's method of inductive theory-building was inappropriate for this study; instead, template analysis (TA) was chosen for its flexibility and use of *a priori* themes (King, 2012; Waring & Wainwright, 2008). Briefly, TA is a qualitative analytic technique whereby the development of themes and the actual coding of text data is guided by a "template" of *a priori* themes (in contrast to open or axial coding). It provides an initial coding structure applied to the data. Rather than discarding data that does not fit, TA encourages modifications to the template, allowing new themes to emerge, or collapsing codes into higher- or lower-order themes, guided by the data and aims of the study. The approach supports feminist research methodologies as it includes non-dominant points of view and honors a marginalized subject's standpoint (Harding, 2004; Reinharz, 1992).

Analysis entailed reading each transcript and coding sections of narratives into *a priori* themes based on IEP/IMBP constructs (i.e., intention, attitude, norms, efficacy, agency). For example, *attitude beliefs* represented participants' perceived benefits/risks of prostitution, *normative beliefs* were the role significant people played in encouraging/discouraging an exit, *efficacy beliefs* were situations that would prompt a return to prostitution, and *agency* referred to whether participants felt forced to engage in prostitution. Also coded were large sections of text containing entry and exit narrative accounts because these often contained key events or catalysts for entering or exiting prostitution and contextualized the theme's relationships to intention.

Once the initial coding was complete, data were reviewed code-by-code to verify assignment to the appropriate theme. Collapsing of codes, identification of new themes, and emerging patterns (e.g., differences by gender or type of prostitution) occurred at this stage. Upon discovery of a new theme, all text was reread and recoded. Two trustworthiness-enhancing strategies were used when coded text did not fit the *a priori* theme: (a) examining previous research to corroborate findings that misaligned with IEP/IMBP, and (b) peer debriefing with an impartial qualitative researcher (no expertise in prostitution) to discuss the meaning of themes and inconsistencies between the findings and IEP/IMBP (Patton, 1999). These methods helped minimize researcher confirmation bias. Data analysis was conducted with Nvivo10 (2012).

Results

Intention

IMBP states that intention to perform a behavior is comprised of a person's attitude, norm, and efficacy beliefs. It is assessed directly (i.e., *"How much do you intend to perform the behavior?"*) or indirectly through semantic differentials (descriptive adjectives). To get at this theme, participants were asked to describe someone who is ready to leave prostitution. Narratives centered on feelings associated with one's desire and readiness to leave prostitution. Becky said, "You gotta want it [to exit] ... that's the only way, because I really haven't seen very many people leave the streets [who didn't want it]." Mara described exiting as an all-or-nothing feeling: "If they're still wanting to [sell sex] a little bit – if they want to at all – they're gonna." She continued: "You have to hate it [prostitution] ... [be] willing to give up everything to not do it again ... down to the clothes on your back." Other sentiments included how beneficial/unbeneficial and necessary/unnecessary it was to prostitute. For example, Sierra recently exited with financial support from her brother, but she always had prostitution to fall back on if it was "necessary". Theresa and Mila were actively selling sex and had no intentions of exiting. Rather, they listed reasons why they are not ready to leave. Quotes from exiters, recent exiters, and non-exiters demonstrate how intentions to exit change over time, by readying oneself to leave.

Attitudes about prostitution: glamorization vs. risk-recognition

Attitudes are (a) outcome beliefs about what will happen if they perform/do not perform the behavior and (b) an evaluation of those outcomes (i.e., whether the outcomes are favorable). For example, believing that prostitution results in violence (outcome) and appraising violence as unfavorable (evaluation) would result in a negative attitude about prostitution's risk of violence. To illuminate this theme, participants were asked to share actual or perceived risks/benefits of prostitution and how those risks/benefits affected their decision to enter or leave prostitution. "Easy money" was the main benefit and motivating factor for getting in, staying in, and returning to prostitution. Donald said: "I did it for money ... that's all it was, just for money." Another benefit was drugs or money for drugs, a truth for on-street workers with drug addictions. "I'd be lying if I said I didn't do \$5 or \$10 blow jobs ... you want the drugs so bad you'll do practically anything," said Becky. The financial lure of prostitution, whether for money or drugs, rarely waned, even after participants exited. Serenity, a successful business owner who exited nearly a decade ago, shared how when her daughter needed money to buy books for college, " ... my mind went straight back to, 'I know how to get this money really quick' ... I was like, 'oh no, where did that [thought] come from?'" Repeat arrests and physical and emotional tolls were other influential outcome beliefs, particularly for on-street workers. Becky was exhausted: "I got so tired of having to be out there … " Mara's "main thing was being arrested … [After] the fourth charge, you get six months [in jail] for each charge. I have 18, so I was in jail constantly."

Attitudes about prostitution changed as the benefits were outweighed by the risks. The main risk was violence. "It goes with the territory … getting beat up, robbed, or raped, you expect that," said Becky. Severe violence – strangulation, rape by weapon, and being thrown from a moving vehicle – was not irregular and most faced violence early on but continued to sell sex anyway. Stephon thought he would be murdered multiple times. "But, here's the other part of that – if you are high enough, you feel like you are 50 feet tall and bulletproof, and it doesn't really matter." Becky also knew the risks, but dismissed its importance initially: "Basically, your life's in your own hands. But it's not because at the time it seems like, 'Well it's okay, I'm doing alright,' but I wasn't." Sierra spoke of a friend who was kidnapped and killed by a customer: "That makes you want to stop, but if you can't stop at that time … you gotta keep working." As the violence inched closer to death, recognition of the risks became harder to deny. "I finally said, you know what – I got to do something. If I don't, I'm going to die," said Becky. "Death was everywhere, that's why I wanted to leave. All I could hear was people dying," said Fiona.

Other benefits were feeling loved and powerful, at least initially. "I thought it was love," said Fiona, "I was fat and ugly when I was little. But with them, people wanting to buy me, that made me feel like I was sexy." Sandy said, " … it makes you feel like you're attractive, but in another way, you feel like a piece of meat, worthless." Sierra mostly enjoyed the lifestyle: "It's like every day you just go to a party." After a while that changed too: "When you're at a certain age you want a certain lifestyle, being gone all day with the pimps and the friends you have … Now that I'm older … I don't party like that no more." Attention, the lifestyle, and other benefits that made prostitution glamorous became less important when risk-recognition increased.

Getting robbed, deserted, or a sexually transmitted disease (STDs) were risks, but more acceptable because they could be managed, ultimately having little impact on attitudes toward prostitution in this sample. Mila learned to collect the money first: "I was putting my pants on … and by the time I got out there, he's gone." Sierra learned not to stray from her neighborhood after a customer took her money, then left her in the middle of nowhere: "You're in a worse predicament than you were first – now you have no money and no ride." Erika said, "Condoms only do so much, and they break, and then there is risk of pregnancy … I've had numerous abortions. That's a risk but that's all part of the job I guess." Becky was "scared of STDs" but didn't care in the face of her addiction: "You want that drug more than you like your life." Erika and Becky "always wore condoms," and even Brian knew to "take some pills." These quotes demonstrate that it is not simply facing a risk or benefit, but how important it is at the time.

Normative beliefs and the role of stigma

Norms refer to (a) significant others' (b) expectations to perform the behavior and (c) one's motivation to comply with those expectations (Figure 2). It focuses on interpersonal interactions, rather than norms embedded in socio-cultural contexts. To understand normative beliefs, participants were asked how important people in their life

Figure 2. *Normative beliefs and role of stigma.* Normative beliefs represent social pressure to engaging in or exiting prostitution.

encouraged or discouraged their involvement in prostitution. They named a cadre of significant persons – partners, friends, family – who, at different times, encouraged, discouraged, or tolerated selling sex. Megan dabbled in prostitution to make ends meet, and briefly stopped after moving in with customer-turned-boyfriend. "He made me feel safe, wanted, protected, and that was everything I was looking for." It changed shortly thereafter. "It didn't matter what I did. I needed to go out and get money … I had to support us. I felt like I had to do it or he wasn't going to care about me as much and be disappointed and upset." Other partners were more overt. Mara's partner would "kick my ass and tell me to make money … it's expected that [you prostitute], not really forced, but it's expected of you after a while." Some partners did not care. A lot of Becky's boyfriends " … didn't say a lot, didn't really care either way." Usually, partners of the off-street workers pressured them to exit. Roxanne married her former client on the condition that she left prostitution: "I may have done one or two calls after him, and he was not happy." Katy's husband supported whatever she decided: "He didn't want me to have to do it … [but] he understood [if I did] … we have an understanding relationship like that."

Generally, participants surrounded themselves with friends who supported their intention, whether it was to stay or exit. Several participants stopped associating with friends who weren't selling sex. The evolution of Roxanne and Beth's friendship demonstrates how friends could encourage and later discourage one's involvement in prostitution. They met at an agency where Roxanne took Beth under her wing, teaching her how to prostitute safely. They quit together, posted ads online, and were each other's bodyguard. After being arrested in a prostitution sting, they exited together. When Beth contemplated returning, she would call Roxanne: "I wanted to go back but didn't because she brought up one of my bad experiences and I was like, 'Yeah, that's not a good idea.'" Other exiters spoke about the dangers of associating with friends who were selling sex. Fiona said, "I thought they were my family … I missed them, that's [why I went back to prostitution]." Even minor contact was problematic: "I've seen the best go out there after they've stopped … they're out there one day to just say 'hello' and they never leave," said Becky.

Family relationships were strained and typically had little effect. Sierra's parents "disowned" her after her teen pregnancy, becoming a catalyst to sell sex. She has no relationship with her parents and lost custody of her child, hence family never factored into her normative beliefs. Megan's family knew what she was doing but did not try to stop her: "They knew that if they couldn't help me with my drug addiction, they couldn't help with anything else I was doing because of it or during it." Other participants lied about or hid their prostitution from family, which diminished any influence, for a time. For years, Stephon hid from his mom until his addiction hit rock bottom: "I didn't want my mother to get a phone call that they found me dead with a needle in my arm in some trick's house." Sandy abandoned her one-year-old twins. She was too "ashamed and uncomfortable" to keep in touch with them: "It makes you feel like a piece of crap because you don't know what to say to your children," those feelings played a part in her reentry. Becky sold sex on the street with her daughters; her eldest daughter even begged her for drug money so she wouldn't have to sell sex. It was the children who found out and judged participants for selling sex that became a catalyst to exit. After Mara was arrested in front of her son, she said, "That was it. I was done. He was four … he still remembers it. He still talks about it to this day." Roxanne's two sons discovered her Backpage.com ad: "My younger son didn't judge me, but my older son judged me very hard … that was a real strong pull to get out."

Stigma

Clearly, these quotes illustrate that IMBP's conceptualization of norms was missing the power of stigma, the identity-damaging social and psychological rejection from being associated with prostitution (Goffman, 1963). Stigma can be *felt/internalized* (e.g., perceived disappointment, feeling judged or embarrassed) like it was for Stephon, or *enacted* (e.g., not allowed to talk to children or family, turned away from places) as in Roxanne's case. Prostitution-related stigma results in social isolation, burnout, and other psychological sequelae (Bradley, 2007; Sallmann, 2010; Tomura, 2009; Vanwesenbeeck, 2005). It has been linked to avoidance of help-seeking behaviors (Lazarus et al., 2012; Weiner, 1996) and even treatment dropout (Roe-Sepowitz, Hickle, & Cimino, 2012), which can make maintaining a prostitution-free life difficult (Mayhew & Mossman, 2007). Hiding or lying, selectively disclosing it to trusted others, or creating an alternative identity ("sex worker self") are ways to deal with stigma (Koken, 2012). While disengaging from significant others helped avoid stigma, it insulated participants from normative pressure to exit. Moreover, it drew some participants closer to friends and partners who encouraged selling sex. Stigma, then, moderates the relationship between norms and intentions (see last construct in Figure 2), which is why Stephon 's fear of his mom finding him dead at a trick's house made him exit, whereas Katy's partner who didn't care and Becky's daughters who also sold sex had no effect. Enacted stigma had the strongest effect as evidenced by Roxanne's oldest son who stopped talking to her; until then, she successfully concealed her sex work.

Efficacy: certainty or resilience?

According to IMBP, efficacy is how much a person believes that he/she can perform the behavior under specific barriers or obstacles, assuming a sense of competence in one's ability. To draw out this theme, participants were asked to describe situations where it would be hard to resist selling sex. Generally, two situations were identified: sex for survival (e.g., food, shelter) or to feed an addiction. These were situations where participants had no choice but to sell sex; hence, instead of certainty and competence, they described diminished agency (e.g., inability to make a behavioral choice, described below). Efficacy did not fit. Post-initial analysis, I returned to the literature for guidance. Several studies described participants hoping and fantasizing about a more positive future (Hedin & Månsson, 2004) or changing their identity to reflect who they wish to become (Baker et al., 2010; Dodsworth, 2011). Fiona echoed this: "until you get that feeling that 'I really can't do this; I want more for myself,' no one can tell you anything [to change your mind]." Peer debriefing helped clarify that these thoughts were be a combination of *resilience*, broadly referring to one's "capacity to deal with, overcome, learn from, or even be transformed by the inevitable adversities of life" (Gortberg, 2003, p. 4) and *self-efficacy*, one's beliefs about his/her capability to change in life (Bandura, 1993). Self-efficacy literature describes highly resilient persons as those who believe they are able to change their environment despite challenges and setbacks (Schwarzer & Warner, 2013); in contrast, people who are plagued with self-doubt lose faith in their abilities and fail to make change (Bandura, 1993). Therefore, what Fiona and others were describing was *resilient self-efficacy*, the notion that in spite of challenging circumstance, I believe I can do better and I deserve better.

Dodsworth's (2011) study on vulnerability to prostitution described a phenomenon that could be characterized as resilient self-efficacy. She found that one's decision to stay in or exit prostitution was based on the meaning they ascribed to adversity/risk and their identity to victimhood, yielding three categories of sex worker-identities: (1) it's who I am, (2) it's what I do, not who I am, and (3) I can't let it be who I am. Those in the last category (i.e., highly resilient self-efficacy) saw "an alternative life as a possibility and themselves deserving it" (*p.* 13). Upon re-analyzing the narratives, all of the exiters exemplified resilient self-efficacy to some degree. Fiona said, "I'm not spending eternity in some shithole … I just wanna be happy." Stephon said, "I have a whole life to live, and I want to live it and see what's out there." Becky said, "I can't get back into that shit … it's not a good life … I know there's something better than this." To confirm that resilient self-efficacy was the appropriate exposition, I sought instances where the opposite was true (i.e., negative case analysis; Lincoln & Guba, 1985). Mila and Theresa, the active sellers, lacked resilient self-efficacy – neither believed they deserved anything else, even after taking steps to change their situation. Theresa, a Certified Nursing Assistant, couldn't find work even at McDonald's:

> … I dressed really nice, had great interviewing skills and I never got a call back once. It was really discouraging because I always worked in hospitals … I always thought people that worked in fast food it must be easy for them to get a job, like anyone could work there. And it made me feel like a piece of crap because I couldn't get a job [at McDonald's]. And I tried for a long time to get a job … just something to pay rent. That was another factor that influenced my decision to go into [prostitution].

The setback diminished her perceived capabilities and self-worth, in spite of her degree and skill.

Agency

An assumption of IMBP is that a person has volitional control to perform the behavior. For a variety of reasons, exiting prostitution may not be within a person's control. To account for this, *agency* was added in IEP. It is defined as to one's capacity to make behavioral choices without force (Cimino, 2012); therefore, agency is independent of intention. To explore this theme, participants were asked whether they felt forced to prostitute. Pimp-controlled prostitution was the most blatant example. A stranger drugged Mara and forced her to prostitute in a hotel room. Serenity was "trapped" in prostitution because her partner beat her, threaten to kill her, and forced her to sell sex: "If I didn't come back [to him], then I was on the run, and he told me he would find me … there was no getting out of there." Choosing to act on their intentions to exit was outside of their control. Others felt forced to prostitute for survival (e.g., food, place to stay, or drugs). Roxanne "had a strong desire to get out [of prostitution] the whole time," but sold sex because she "just had to survive." After a close call, Katy had strong reservations against seeing a new client: "I did it anyway because I had 5 cents on my debit card." Serenity broke two years of prostitution sobriety for "just enough money to pay rent." Stephon's drug addiction was "an internal force." He said " … if you want to support this habit, you have to [sell sex], so I did." Becky agreed: " … my pimp was my addiction." Those who did not have pimps, addictions, or face housing instability had more agency. Theresa sold sex for "miscellaneous financial obligations," saying: "I definitely feel like it's up to me when I want to stop. There's nothing to make me not stop … with a pay-as-you-go phone, I can just turn it off."

It is important to note that agency differs from norms because it refers to one's actual ability to stop prostituting, not merely a motivation to comply with social expectations. Mara illustrated this key point. She escaped the stranger who drugged her and forced her to sell sex in a hotel room but decided to sell sex on her own. As her prostitution career progressed, she remarked that her son's father and friends expected her to prostitute: " … they start depending on you a little bit for this and that and the next thing you know it's expected of you." Mara was *expected* to sell sex, *not forced*, demarking a clear contrast from her earlier experience.

A theory of intentions to exit prostitution: the full theoretical model

Thus far, each IEP construct related to intention and its nuances have been described. Some aspects may more strongly influence one's intentions to exit, but it is the coalescence of factors in the full model that facilitate an actual exit from prostitution (see Figure 3). We can see this in Megan's story. Her friends "brought up the idea" of selling sex (norms). Megan got money, attention, drugs, plus "mak[ing] other people happy" felt good (glamorizing attitudes). She didn't experience stigma – her family knew but didn't stop her and her boyfriend drove her to see clients. "Of course there were risks," but " … that will never happen to me … I'm smarter than that." Then she was at client's house in middle of nowhere when he became hostile: "No one will know I am here or what I am doing, and that was the first time I had ever experienced that fear" (risk-recognition). Her boyfriend became mentally and physically abusive, eventually pimping her. She wanted to

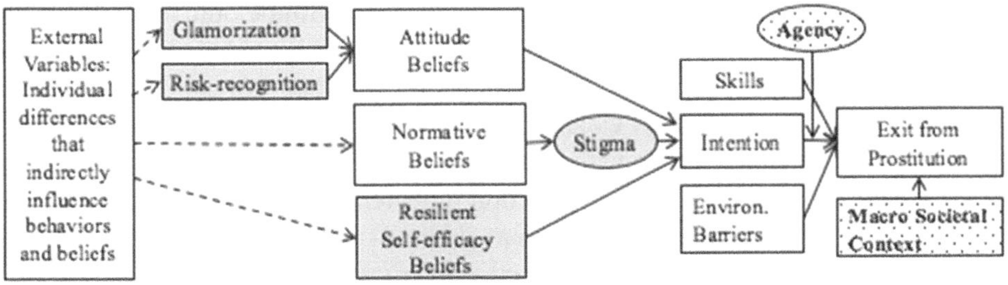

Figure 3. *The revised intentions to exit prostitution theoretical model.* Constructs in white are from IMBP (Fishbein, 2000), dotted constructs are from preliminary theoretical work (Cimino, 2012), and those in gray are from the current study.

quit but couldn't (agency). Unbeknownst to Megan, he was arrested for forgery. She feared running into him and having to sell sex: "I wasn't willing to go back into the lifestyle I was living" (risk-recognition). "I know my life is valuable and I don't need somebody to validate who I am and what I need to be doing with my life ... I do have a life worthy of living" (resilient self-efficacy). Megan now lives in transitional housing, no longer relying on friends or boyfriend-pimps (environmental barrier). She finished a drug treatment program and enrolled in a jobs program that helped her secure legal employment (skills).

Appropriateness for women attempting to exit street-level prostitution

This study was designed primarily with women engaged in street-level prostitution; outcome beliefs and motivations may differ for different populations. For instance, off-street vs. on-street workers make emotional investments with customers (Lever & Dolnick, 2000). Off-street workers in this study like Mila, glamorized being "treated like a princess" by from gifts, fine dining, and exotic travel, whereas on-street workers had quick and anonymous customer contact. Street workers also experience more extreme and frequent violence (Plumridge & Abel, 2001; Raphael & Shapiro, 2004; Seib et al., 2009), and risk of murder vastly influenced their intentions to exit. Off-street workers tended to acknowledge violence as a possibility, but most downplayed its significance; for them, stigma and emotional risks were omnipresent. Gender differences also emerged. Male participants enjoyed the physical act of sex, which never faded. Women enjoyed the emotional aspects, namely feeling wanted and valued, which did fade. A more demographically diverse sample would likely yield other outcome beliefs. For instance, transwomen of color may perceive risks and benefits differently because they face higher levels of violence and stigma and have less mobility to exit prostitution than persons included in this study (Sausa, Keatley, & Operario, 2007). Regardless, the data here show that evaluative aspects of one's attitudes, motivation to comply with significant persons, and resilient beliefs all play a role in increasing one's intentions to exit and change over time.

Discussion

The aim of this study was to provide qualitative evidence testing a theory of intentions to exit prostitution. Participants described intention as an all-or-nothing desire to leave prostitution. Narratives revealed that intention to exit was brought on by disillusionment with the glamorizing or positive benefits of prostitution as the risks and negative outcomes became more evident. Existing literature corroborates the attitude outcome beliefs identified here (e.g., money, violence, lifestyle, etc.) but this study added that a person can simultaneously acknowledge a risky behavioral outcome but disregard its impact and importance (or vice versa) – e.g., violence happens, but not to me; STDs and unwanted pregnancies happen but it "goes with the territory." Sexual health risks were not universally salient as touted in harm reduction interventions (Rekart, 2005); therefore, messaging on risk should be carefully presented based on underlying beliefs.

Existing literature highlights the role social supports have on increasing one's ability to exit (Hedin & Månsson, 2004; Sanders, 2007). However, participants in this study surrounded themselves with significant others who supported their current action, whether that was to remain selling sex or to exit, making norms fluid and inconsistent. Other studies adapting IMBP also found this inconsistency (Ajzen, 1991). Stigma was an essential element of norms as participants were largely unaffected by normative beliefs to exit until they faced stigma. This finding diverged from literature on prostitution-related stigma as it suggests a positive effect of stigma – increasing one's intention to exit. Research on the relationship between stigma and intention to exit is needed as other evidence suggests that stigma diminishes one's ability to exit and affects other help-seeking behaviors (Lazarus et al., 2012; Weiner, 1996).

Finally, two new constructs – agency and resilient self-efficacy – were added to address adaptations of IMBP to prostitution-exiting. Agency, an IEP construct that accounts for a lack of volitional control, reflected an inability to act on one's intention because of pimp-control, addiction, or survival needs (Cimino, 2012). Pimps use a variety of tactics including love, debt, drugs, brute force/violence, and authority to maintain control (Kennedy, Klein, Bristowe, Cooper, & Yuille, 2007); identifying these techniques are needed to properly address lack of agency due to pimp control. Exiting interventions offering housing and substance use treatment can alleviate agency-related barriers (Arnold et al., 2000). Resilient self-efficacy, the notion that in spite of challenging circumstance, I believe I can do better and deserve better, was added to address shortcomings of IMBP's conceptualization of efficacy. Resilient self-efficacy reflects prostitution literature that notes the importance of a desire to change one's identity and life to something more positive among women who have exited (Baker et al., 2010; Dodsworth, 2011; Hedin & Månsson, 2004). These modifications helped fine tune the IEP theoretical model; future quantitative studies based on these concepts with larger samples are needed and can offer more valid and reliable conclusions.

Implications for research

This study fills a gap in the literature calling for a theoretical and process-orientated model to explain exiting (Gerassi, 2015). The IEP model includes the individual, relational, and structural factors related to exiting described throughout extant literature. This study's qualitative test case of the model offers operationalized constructs that can inform a quantitative assessment that weighs the degree to which these factors are associated with an actual exit from prostitution. Research is needed to create and validate items measuring the constructs identified in the current study. The wording of questions and ways to scale each of the IMBP constructs include the use of complex, two-part unipolar and bipolar evaluative scales (Ajzen & Fishbein, 1980; Fishbein et al., 2001) that need extensive field testing to ensure readability for women in prostitution who may struggle with literacy. Instrument validation studies require large sample sizes for statistical power that may be difficult to obtain given the hidden and stigmatized nature of prostitution. Regardless of logistical barriers, a quantitative readiness to exit assessment could have far-reaching theoretical and clinical implications for this group of highly vulnerable women.

Implications for practice

Currently, there are no valid measures to assess readiness to exit prostitution, rendering programs serving this population with two serious disadvantages: first, they could be providing the wrong type of services, and second, they may be expending resources on participants who are not ready to leave prostitution. A thoroughly tested and validated assessment based on IEP can help identify which beliefs to target (i.e., attitudes, norms, efficacy, etc.) in an intervention, such as a communication campaign (Ajzen, 2011; Yzer, 2012) or decision aids (Stacey et al., 2014). Communication campaigns use underlying beliefs to inform behavioral change, for instance, to challenge glamorizing attitudes towards prostitution, combat normative pressure, and/or address low resilient self-efficacy beliefs. Some outcome beliefs, like the monetary value of selling sex, may never change, but communication campaigns are designed to increase cognitive dissonance between benefits and risks. Likewise, decision aids can help weigh the benefits and harms of a particular decision. For instance, decision aids created for intimate partner violence (IPV) help victims understand their risk for repeat and near-lethal IPV, clarify safety priorities, and develop a customized action plan to meet these priorities (Eden et al., 2015). A similar tool based on the IEP could be developed for street-level prostitution. Moreover, a thoroughly tested and validated IEP instrument may function as a readiness to exit assessment, helping practitioners assess where a person is on a continuum of readiness to exit prostitution. Administering the assessment before and after an intervention could help criminal justice departments and social services assess incremental changes in underlying beliefs, assist in treatment planning, and demonstrate a program's effectiveness and accountability (Cimino, 2012).

Limitations

A limitation of qualitative research is that there are no quantitative criteria to measure quality and draw generalizable conclusions. Qualitative studies cannot achieve validity and reliability as in quantitative research, but rather seek rigor and accountability in how the data were collected and interpreted ("trustworthiness"; Lincoln & Guba, 1985; Patton, 1999). This study used a small and varied sample; comparing results to active, male, and off-street sex workers (negative case analysis) may have increased study rigor and transferability, showing that the findings fit as intended with street-level prostitution. However, more research is needed with larger homogeneous samples, which could yield more replicable or consistent findings. Evidence for IEP was based on literature and interviews focused primarily on US street-level prostitution and may not be generalizable to international sex trafficking or sex work in countries where cultural and social mores likely affect attitudes and behaviors. For example, in Taiwan prostitution includes flirting, dancing, and sharing drinks (Hwang & Bedford, 2004). Other differences may emerge where sex work is legalized or culturally legitimized. Future research should be conducted with more diverse samples (e.g., transgender) as the exiting process may be different. These limitations should not deter scholars from applying a similar model to other populations. Another limitation of this study is that the results focus on the perspective of persons who have exited prostitution and may not be comprehensive of all beliefs, particularly those who have not exited. Regardless, findings showed support for IEP's basic constructs and their relationships. Relatedly, because only the author coded the data, credibility (internal validity) of findings may be threatened; future studies should have multiple coders or use member checking to reduce confirmation bias in the author's interpretation (Patton, 1999).

Conclusion

This study extends current evidence on the prostitution exiting process by offering a process-oriented and nuanced understanding of the gradual psychosocial shifts preceding one's decision to leave street-level prostitution. Understanding why women cycle in and out of prostitution is integral to reducing the number of unsuccessful exiting attempts made by most women engaged in street-level prostitution. Each failed exiting attempt means a person is selling sex longer, and therefore exposed to more risks. If a person chooses to exit prostitution, then providing them with the best possible intervention is a professional responsibility. Understanding the exiting process is essential to designing evidence-based interventions for this highly vulnerable group and addresses a significant gap in the field.

Note

1. The term "prostitution" (vs. "sex work") is intentionally used throughout this study to refer to oppressive and exploitative commercial sex trade markets (specifically, street-level) instead of indoor sex work markets where the term "sex work" is commonly used. This is because street-level prostitution has highest rates of violence, illegality, and diminished agency/autonomy, whereas the term "sex work" implies workers have the ability to enter/exit more easily than women engaged in street-level prostitution. See Cimino (2018) and Sanders et al. (2009) for philosophical distinction and delineation of sex trade markets.

Disclosure statement

No potential conflict of interest was reported by the author.

Funding

This research was supported by the Arizona State University Graduate College's Doctoral Dissertation Fellowship (2012–2013) and the Arizona Board of Regents' Doctoral Research Grant (2013).

References

Ajzen, I. (1991). The theory of planned behavior. *Organizational Behavior and Human Decision Processes, 50*, 179–211. doi:10.1016/0749-5978(91)90020-T

Ajzen, I. (2010). *The theory of planned behavior: A bibliography complied by Icek Ajzen*. Retrieved from http://www.people.umass.edu/aizen/tpbrefs.html

Ajzen, I. (2011). Behavioral interventions: Design and evaluation guided by the theory of planned behavior. In M. M. Mark, S. I. Donaldson, & B. C. Campbell (Eds.), *Social psychology for program and policy evaluation* (pp. 74–100). New York, USA: Guilford.

Ajzen, I., & Fishbein, M. (1980). *Understanding attitudes and predicting social behavior*. Englewood Cliffs, NJ: Prentice-Hall.

Arnold, E. M., Stewart, J. C., & McNeece, C. A. (2000). The psychological treatment need of street-walking prostitutes: Perspectives from a case management program. *Journal of Offender Rehabilitation, 30*(3), 117–132. doi:10.1300/J076v30n03_06

Baker, L. M., Dalla, R. L., & Williamson, C. (2010). Exiting prostitution: An integrated model. *Violence Against Women, 16*(5), 579–600. doi:10.1177/1077801210367643

Bandura, A. (1993). Perceived self-efficacy in cognitive development and functioning. *Educational Psychologist, 28*(2), 117–148. doi:10.1207/s15326985ep2802_3

Benoit, C., & Millar, A. (2001). *Dispelling myths and understanding realities: Working conditions, health status, and exiting experiences of sex workers*. Funded by BC Health Research Foundation, Capital Health District, and BC Centre of Excellence on Women's Health. Retrieved from http://dspace.library.uvic.ca/bitstream/handle/1828/7473/Benoit_Cecilia_DispellingMyths_2001.pdf?sequence=1&isAllowed=y

Betts, K. R., Hinsz, V. B., & Heimerdinger, S. R. (2011). Predicting intentions of romantic partner abuse with the theory of planned behavior. *Current Psychology, 30*(2), 130–147. doi:10.1007/s12144-011-9105-2

Bradley, M. S. (2007). Girlfriends, wives and strippers: Managing stigma in exotic dancer romantic relationships. *Deviant Behavior, 28*, 379–406. doi:10.1080/01639620701233308

Burnette, M. L., Lucas, E., Ilgen, M., Frayne, S. M., Mayo, J., & Weitlauf, J. C. (2008). Prevalence and health correlates of prostitution among patients entering treatment for substance use disorders. *Archives of General Psychiatry, 65*(3), 337–344. doi:10.1001/archpsyc.65.3.337

Byrne, C. A., & Arias, I. (2004). Predicting women's intentions to leave abusive relationships: An application of the theory of planned behavior1. *Journal of Applied Social Psychology, 34*(12), 2586–2601. doi:10.1111/jasp.2004.34.issue-12

Cimino, A. N. (2012). A predictive theory of intentions to exit street-level prostitution. *Violence against Women, 10*(8), 1235–1252. doi:10.1177/1077801212465153

Cimino, A. N. (2013). *Developing and testing a theory of intentions to exit street-level prostitution: A mixed methods study* (Doctoral dissertation). Arizona State University, Tempe, AZ. Retrieved from ProQuest.

Cimino, A. N. (2018). Sex work and adult prostitution: From entry to exit. In M. Bourke & V. Van Hasselt (Eds.), *Handbook of behavioral criminology: Contemporary strategies and issues*. New York, NY: Springer Publishing.

Creswell, J. W., & Plano Clark, V. L. (2011). *Designing and conducting mixed methods research*. Thousand Oaks, CA: Sage Publications.

Cronley, C., Cimino, A. N., Hohn, K., Davis, J., & Madden, E. (2016). Entering sex work in adolescence: Youth homelessness predicts earlier entry into prostitution. *Journal of Aggression, Maltreatment & Trauma, 25*(9), 893–908. doi:10.1080/10926771.2016.1223246

Dalla, R. L. (2006). *Exposing the "pretty woman" myth: A qualitative investigation of street-level prostituted women*. Lanham, MD: Lexington Books.

Davis, N. J. (2000). From victims to survivors: Working with recovering street prostitutes. In R. Weitzer (Ed.), *Sex for Sale* (pp. 139–155). New York, USA: Routledge.

Denzin, N. K. (1989). *Interpretive interactionism*. Newbury Park, CA: Sage Publications.

Dodsworth, J. (2011). Pathways through sex work: Childhood experiences and adult identities. *British Journal of Social Work*, 1–18. doi:10.1093/bjsw/bcr077

Eden, K. B., Perrin, N. A., Hanson, G. C., Messing, J. T., Bloom, T. L., Campbell, J. C.,... Glass, N. E. (2015). Use of online safety decision aid by abused women: Effect on decisional conflict in a randomized controlled trial. *American Journal of Preventive Medicine, 48*(4), 372–383.

Farley, M., Cotton, A., Lynne, J., Zumbeck, S., Spiwak, F., Reyes, M. E., ... Sezgin, U. (2003). Prostitution and trafficking in nine countries: Update on violence and posttraumatic stress disorder. *The Journal of Trauma and Practice, 2*(3/4), 33–74. doi:10.1300/J189v02n03_03

Felini, M., Qualls-Hampton, R., Ryan, E., Kader, E., Coleman, M., & Costa, J. (2011). *Prostitution diversion initiative annual report: 2010–2011*. Dallas, TX: Dallas Police Department. Retrieved from http://www.pdinewlife.org/wp-content/uploads/2012/05/PDI-Annual-Report-2010-2011f.pdf

Fishbein, M. (2000). The role of theory in HIV prevention. *AIDS Care, 12*(3), 273–278. doi:10.1080/09540120050042918

Fishbein, M., & Ajzen, I. (1975). *Belief, attitude, intention, and behavior: An introduction to theory and research*. Reading, MA: Addison-Wesley.

Fishbein, M., Triandis, C. H., Kanfer, F. H., Becker, M., Middlestadt, S. S., & Eichler, A. (2001). Factors influencing behavior and behavior change. In A. A. Baum, T. A. Reveneson, & J. E. Singer (Eds.), *Handbook of health psychology* (pp. 3–17). Mahwah, NJ: Lawrence Erlbaum.

Francis, J., Eccles, M. P., Johnston, M., Walker, A., Grimshaw, J., Foy, R., … Bonetti, D. (2004). *Constructing questionnaires with the theory of planned behaviour*. Retrieved from http://www.gvo.unimaas.nl/Onderwijs/Francis2004.pdf

Gerassi, L. (2015). From exploitation to industry: Definitions, risks, and consequences of domestic sexual exploitation and sex work among women and girls. *Journal of Human Behavior in the Social Environment, 26*(6), 591–605. doi:10.1080/10911359.2014.991055

Goffman, E. (1963). *Stigma: Notes on the management of spoiled identity*. Englewood Cliffs, NJ: Prentice-Hall.

Gortberg, H. (2003). *Resilience for today: Gaining strength from adversity* (pp. 4–5). Westport, CT: Praeger Publisher.

Harding, S. (2004). *The feminist standpoint theory reader: Intellectual and political controversies*. New York, NY: Routledge.

Hedin, U. C., & Månsson, S. A. (2004). The importance of supportive relationships among women leaving prostitution. *Journal of Trauma Practice, 2*(3), 223–237. doi:10.1300/J189v02n03_13

Hwang, S. L., & Bedford, O. (2004). Juveniles' motivations for remaining in prostitution. *Psychology of Women Quarterly, 28*(2), 136–146. doi:10.1111/j.1471-6402.2004.00130.x

Kennedy, M. A., Klein, C., Bristowe, J. T. K., Cooper, B. S., & Yuille, J. C. (2007). Routes of recruitment: Pimps' techniques and other circumstances that lead to street prostitution. *Journal of Aggression, Maltreatment & Trauma, 15*(2), 1–19. doi:10.1300/J146v15n02_01

King, N. (2012). Doing template analysis. In C. Cassell & G. Symon (Eds.), *Qualitative organizational research* (pp. 426–450). London, UK: Sage.

Koken, J. A. (2012). Independent female escort's strategies for coping with sex work related stigma. *Sexuality and Culture, 16*(3), 209–229. doi:10.1007/s12119-011-9120-3

Lazarus, L., Deering, K. N., Nabess, R., Gibson, K., Tyndall, M. W., & Shannon, K. (2012). Occupational stigma as a primary barrier to health care for street-based sex workers in Canada. *Culture, Health & Sexuality, 14*(2), 139–150. doi:10.1080/13691058.2011.628411

Lever, J., & Dolnick, D. (2000). Clients and call girls: Seeking sex and intimacy. In R. Weitzer (Ed.), *Sex for sale* (pp. 85–100). New York, NY: Routledge.

Lincoln, Y., & Guba, E. (1985). *Naturalistic inquiry*. Beverly Hills, CA: Sage.

Månsson, S. A., & Hedin, U. C. (1999). Breaking the Matthew Effect on women leaving prostitution. *International Journal of Social Welfare, 8*, 67–77. doi:10.1111/1468-2397.00063

Matthews, R., Easton, H., Young, L., & Bindel, J. (2014). *Exiting Prostitution: A study in female desistance*. New York, NY: Palgrave MacMillan.

Mayhew, P., & Mossman, D. (2007). *Exiting prostitution: Models of best practice*. Wellington, New Zealand: Crime and Justice Research Centre, Victoria University of Wellington.

Mueller, D. (2012). *Treatment courts and court-affiliated diversion projects for prostitution in the United States: A report from the prostitution alternatives roundtable of the Chicago coalition for the homeless*. Chicago, IL: Chicago Coalition for the Homeless.

NVivo qualitative data analysis software. (2012). *QSR international Pty Ltd. Version 10*. QSR International Pty Ltd. Retrieved from https://www.qsrinternational.com/nvivo/support-overview/faqs/how-do-i-cite-qsr-software-in-my-work

Oselin, S. S. (2010). Weighing the consequences of a deviant career: Factors leading to an exit from prostitution. *Sociological Perspectives, 53*(4), 527–549.

Patton, M. (1990). Purposeful sampling. In M. Patton (Ed.), *Qualitative evaluation and research methods* (pp. 169–186). Beverly Hills, CA: Sage.

Patton, M. Q. (1999). Enhancing the quality and credibility of qualitative analysis. *Health Services Research, 34*, 1189–1208. doi:10.4135/9781412985727

Plumridge, L., & Abel, G. (2001). A 'segmented' sex industry in New Zealand: Sexual and personal safety of female sex workers. *Australian and New Zealand Journal of Public Health, 25*(1), 78–83.

Polkinghorne, D. E. (2010). The practice of narrative. *Narrative Inquiry, 20*(2), 392–396.

Preble, K., Aguirre, R. T. P., & Cimino, A. N. (2015). Supportive exits: A best practices report for a sex worker intervention. *Journal of Human Behavior in the Social Environment, 26*(2), 162–178. doi:10.1080/10911359.2015.1082852

Raphael, J., & Shapiro, D. L. (2004). Violence in indoor and outdoor prostitution venues. *Violence Against Women, 10*(2), 126–139. doi:10.1177/1077801203260529

Reinharz, S. (1992). *Feminist methods in social research.* New York, NY: Oxford University Press.

Rekart, M. (2005). Sex-work harm reduction. *The Lancet, 366*, 2123–2134.

Roe-Sepowitz, D., Hickle, K., & Cimino, A. N. (2012). The impact of abuse history and trauma symptoms on successful completion of a prostitution-exiting program. *Journal of Human Behavior in the Social Environment, 22*(1), 65–77. doi:10.1080/10911359.2011.598830

Sallmann, J. (2010). Living with stigma: Women's experiences of prostitution and substance use. *Affilia: Journal of Women and Social Work, 25*(2), 146–159.

Sanders, T. (2007). Becoming an ex-sex worker: Making transitions out of a deviant career. *Feminist Criminology, 2*, 74–95. doi:10.1177/1557085106294845

Sanders, T., O'Neill, M., & Pitcher, J. (2009). *Prostitution: Sex work, policy & politics.* Thousand Oaks, CA: Sage.

Saphira, M., & Herbert, A. (2004). *Exiting commercial sexual activity.* Retrieved from http://www.ecpat.org.nz/Other/Researches/ExitingCommercialSexualActivity.asp

Sausa, L. A., Keatley, J., & Operario, D. (2007). Perceived risks and benefits of sex work among trans women of color in San Francisco. *Archives of Sexual Behavior, 36*(6), 768–777.

Schwarzer, R., & Warner, L. M. (2013). Perceived self-efficacy and its relationship to resilience. In S. Prince-Embury & H. D. Saklofske (Eds.), *Resilience in children, adolescents, and adults: Translating research into practice* (pp. 139–150). New York, NY: Springer.

Seib, C., Fischer, J., & Najman, J. M. (2009). The health of female sex workers from three industry sectors in Queensland, Australia. *Social Science and Medicine, 68*, 473–478.

Stacey, D., Légaré, F., Lewis, K., Barry, M. J., Bennett, C. L.,Eden, K. B., ... Trevena, L. (2014). Decision aids for people facing health treatment or screening decisions. *Cochrane Database of Systematic Reviews, 2017*(1), Art. No. CD001431. doi:10.1002/14651858.CD001431.pub5

Surratt, H. L., Inciardi, J. A., Kurtz, S. P., & Kiley, M. C. (2004). Sex work and drug use in a subculture of violence. *Crime and Delinquency, 50*(1), 43–59.

Tolman, R. M., Edleson, J. L., & Fendrich, M. (1996). Applicability of theory of planned behavior to abusive men's cessation of violent behavior. *Violence & Victims, 11*, 341–354.

Tomura, M. (2009). A prostitute's lived experiences of stigma. *Journal of Phenomenological Psychology, 40*(1), 51–84. doi:10.1163/156916209X427981

Vanwesenbeeck, I. (2005). Burnout among female indoor sex workers. *Archives of Sexual Behavior, 34*(6), 627–639. doi:10.1007/s10508-005-7912-y

Waring, T., & Wainwright, D. (2008). Issues and challenges in the use of template analysis: Two case studies from the field. *Electronic Journal of Business Research Method, 6*(1), 85–94.

Webb, T. L., Sniehotta, F. F., & Michie, S. (2010). Using theories of behaviour change to inform interventions for addictive behaviours. *Addiction, 105*(11), 1879–1892.

Weiner, A. (1996). Understanding the social needs of streetwalking prostitutes. *Social Work, 41*, 457–479.

Williamson, C., & Folaron, G. (2003). Understanding the experiences of street level prostitutes. *Quaitative Social Work, 2*(3), 271–287. doi:10.1177/14733250030023004

Yzer, M. (2012). The integrated model of behavioral prediction as a tool for designing health messages. In H. Cho (Ed.), *Health communication message design* (pp. 21–40). Los Angeles, CA: Sage.

"It's like Being an Electrician, You're Gonna Get Shocked": Differences in the Perceived Risks of Indoor and Outdoor Sex Work and Its Impact on Exiting

Kathleen Preble, Karen Magruder, and Andrea N. Cimino

ABSTRACT

This study sought to understand differences in risks of indoor versus outdoor sex work and how perceptions of risk influenced sex workers' motivation to exit. Among the 19 indoor and outdoor sex workers included in this qualitative study, themes of risks included: violence versus death, discovery, romantic relationships, arrest, health risks, loss, and "the unknown". Results of this study show that sex workers have a nuanced perceptions of risks and exiting motivations dependent upon the sex trade market. These results officer suggestions for policy and intervention practices uniquely tailored for indoor and outdoor sex workers.

Background

Understanding how perceptions of risk differ between indoor and outdoor sex trade markets is important because risks influence behavioral change, such as exiting. Unfortunately, there is a dearth of literature examining risks and its impact on exiting. The myriad of terms used to describe the sex trade (e.g., sex work, trafficking, prostitution, commercial sexual exploitation, etc.) further obfuscates nuanced understanding of this topic. All forms of sex work incur occupational risks, whether they are physical, emotional, or legal. Scholarly literature tends to highlight the physical health consequences of sex work, in part because outdoor sex work is notoriously more violent and risky than indoor sex work (see Plumbridge & Abel, 2001; Raphael & Shapiro, 2004; Seib, Fischer, & Najman, 2009). With the advent of the Internet, sex work has become more accessible, promising a new level of anonymity and ability to screen clients, thereby decreasing risks and increasing perceived safety (Agresti, 2009; Sanders, 2005). The reality of this perception is wrought with controversy, conflicting evidence, and ill-conceived policies (Hughes, 2004; Jackson & Heineman, 2018). The goal of this study is to explicate the unique risks faced by indoor (i.e., Internet-based, brothel, escort) and outdoor (i.e., street prostitution) sex workers and to understand to what extent risks impact their decision to exit the sex trade. Understanding perceived risks of the sex trade is integral to changing behaviors and can lead to targeted interventions meaningful to persons working in specific sex trade markets (Cimino, 2012).

Variations in the sex trade

The sex trade encompasses direct (e.g., fellatio, intercourse) and indirect (e.g., stripping, phone sex) sexual exchanges that occur in indoor (e.g., escorts/call girls, brothels, massage parlors) or outdoor settings (e.g., on the streets, cars, etc.). The sex trade's many nuances have been explained elsewhere (Sanders, O'Neill, & Pitcher, 2009; Weitzer, 2005). Crucial differences in sex trade markets include workers' socioeconomic background (e.g., poverty, education), exposure to violence and risk for murder, earning potential and control over working conditions (e.g., when/how often to work, condom use; Alexander, 1987), access to technology to facilitate exchanges (e.g., websites, credit cards), and visibility/stigma (i.e., inability to hide on-street sex work; Weitzer, 2010). As a result, the sex trade has been described on a continuum of increasing danger, illegality, and oppression/agency (Buke, Sitter, & Boggan, 2018), with indoor sex work seen as a personally empowering career choice (Blissbomb, 2001, Weitzer, 2010) and outdoor sex work, often pimp-controlled, viewed as oppressive with greater risks to one's health and safety (Farley et al., 2003; Weitzer, 1991, 2010). These descriptions should not be confused with sex trafficking, referring to non-consensual sexual exchanges through threats of force, fraud, or coercion (Alvarez & Alessi, 2012; Jackson & Heineman, 2018). In this paper, we use the words "sex trade" and "sex work" interchangeably to refer to non-sex trafficking situations, though it can include pimp-controlled situations; the term "outdoor" refers to street-based sex work; "indoor" refers to sex work occurring in strip clubs, massage parlors, or Internet-facilitated means; and "mixed" refers to sex workers who engaged in both indoor and outdoor sex work.

Sex work is a continuum of risks

The few studies comparing indoor and outdoor sex work show that violence and health risks sharply differ, suggesting there may be a "continuum of risks" that vary by sex trade market (Sanders, 2004). For example, as few as 3% to as many as 48% of indoor sex workers have been physically or sexually assaulted compared to 52% to 81% of outdoor sex workers (see studies by Plumbridge & Abel, 2001; Raphael & Shapiro, 2004; Seib et al., 2009). The murder rates for outdoor sex workers is nearly 18 times higher than non-sex workers (Potterat et al., 2004) with customers being responsible for 57–100% of homicides (Brewer et al., 2006). One study comparing outdoor versus indoor sex work homicides in the United Kingdom showed outdoor sex workers were murdered three times more frequently than indoor workers (85 outdoor vs. 24 indoor of 109 sex worker homicides; Sanders, Cunningham, Platt, Grenfell, & Macioti, 2017). Most studies on sex workers' sexual health focus on HIV/STI prevalence, with little delineation by sex work market, muddying a nuanced understanding of risks. Worldwide estimates show that sex workers are 13.5 times more likely to have HIV than non-sex working women (Kerrigan et al., 2012). Yet, Weitzer (2007) suggests that HIV/STIs are lower among indoor sex workers where condom use is more likely mandated. Other studies consistently demonstrate that sexual health risks increase with violence and drug use, two factors more commonly associated with outdoor versus indoor sex work (Edwards, Halpern, & Wechsberg, 2006; Jeal & Salisbury, 2004).

While health and safety risks are important, less visible risks, like emotional health and stigma, can be overlooked. Moreover, evidence suggests that health concerns are not universally salient as touted in many sex work studies (Cimino, 2013; Buke, Sitter, & Boggan, in press; Sanders, 2004). For instance, indoor sex workers place more emphasis on emotional risks of selling sex and less on physical health and violence risks (Koken, 2012; Sanders, 2004). Lever and Dolnick's (2000) comparison of sex markets found that indoor sex workers spend significantly more time with clients and provide more emotional labor (i.e., feigning desire, illusion of intimacy) than outdoor sex workers, leading to higher rates of mental fatigue and exhaustion. Stigma is a consistent concern among indoor sex workers who experience social isolation, burnout, and other psychological sequelae (Blissbomb, 2001; Bradley, 2007; Sallmann, 2010). Outdoor sex workers also face stigma and similar risks, but evidence suggests they face additional consequences such as diminished access to healthcare, fewer protections and increased risk of arrest from law enforcement, and being denied social services, which has led to underreporting (Preble, 2015; Benoit, Jansson, Smith, & Flagg, 2018; Lazarus et al., 2012).

Perception of risk can impact motivation to exit

Regardless of whether there exists a continuum of risks by sex trade market, the impact of perceived risks on exiting is understudied. Exiting is a process whereby women take steps to disengage from the sex trade; exiting is notably arduous, requiring a whole life transformation (Månsson & Hedin, 1999). Sanders (2004) argues that sex workers essentially balance their desire to make money against risks to their physical and emotional wellbeing. When the risks outweigh the benefits, they become motivated to exit. Much of the literature on exiting outlines barriers to exiting (e.g., poverty, addiction, etc.) or describes exiting pathways, such as a reactionary transition due to a traumatic or eye-opening event (Baker, Dalla, & Williamson, 2010; Dalla, 2006; Oselin, 2010; Sanders, 2007). Few studies examine motivation to exit, and none have systematically compared reasons for exiting by sex trade market. Only Manopaiboon et al.'s (2003) study on sex workers in Thailand identified risks as reasons to exit, which were economics, relationships, the threat of HIV/STIs, and changing attitudes toward sex work.

Risk management through misguided practice and policy

Another reason to study sex workers' risks and their impact on exiting is because risks shape and are shaped by policies and practices intended to curtail sex work. For instance, the history of U.S. anti-prostitution policies was born from an attempt to eradicate the unsightly vice and establish a moral standard of womanhood, a notion that persists throughout modern criminalization laws (Smolak, 2013). Criminalization policies have driven prostitution deeper underground and arguably created more danger for buyers and sellers alike (Musheno & Seeley, 1987; Weitzer, 1991). More contemporary policies recognize the harms associated with sex work focusing on its public health consequences. This perspective on risk has led to harm reduction interventions that increase access to condoms, HIV/STI testing, and safety planning to prevent STIs and violence (Cusick, 2006; Rekart, 2005).

An added complexity to this discussion is a recent law, the Fight Online Sex Trafficking Act (FOSTA)-Stop Enabling Sex Trafficking Act (SESTA), intended to reduce demand by holding online platforms accountable for material its users post that promote prostitution, pornography, and/or sex trafficking. FOSTA-SESTA effectively banned online sex trade markets, resulted in the complete dissolution of Backpage.com and other websites sex workers use to access and screen clients. As noted earlier, sex workers and customers alike perceive online sex markets as "safer" due to its ease, anonymity, and screening potential (Agresti, 2009; Sanders, 2005). One study showed that FOSTA-SESTA increased sex workers' risks, finding that 60% took on "less safe" clients due to fewer outlets to advertise and 30% lowered their standards of safety (Jackson & Heineman, 2018). A recent commentary suggested that FOSTA-SESTA may have increased physical and financial harms to sex workers and may exacerbate sex trafficking as the law took away a safety mechanism without offering other stabilizing resources to help women exit the sex trade (Higgins, 2019).

Study purpose

While risks to one's physical, sexual, and emotional health may be evident to sex workers, what is not well understood by researchers and other professionals (e.g., police, social workers, clinicians, etc.) is how sex workers prioritize those risks and to what extent perceived risks and sex trade markets should influence intervention approaches (i.e., harm reduction models, criminalization policies, and other social services). This study seeks to understand, from the sex workers' point of view, differences in perceived risks associated with indoor and outdoor sex work and its impact on exiting and other behaviors. In exploring these differences, we consider their meaning in the context of policies, interventions, and direction for future areas of study.

Methodology

Data for the current study come from three rounds of interviews with indoor and outdoor sex workers from Arizona (January-May 2012) and Texas (June-December 2013 and July-September 2014). Combining these data sets allowed the researchers to broaden their understanding of the phenomena and may have increased transferability of the findings (Patton, 1990). The overall purpose of each of the studies was to understand how and why women exit the sex industry, including their interaction with exiting service providers. The interviews followed the same methodological protocols and were guided by phenomenological and narrative traditions, which seek to explore one's life and understand their experiences (Lincoln & Guba, 1985; Moustakas, 1994). These methodologies support feminist research methods that encourage non-dominant points of view and the ability to discuss and clarify participants' reality through free interaction between researcher and subject (Harding, 2004; Reinharz, 1992). All protocols were approved by the authors' respective university Institutional Review Board.

Procedure

The each of the studies used a combination of flyers, online ads (i.e., Backpage.com), and agency-based referrals to recruit participants. Those who responded to flyers or online ads were instructed to call the researchers for screening and to set up an interview time. Screening involved verbal confirmation that the participant ever sold or traded sex for money or other goods, regardless of sex trade market and whether they exited. Those referred from an agency were first approached by agency staff, then referred to a researcher for an interview. Upon providing informed consent, participants were interviewed face-to-face at the referring agency, another location, or via phone. Compensation was a $15 gift card.

The interviews were conducted by all three authors who were trained in qualitative methodologies and had experience working with women with histories of physical/sexual assault, prostitution, and/or incarceration. The interviews lasted 60–90 minutes and were audio recorded, then transcribed. The semi-structured interview guide focused on reasons for exiting but included open-ended questions about how they first got involved in the sex trade and the pros (benefits) and cons (dangers/risks) of the sex trade for context to understand their experiences. Participants were probed about how specific events (e.g., violence, pregnancy, arrest, etc.) and access to support services affected their ability to exit. Multiple interviewers and open-ended questions may have minimized reactivity and researcher bias (Denzin, 1989).

Participants

Intensity sampling was used to select a subsample of 19 of 46 total participants who yielded information-rich, yet typical (vs. extreme) explanations of risks in the sex trade (Patton, 2010). Participants not selected for the current study ($N = 27$) were indirect sex workers (i.e., strippers/exotic dancers, phone sex workers; $n = 8$), male/gender non-conforming sex workers ($n = 3$), those who never exited ($n = 3$), and those who did not explain risks or its impact on exiting in great detail ($n = 17$). Of the 19 participants included in the study, nine were indoor sex workers only, four were outdoor sex worker only, and six had participated in both types of sex work. Participants were between ages 19 and 57 years old ($M = 35.4$, $SD = 12.1$) and spent an average of 7.9 years in sex work and 2.2 years out of sex work. Six participants previously exited but were actively selling sex indoors at the time of the interview. All names were changed to pseudonyms to protect participants' identity. See Table 1 for more details.

Analysis

The analytic strategy employed in this study was descriptive/interpretive qualitative research (Elliott & Timulak, 2005; Hunt, 2009; Thorne, Kirkham, & O'Flynn-Magee, 2004). Born from nursing science, this methodology's purpose is to describe a phenomenon with an interpretative or explanatory lens that yields clinical applications or implications. Therefore, the descriptive/interpretive qualitative approach matched the study's purpose, which was to identify risks in indoor and outdoor sex work and its impact on exiting. A benefit of interpretive description is that organization of data and

Table 1. Participant demographics (N = 19).

Pseudonym	Type of sex work	Race/ Ethnicity	Age of entry	Years in prostitution	Years out of prostitution
Arizona Sample					
Theresa	Indoor*	Hispanic	26	0.25	Active
Becka	Outdoor	Hispanic	37	19	1
Serenity	Outdoor	White	10	24	9
Fiona	Outdoor*	White	15	4	.04
Cat	Indoor*	White	23	4	.25
Mila	Indoor	White	20	1	Active
Roxanne	Indoor	White	46	3	1
Beth	Indoor*	White	19	4	1
Hoodia	Outdoor	Hispanic	17	3	2
Texas 1 Sample					
Lacy	Mixed	White	20	10	.5
Megan	Mixed	Black	25	5	.5
Katie	Mixed	White	15	7	12
Jenny	Mixed	White	18	20+	.5
Ashley	Mixed	White	14	20+	.5
Texas 2 Sample					
Molly	Indoor	White	39	3.5	Active
Greta	Indoor	White	18	3	.5
Dani	Mixed	Black	37	17	Active
Val	Indoor	White	40	.5	Active
Elyse	Indoor	Black	18	2	Active
Mean (*SD*)			23.2 (10)	7.9 (7.8)	2.2 (3.8)

*Indicates telephone interview

its analysis are guided by a coherent logic and structure. Specific to this study, the framework for analysis follows this structure: a description of risk → relevant context within indoor vs. outdoor sex trade markets → its impact on exiting. A critique of interpretive description is that it can be biased (Hunt, 2009); however, reflexivity, merging the three sets of data, and using multiple coders may have increased trustworthiness via methodological and analytic triangulation (Patton, 1999). Where relevant, we indicated the percent of participants who endorsed a particular risk, but we caution the reader from overinterpreting the counts as a statement of generalizability, inference, or causality; rather, the counts represent evidence, patterns, and diversity of perceptions within this particular set of data (see Maxwell, 2010 for a discussion on numerical data in qualitative research).

Analysis began with the authors reading each transcript and memo-ing any initial insights about emerging patterns. Next, we selected specific sections of the narrative that focused on risks and exiting, and identified "meaning units," parts of the data that stood out and sufficiently communicated meaning without additional context (Wertz, 1983). Once these sections were identified and agreed upon, the authors organized the risks into themes. Using participants' own words, we interpreted to what extent risks impacted reason for exiting (not all risks contributed to one's decision to exit) by sex trade market (i.e., indoor vs. outdoor) through a constant comparison of the data to the themes and vice versa. Reflexivity and peer debriefing about the themes and their significance helped ensure that themes were accurately extracted and closely followed the participants' intended meaning, thereby increasing credibility/reliability and minimizing confirmation bias (Patton, 1999). Data analysis was conducted with Nvivo 10 (QSR International, 2012).

Results

Analyses yielded a descriptive account of the risks associated with sex work along seven themes: violence versus death, discovery, arrest, romantic relationships, health risks, loss, and "the unknown." Following a description of each risk, we use the participants' quotes to highlight prominent differences that emerged regarding how indoor and outdoor sex workers weighed the significance of those risks against their decision to exit the sex trade. Following the participants' pseudonym is they type of sex trade market they participated in. We summarize our results in Table 2, which outlines the risk and its definition, type of sex trade market, the risk's impact on exiting, and citations to supporting literature (complied post analysis). It is important to note that the risks identified here likely impact individuals differently and accumulate over time. As such, they should not be thought of as having a direct relationship to exiting or as a sole reason for exiting.

Risk of violence vs. death

All of the participants said violence was a major risk of selling sex, that "it goes with the territory." Being raped, hit, or beat up by customers or boyfriend-pimps were common among indoor and outdoor sex workers. Tara (indoor) was hit in the face so hard that her tooth came loose. Megan (mixed) was "made to do a lot of things I didn't wanna do" alluding to rape. More severe violence included being thrown from a moving vehicle and being beaten with a weapon or threatened with a weapon while raped (i.e., gun, knife, screwdriver to the temple). Extreme violence is typical in outdoor sex work (Weitzer, 2009). On multiple occasions, Becka (outdoor) "talked her way out of being killed." Holli (outdoor) estimated she had "bad incidents, I'd say about ten, ten a year. Really bad incidents, like death incidents, probably one a year." The last time, she remembered being punched in the face by a customer then waking up in the hospital "with a neck brace and tubes in my nose." She had been tied by the neck to a pick-up truck and dragged along the road. Dani (mixed) exited twice after being shot at both times. "The street is a dangerous place, 'cause you don't know. You don't know what car you're jumping in. You don't know who is behind the wheel, what monster that you're gonna run into," she said.

Because the severity of violence faced by outdoor sex workers was more extreme, they expressed more powerful concerns of being killed than indoor sex workers. Many (7 of 10) outdoor/mixed sex workers legitimately escaped murder. "Why I wanted to leave – because we knew death is coming … girls started dying and after I got back from that trick that wanted to kill me … all I could hear was people dying," said Fiona (outdoor). Outdoor sex work was like "playing Russian roulette" with your life for Jenny (mixed) who knew "many girls that were killed and died." Serenity (outdoor) felt her "number was going to be up" – a sentiment shared by most outdoor sex workers – when a customer chased her with a knife: "I just felt more and more that my time was coming." Indoor sex workers, on the other hand, were afraid of being killed if only hypothetically: "I was very worried about meeting a crazy guy who was gonna try to kill me or kidnap me or something like that," Molly (indoor) said.

The frequency of violence was also less for indoor sex workers compared to outdoor sex workers. For instance, Cat, Roxanne, and Beth (all indoor) had one or two rapes, whereas

Table 2. Identification and Definition of Risks.

Risk and Definition	Sex Trade Market	Impact on Exiting	Supporting Literature
Risk of Violence vs Death: The risk of experiencing violence or near death	Indoor and outdoor	Outdoor sex workers experienced more frequent severe violence, often life-threatening, that prompted an exit. Indoor sex workers feared violence but downplayed its significance and had more resources to protect themselves.	Cobbina & Oselin, 2011; Plumbridge & Abel, 2001; Potterat et al., 2004; Raphael & Shapiro, 2004; Sanders et al., 2017; Sanders, 2004; Seib et al., 2009
Risk of Discovery: The risk of being "found out" by friends, family, children, employers	Indoor and outdoor	Outdoor sex workers were less concerned about discovery until after they exited. Indoor sex workers were concerned with both the threat of and actualized discovery, which was a motivation to exit. They went to great lengths to hide their involvement from loves ones, including engaging in risky or potentially dangerous encounters.	Preble, 2015; Benoit et al., 2018; Lazarus et al., 2012
Risk of Arrest: The risk of becoming involved with the criminal justice system	Indoor and outdoor	Outdoor sex workers had more prostitution arrests and other criminal histories, but this was not a strong motivation to exit. Indoor sex workers were motivated by the threat of arrest and engaged in risky or potentially dangerous encounters to avoid arrest.	Preble, 2015; Benoit et al., 2018; Lazarus et al., 2012; Musheno & Seeley, 1987; Weitzer, 1991
Risk to Romantic Relationships: The risk to current or future intimate relationships	Indoor and outdoor	Some outdoor and indoor sex workers and their partners were unaffected by this risk (partners were complicit), and it had no impact on exiting. Mostly indoor sex workers were affected by this risk, both while trading sex and after exiting; no one reported exiting because of this risk.	Pyett & Warr, 1997; Preble, 2015
Health Risks: Risk to physical, sexual, and emotional health	Indoor and outdoor	Both outdoor and indoor sex workers were concerned about physical and sexual health risks but did not exit upon experiencing these risks. Emotional health risks were experienced by both types of sex workers and was a motivation to exit when they were overwhelmed with shame, guilt, and depression.	Kerrigan et al., 2012; Koken, 2012; Edwards et al., 2006; Jeal & Salisbury, 2004; (Cimino, 2013; Buke, Sitter & Boggan, in press; Sanders, 2004
Risk of Loss: The risk of losing money, meaningful relationship, and children	Indoor and outdoor	Indoor and outdoor sex workers expected some level of loss (i.e., being robbed, losing friendships), but this was not a strong motivator to exit and, in some cases, loss made exiting more difficult.	Baker et al., 2010
Risk of the "Unknown": The risk of leaving sex trade for the unfamiliar	Indoor and outdoor	Indoor and outdoor sex workers feared leaving the sex trade and continued selling sex despite experiencing risks. When other risks were too much, fear of the unknown subsided and participants were able to exit.	Preble, 2015

Jenny (mixed) was gang raped by three men and Serenity (outdoor) was raped at least eight times. Rape marginally influenced indoor and outdoor sex workers' motivation to exit. Beth (indoor) "figured once I got raped, it couldn't get worse than that," and continued to work independently. Some indoor sex workers simply didn't think violence would happen to them. Val (indoor) only sees "educated, high-level men," which she believes helps her filter out guys who are "gonna kill you." When confronted with violence, indoor sex workers tended to rationalize it away. For example, Theresa (indoor) "wasn't very smart at first," which lead to a customer stalking her and attempting to rape by gunpoint. She "took it as a learning experience" and insists she won't experience violence "because I'm not seeing anyone new." Outdoor sex workers adopted a less naïve approach and developed safety strategies as Holli (outdoor) explained:

> I learned from my mistakes ... when you get in the car, make sure the window rolls down. Make sure the door opens. Make sure they can't have it locked to where I can't get out ... Look around. If he looks and looks, it's big – I like to see if they look in the rearview mirror too much.

One difference that may have tempered the perceived risk of violence for indoor sex workers was whether they had access to a bodyguard, driver, or friend/partner to help them. Dani (mixed) said, "Stripping's more covered up ... they have the bouncer ... escort, same thing, there's a business behind you." She feels safer at agencies that check IDs and take credit cards. Roxanne (indoor) was raped on her very first call, "but after that, I got smart, and I got a driver. I got this big black dude to come along with me." Independent sex workers "couldn't afford" bodyguards or were discouraged from using them: "Nobody helps me ... a lot of [clients] get really freaked out with that sort of thing ... they don't want you to have a driver," said Cat (indoor). Elyse (indoor) and Katie's (mixed) partners saved them from being attacked by a customer. Working indoors with a bodyguard did not guarantee safety. Mila (indoor) was forced to have anal sex despite her boss monitoring her on closed-circuit television. Beth (indoor) was raped at an escort agency to which her boss replied, "It's like being an electrician, you're gonna get shocked." Mila and Beth's rape did not spur their exit from sex work, but prompted them to leave the agency to work independently.

Risk of discovery

Discovery – the risk that a friend, family member, your child, or an employer finds out you're selling sex – made some participants, primarily indoor sex workers, attempt to hide their involvement in sex work from others. Theresa (indoor) is a nanny and would lose her job if she were discovered. Val's (indoor) veterinarian license was already suspended because of her drinking problem. She doesn't worry about discovery because only her customers know, including doctors and a banker: "I don't really fear that they would tell someone because they're not gonna tell on themselves in the process." Greta (indoor) had a "druggie" reputation before she began dancing and selling sex at a strip club. "It wasn't a secret that I was dancing," she said, because it offered her a cover story: "I always try to keep that – my trickin' a secret." Cat (indoor) was one of a few indoor sex workers whose family knew she was selling sex. Only one of her friends would be disappointed: "I can't sit and worry about it. If [her friend] did find out, the result is going to be what it is going to be ... if you can't handle it, well sorry."

Linked to the risk of discovery (or lack thereof) was stigma, whether it was internalized or came from others. Elyse (indoor) and Theresa's (indoor) "biggest fear" was having friends and family find out they sold sex. Molly (indoor) said, "It would destroy my son if he knew what I was doing, especially if he thought it's because I was doing it for [him]." She feels that if people knew, their "whole opinion" of her would change: "There's no doubt that people would yell at me, tell me all the horrible aspects of this, and that I'm a terrible mother … " Elyse (indoor) wasn't proud of selling sex, but would "own up to it" because no one was there for her: "You can't really judge me for taking care of me when you wasn't trying to take care of me." Val (indoor) can "just let it roll off my back." Dani and Holli were the only outdoor sex workers to express shame. Dani (mixed) let judgement from others "blow over my head or [go] in one ear and out the other." Holli (outdoor), who proudly wears "hootchie shorts" even after exiting, cried as she recalled no longer receiving invitations to family gatherings. Although many participants worried about discovery, internalized stigma did not motivate any sex workers to exit. Molly (indoor) "would probably stop immediately" if her family figured out she was selling sex. Only Roxanne (indoor) exited when her sons "judged her hard" after finding her ad on Backpage.com.

By virtue of being visible on the street, discovery was less of a concern for outdoor sex workers. Becka (outdoor) sold sex to support herself and her partner, often with friends and occasionally her daughters. Fiona (outdoor) was "16 and selling my pussy … nobody wanted their kid handing out with me." Being less concerned with discovery, outdoor sex workers could harness their visibility to keep safe. Becka (outdoor) and Jenny (mixed) had "buddies" who protected them from dangerous customers or pimps looking to exploit them: "The street people … other girls would look out for you," said Jenny (mixed). Not fearing discovery allowed Jenny (mixed) to take steps to increase her safety.

> …these girls are so stupid they'll tell a guy, "Oh, I don't have a pimp" or "I don't have anybody." … The first thing I would do when I got to a call [to see a customer] was to make a phone call, 'cause I had a girlfriend who always knew where I was at. And I would tell the client, "Look, I just have to check in with my girlfriend to tell her that I'm okay 'cause, you know, just let somebody know where I'm at." And most of 'em were okay with that.

Outdoor sex workers were largely unphased with discovery unless they recently exited, wherein discovery by an employer impacted their ability to secure gainful employment. Jenny (mixed) was working on her real estate license and "didn't want to mess up my options with the Texas Real Estate Commission". Elyse's (indoor) worries of discovery were more prominent when she started a new job at a prestigious company:

> I just wonder, is someone from Backpage.com gonna recognize my face? Does one of my customers work here? It's just not a good feeling when you feel like someone in the store is staring at you because, hey, I know that girl from such-and-such, or maybe one of my brother's friends seen me, or maybe one of my husband's friends seen me on it.

Indoor workers tended to list fear of discovery as a major factor in their decision to exit. Beth (indoor) said, "Trying to live your life afraid of running into these guys on the street … in public with their families," and she eventually exited because of the emotional toll fear of discovery took on her. Theresa (indoor) said, "I feel like the only way that I would stop would be if something drastic happens … that would be my family finding out." For her, risk of discovery was even greater than the risk of violence. "My biggest fear is that if [a client is violent] then I'll have to use self-defense and the police would become involved and lead to my family figuring it out," said Theresa (indoor). In trying to avoid "being found out," Theresa made decisions that jeopardized her physical safety: "I just go to their [customers'] house … I don't do hotels because they could be a trap with law enforcement and I don't meet up in a car because I know too many people and someone would see me." Molly (indoor) at least recognized that her fear of discovery impacted her safety: "There's nobody you can call and say, 'Hey, if you don't hear from me in two hours, then this is the address I'm going to. Please call someone.'"

Risk of arrest

Prostitution is illegal in most the U.S.; therefore, being arrested is a major risk factor. Risk of arrest was certainly linked to fear of discovery. Jenny (mixed) contemplated returning to sex work but feared that an arrest would derail her exiting plans: "All I need to do is catch another [prostitution arrest] and I can kiss that [real estate] stuff goodbye." Cat (indoor) said, "The biggest concern for me is having that on my record … that was one of the things that actually lead me to quitting all together … I came close enough [to being arrested]." She even admitted that the legal consequences were more important than violence: "I was scared of being arrested, probably more than getting raped or hurt or sold into slavery. Those are the kind of things I should've been worried about, but I was more worried about someone being an undercover cop."

Outdoor sex workers were less afraid of discovery due to arrest because most had multiple prostitution charges, whereas indoor sex workers had none (7 of 9 indoor) or managed to get them expunged (2 of 9 indoor) from their record. Being visible on the street meant coming to terms with being arrested. Holli (outdoor) was arrested four times in two months: "If you're working, you're bound to go to jail … I can guarantee you, everybody gets caught within six months." Some (5 of 10) outdoor/mixed sex workers felt being arrested was a "vacation." Serenity (outdoor) said, "Even though the food is shitty, you get rest, you get exercise, walking around. You get better, you get healthy. You get healthy again just to get out and go back." The deterrent effect of arrest for outdoor sex workers was related to the time it took them to re-figure out the landscape once released: "There is always a fear of [arrest] because you also don't want to leave the streets … stop the addiction … dope houses move … it's a lot of change to get back into the swing of things," said Serenity (outdoor). When Holli (outdoor) was released from six months in jail, her pimp's house was gone, so she "didn't have a place to go" and so were her belongings: "They [pimps] will save your clothes for the next girl." In her experience, being locked up for more than seven days meant "you're gonna start all over … you're gonna lose everything."

Risk to romantic relationships

Current and future romantic relationships were impacted by sex work. Some partners of indoor sex workers (4 of 9), like Cat's (indoor) husband, knew and accepted that she was selling sex, which had no impact on her motivation to exit. Mila (indoor) resented her boyfriend's acceptance of her selling sex: "He was like, 'Okay, as long as it wasn't a scam.' I wish he'd fight for me and say he'd take care of me," Mila (indoor) said. Even getting an

STD didn't change things: "He wasn't angry but really frustrated that I got genital warts so we both had to get checked out."

Katie (mixed) told her partner what she "did on the side and he just accepted me." The past year of their relationship has been in turmoil because she asks too much of her partner:

> He babysat the kids, he wasn't working because he was supporting me in a way as far as the kids and being there whenever I got robbed or, you know, something bad went down he would be there to come save me in a way. And he's always told me that this isn't something that I should be doing but he never stopped me and he never left me because it's what I was. But it's caused a lot of problems in our relationship because I've lied to him. I've done a lot of things that normal girlfriend probably wouldn't do. And he's had to deal with men stalking me and showing up at our house. And then me being gone for two, three weeks at a time he'd have to deal with the kids. Whenever I decided to finally get out it was real tough on him too because all of our money was gone. So the lifestyle he'd been accustomed to was no more.

Elyse's (indoor) fiancé "understands it to a level," but they regularly argue about sex work. He said, "If you want to keep doing it, I can't stop you from doing it, but I don't want to be a part of it anymore." She was frustrated because he "don't complain when I'm paying bills or spending money, but you want to complain when you know I'm in the act of doing it." No one exited because it impacted their current relationship, but Val (indoor) would exit if her new boyfriend wanted a "permanent relationship" with her and she had the means to support herself.

Another way that sex work posed a risk to romantic relationships dealt with sex workers' ability to develop romantic connections and sexual intimacy. Sex was "the furthest thing from my mind," said Elyse (indoor) whose partner "feels like [sex work is] taking away from his sex life." Dani (mixed) struggles to turn on her emotions, so she has to remind herself she's "with somebody that loves you. You're not with somebody that wants to take advantage of you. They're not here for business." The sex trade made Ashley (mixed) act "cold-hearted" toward her partners. She goes into "robot mode" and says sex feels "mechanical." She wonders, "Is [sex] ever going to be good for me again?" Molly (indoor) wants a relationship but knows that if she is selling sex "a relationship's not gonna happen 'cuz I don't know any guy that would be okay with it." Megan (mixed) simply questioned, "What is a relationship? I don't know." Her partners complained that she treats them "like they're a trick." She avoids relationships because it's her "mentality" to ask them for money and withhold sex.

Health risks

Indoor and outdoor sex workers alike experienced physical, emotional, and sexual health risks. Dani (mixed) has bipolar disorder and has panic attacks from trauma: "They still stick in my head like someone's out to get me. I have a hard time sleeping." Many worried about health risks. "Am I gonna go out here and end up with HIV? Or am I gonna go out and get raped this time? Am I not gonna make it out because I promised God I wasn't gonna go do this anymore?" questioned Megan (mixed). All continued to sell sex to support themselves, their partner and child, or a drug habit anyway. Only when the health risks became undeniable, particularly the physical and mental exhaustion, did it impact their decision to exit. Greta (indoor) said, "Emotionally and physically, my body couldn't take it." Becka (outdoor) "finally got so tired of having to be out there … when I got out I was like, 'What am I doing – I'm old, I'm tired.' … Your body can't withstand all that abuse." Beth (indoor) said, "A million dollars wouldn't be worth it, it's degrading, your self-esteem goes really, really low and you feel like crap. You feel like you're below everyone else in society. You're low, you're dumb. I got really depressed and started drinking." Megan (mixed) "never [had] good days. They were all filled with worry, exhaust, pain, misery … " Lacy (mixed) was "grossed out" with herself and didn't "wanna be looked at like a piece of meat anymore, like a sex object … " At one time, Fiona (outdoor) liked being desired by men; now, the objectification feels "disgusting," which factored into her decision to exit.

Indoor and outdoor sex workers also struggled with shame and guilt. They had to reconcile having sold sex despite not being "brought up that way." Greta's (indoor) shame made her wonder, "If I have kids, am I gonna give them a shitty life? Even if I don't, are they gonna make the wrong choices like I made and make it shitty for everybody?" Some numbed themselves with drugs to avoid these uncomfortable feelings. "My emotions tell me, 'Just die,' and I want to," said Greta (indoor). When she shoots up, "I realize that I really don't want to, and it feels good." When Megan (mixed) returned to sex work "with no drugs, I was able to feel everything … feel the guilt … oh it's just nasty, it was just nasty to me … terrible."

Interestingly, indoor and outdoor sex workers regarded STIs as a reality, more than a risk. Ashley (mixed) said, "It was already stressful enough to think, ok well is this guy gonna kidnap me or rape me today? … Now, you gotta worry about catching AIDS and gonorrhea and herpes, it's just too much." The majority of participants (8 of 9 participants, 10 did not disclose) contracted an STI, often multiple times, and some nearly died. Serenity (street) had syphilis: "[The doctor] told me there are three stages to this disease and you're fixing to go into the third stage." Greta (indoor) isn't even sure whether she could have children "cuz of how many STDs I've had." Participants were certainly "afraid" of HIV/STIs, but no participants in this study had HIV. Holli (outdoor) "know[s] a lot of girls who have AIDS and who are still out there working." Becka felt "blessed" she didn't get HIV despite not always using protection:

> I was always very scared [of HIV]. And, of course, we all say you are going to use condoms, but that's not the case, that's not true. We don't always because sometimes the guy doesn't want to use them, or you don't have them or it's something. So, you always put yourself in a dangerous position.

Risk of loss

Indoor and outdoor sex workers alike spoke about the risk of loss from being robbed or cheated out of money. Only seven participants reported being robbed, but the rest "expected" it. Mila (indoor) was "burned" by a few customers, including one who disappeared to get money he kept in his car "because he didn't know if he was going to get robbed" by her. Loss marginally impacted participants' decision to exit. Theresa (indoor) said, "I've been robbed before – once with a knife … the risks definitely outweigh the benefits, but the money is like – that's it. " Many took getting robbed as a learning lesson, like Jenny (mixed) who explained:

> I think a worst day in the sex industry is when you don't make any money or you have a guy – or you get counterfeit money. That pisses you off … And you look in the envelope, 'cause when he came in, he flashed the envelope … and it's 20s and it's dark in the room. So he hurries up, puts the money back in the envelope, and you're like, "Okay, I saw it. It's 20s. Whatever." And he leaves, and you look at the envelope, and it's only 20s on one side, because he made color copies, and you're so – I was so fucking pissed, 'cause he got me. He stole from me. He stole my time. He stole my energy. He was a thief.

Selling sex didn't guarantee a customer, resulting in lost money and time. "You might post ads all day long, but no money comes," said Katie (mixed). Katie managed to break even, but Mila (indoor) actually lost money on one occasion: "I'd spend money on a room and I still won't get anybody." This gave Mila (indoor) pause: "This isn't really fun; I just want a regular job where I know I am going to get paid." Another way to lose money in sex work was by getting arrested. Katie (mixed) said, "[The police] took everything. Then I didn't get any of my belongings back. I paid couple thousand dollars in a bond and I guess the fines was only $300."

There were other forms of loss. Molly (indoor) "would probably lose a lot of friendships" if people found out she was selling sex. Drugs magnified the risk of loss. Greta (indoor) is "scared to get caught [using drugs]" by her boyfriend: "I would be lost. I wouldn't know where to go. I mean, he feeds me, and he clothes me, and he just takes care of me." Despite the risk of loss, she's "not gonna stop [drugs] 'cuz it's just – I guess, feelin' like shit and being treated like shit all the time is worth it to me if I can get high. I'll fuck for money if I can get high." Following her prostitution arrest, Child Protective Services (CPS) took Ashley's (mixed) children from her:

> … its just been a horrible struggle ever since. I pretty much lost my will for anything else in life when they took my kids from me. I really did. I didn't care. Especially, after I did everything they told me to do and they still sat there and said, "Well, we're sorry you still can't have your kids." Because they knew the lifestyle that I was living, and I even tried to get out of it then, and when they still, no still can't have your kids.

Serenity (outdoor) relinquished her children to child welfare so that she could keep selling sex and struggled with guilt over this decision post-exit. Elyse's (indoor) brother reported her to CPS and she lost her children, job, and apartment. Ultimately, losing friends, family, children, jobs, and homes damaged Ashley and Elyse's self-esteem and made it more difficult for them to exit.

Risk of "the unknown"

Selling sex was risky, but leaving sex work was risky, too. Despite "death being everywhere," Fiona (outdoor) continued to sell sex because she was scared of "the unknown … I don't know any other way … I have no experience." Leaving behind the lifestyle and people indoor and outdoor sex workers knew and trusted for decades was difficult. Exiting sex work for an unknown life *was the risk*. Roxanne (indoor) thinks the majority of sex workers "do not know how to get out" and are scared to leave because they'll have to deal with their addictions. "They have to get clean," Roxanne said. "Nobody's gonna hire them if they're gonna be doing crystal meth. So, it's a twofold problem to get out of prostitution." Fears of not being able to support themselves and their families factored into decisions to exit. Becka (outdoor) said a lot of the outdoor sex workers she knows "think about getting out but then they think, 'What am I going to do? I don't have any skills, I've never worked, or I don't want to work.'" Some worried about whether they would be accepted by their families and broader society. Holli (outdoor) said, "It's a lot better to be around people who accept what you're doing, than be around people like that." Serenity (outdoor) recognized, "Everyone isn't going to accept me for who I am, but as long as I accept myself and I am doing the best I can for myself, than that is enough for me."

Exiting was worth the unknown risk when participants simply could not face another day in sex work. Lacy (mixed) was "living a very wild life for a long time." "You just get tired," she said, "want something better." Ashley (mixed) was scared after exiting: "I was still only [working] 4–8 hours a week at my real job. I was like, 'I don't care anymore. I can't do this anymore. I don't care if I lose money, I can't take it anymore.'" For these women, the unknown was a risk worth taking for anything better than what sex work offered.

Discussion

The purpose of this study was to understand differences in perceived risks of indoor versus outdoor sex work and its impact on exiting. As a whole, findings in this study and other literature suggest that sex workers exit once the risks outweigh the benefits (Author, 2013; Sanders, 2004; Williamson & Folaron, 2003). Ultimately, this study showed that indoor and outdoor sex workers exit for a variety of reasons based on their experiences and what risks they deemed unacceptable. No single risk "predicted" an exit for either group; rather, it was the severity, frequency, and accumulation of risks that prompted one's decision to exit. This study supports existing literature showing that both indoor and outdoor sex workers experience similar risks, but experience them differently (Armstrong, 2017; Plumbridge & Abel, 2001; Sanders, 2004). Moreover, risks that scholarly literature identifies as important minimally increased motivation to exit for both indoor and outdoor sex workers (i.e., HIV/STI risks over discovery and exhaustion). Because this was the first study to compare risks between sex trade markets and their impact on exiting, future studies can use our findings to develop a theoretical model with a larger and more diverse sample to make generalizable claims.

This study found that both indoor and outdoor sex workers experienced violence. Frequent and severe violence motivated outdoor sex workers to exit, particularly after a near death experience. Indoor sex workers were still concerned about violence, but other risks such as discovery, arrest, and romantic relationships were more pertinent, which align with social bond/control theory (Hirschi, 2017). Moreover, we found that indoor sex workers put themselves in riskier situations in order maintain anonymity, avoid arrest, and conceal their involvement in sex work from friends and family. Literature supports the notion that outdoor sex work is more violent than indoor sex work (Raphael & Shapiro, 2004; Seib et al., 2009); murder among indoor sex workers does occur, albeit at lower rates than in outdoor sex work (DeLateaur, 2016). However, a recent study found indoor murder rates are increasing as outdoor sex workers transition to online markets (Sanders et al., 2017).

The link between violence and exiting has important implications for practice and policy. First, indoor sex workers in this study did not perceive their risk for violence as strongly as they should, perhaps demonstrating a false sense of safety from online forums. Dispelling this myth, and offering indoor sex workers who do not want to exit harm reduction interventions, such as safety planning to avoid violence, may reduce violence and save lives (Cusick, 2006; Rekart, 2005). Other ways sex workers can keep safe are through digital communities where sex workers share reviews of customers, tips, and other resources (Gow et al., 2015). Unfortunately, FOSTA-SESTA effectively outlawed this kind of information sharing, likely pushing sex workers onto the streets or to increasingly dangerous situations (Finn & Stalans, 2016; Heil & Nichols, 2014). Additionally, participants in this study were interviewed before FOSTA-SESTA, so there is more to learn regarding whether this policy, which increased the risk of arrest, caused more indoor sex workers to exit the sex trade, as suggested in recent commentary (Higgins, 2019).

If an intervention's goal is to increase intentions to exit sex work, then harm reduction interventions may not be the best strategy. For instance, outdoor sex workers in this study overwhelmingly exited because they were nearly murdered. Therefore, teaching outdoor sex workers ways to keep safe on the streets may keep them selling sex longer. Literature shows that the longer a woman is involved in sex work, her risk for violence increases (Cobbina & Oselin, 2011). Instead, exiting interventions should focus on helping outdoor sex workers recognize dangers while being mindful to address their survival needs and make strategic exiting plans (some women cannot or choose not to exit). Risk assessment and decision aid tools, such as the Danger Assessment and myPlan, have been used to predict lethality/near lethality in domestic violence situations and for safety planning (Alhusen, Bloom, Clough, & Glass, 2015; Campbell, Webster, & Glass, 2009). The Danger Assessment has a calendar to track the frequency and severity of violent incidents, potentially reducing sex workers' ability to ignore this risk. The myPlan app is a safety decision aid that can be a useful starting point to plan an exit strategy.

Specific to indoor sex workers in this study, the risks of discovery and arrest more heavily factored into their motivation to exit, potentially due to stigma (Benoit et al., 2018). Although arrest is disproportionally used to deter street-based prostitution (Parmigiani, 2013), the mere threat of arrest prompted indoor sex workers worried about the risk of discovery to exit. Our study revealed that the tangible effect of discovery and arrest – namely, the loss of friends, family, children, jobs, and homes – increased barriers to exiting for indoor and outdoor sex workers alike, consistent with other research (Baker et al., 2010). This finding problematizes criminalization policies that are ultimately harmful to sex workers (Jackson & Heineman, 2018). Moreover, arrest did little to discourage outdoor sex workers from selling sex as some felt that being arrested offered a reprieve from selling sex. On the other hand, incarceration is an avenue by which sex workers can gain access to formal rehabilitative services or other criminal justice-initiated interventions (Mueller, 2012). Perhaps a middle ground is advocating for the decriminalization of sex work (Weitzer, 1999), which has an added benefit of addressing sex trafficking by inviting sex workers to partner in the anti-trafficking movement (Preble & Black, 2019; Preble, 2019).

One of the most significant findings regarding sex work's impact on romantic relationships was how it affects their ability to develop intimate connections post-exit. It was not clear whether participants foresaw this risk prior to entering sex work, but all must deal with its aftermath, supporting earlier research on this topic (Pyett & Warr, 1997).

Relatedly, emotional health consequences of sex work led indoor and outdoor sex workers to contemplate suicide and to self-medicate with drugs, supporting extant literature (Burnette et al., 2008). At the core of these issues is trauma, suggesting the need for therapeutic interventions to reduce PTSD and increase positive connections with others. Ideally, these interventions should foster non-judgmental interactions that build trust between sex worker and service providers (Preble, 2015; Smolak, 2013) with a trauma-informed approach (Clawson, Salomon, & Grace, 2008).

Participants in this study feared "the unknowns" of life without sex work and whether they would survive, which was actually a deterrent to exiting, found in this and other studies (Preble, 2015). Recognizing and building upon sex workers' strengths and resilience may make exiting less overwhelming. This finding also underscores the importance of addressing the root causes of why women enter sex work in the first place (Sanders, 2007). Diversion programs and other exiting interventions that force or mandate women to stop selling sex before they desire to may be a misguided approach. Requiring sex workers to stop engaging in behaviors necessary for their survival is unethical, coercive, and disempowering (Wahab & Panichelli, 2013). Moreover, the effectiveness of arrest alternative diversion programs show poor results (Roe-Sepowitz, Gallagher, Hickle, Pérez Loubert, & Tutelman, 2014). Failing to remedy the structural issues that allow the sex trade to exist, such as unaffordable housing, lack of employment, and coercive sexual environments (Sanders, 2007), ultimately does little to prevent others from being commercially sexually exploited.

Limitations

This study's small, primarily White (68.4%, n = 13 of 19) cisgender sample may have resulted in an underrepresentation of risks based on race and gender, limiting the transferability/validity of the study findings to other populations. Literature shows that transgender persons of color face more risks that other sex workers (Sausa, Keatley, & Operario, 2007). Future studies on risk in sex work should examine differences by race and gender. Another limitation is that none of the three studies were designed to gather a comprehensive list of risks; rather, the themes reported here emerged from the data. Future studies that have a larger and more diverse sample would increase generalizability. Regardless of these limitations, we found evidence that risk differs among sex trade markets and makes a distinctive impact on exiting behavior.

Conclusion

Aligning risks with one's motivation to exit helps ensure proposed interventions meet the intended goal and not induce further harm. This and other studies show that risks vary among sex trade markets and in their impact on exiting. While pro- and anti-sex work advocates seek to achieve similar goals – empowering women and reducing harms – failing to recognize nuances in sex trade markers increases the risk of missed opportunities to engage with sex workers. Sex work has not abated despite heavy-handed criminalization approaches like FOSTA-SESTA, and likely will prevail until the underlying conditions that support the existence of the sex trade are addressed (see

Razack, 1998 and Weitzer, 2010); however, a clear finding of this study is the need for interventions focused on the identified risks and motivations perceived by sex workers. This study highlighted these nuances and linked them to practice and policy interventions with sex workers. Moreover, it demonstrates the power in sex workers' voices. We simply have to listen.

Acknowledgement

This research was supported by the Arizona State University Graduate College's Doctoral Dissertation Fellowship (2012-2013) and the Arizona Board of Regents' Doctoral Research Grant (2013).

Disclosure statement

No potential conflict of interest was reported by the authors.

Funding

This research was supported by the Arizona State University Graduate College's Doctoral Dissertation Fellowship (2012-2013) and the Arizona Board of Regents' Doctoral Research Grant (2013).

References

Agresti, B. T. (2009). *E-prostitution: A content analysis of internet escort websites.* Ann Arbor, MI: Thesis Proquest.

Alexander, P. (1987). Prostitution: A difficult issue for feminists. In F. Delacoste & P. Alexander (Eds.), *Sex work: Writings by women in the sex industry* (pp. 184–214). San Francisco, California: Cleis Press.

Alhusen, J., Bloom, T., Clough, A., & Glass, N. (2015). Development of the myplan safety decision app with friends of college women in abusive dating relationships. *Journal of Technology in Human Services, 33*(3), 263–282. doi:10.1080/15228835.2015.1037414

Alvarez, M. B., & Alessi, E. J. (2012). Human trafficking is more than sex trafficking and prostitution: Implications for social work. *Affilia, 27*(2), 142–152. doi:10.1177/0886109912443763

Armstrong, L. (2017). From law enforcement to protection? Interactions between sex workers and police in a decriminalized street-based sex industry. *The British Journal of Criminology, 57*(3), 570–588. doi:10.1093/bjc/azw019

Baker, L. M., Dalla, R. L., & Williamson, C. (2010). Exiting prostitution: An integrated model. *Violence Against Women, 16*(5), 579–600. doi:10.1177/1077801210367643

Benoit, C., Jansson, M. S., Smith, M., & Flagg, J. (2018). Prostitution stigma and its effect on the working conditions, personal lives, and health of sex workers. *The Journal of Sex Research, 55* (4–5), 457–471. doi:10.1080/00224499.2017.1393652

Blissbomb, L. (2001). Sex work for the soul: Negotiating stigma as a feminist activist and closeted sex worker. *Wagadu, 8*, 292–311.

Bradley, M. S. (2007). Girlfriends, wives and strippers: Managing stigma in exotic dancer romantic relationships. *Deviant Behavior, 28*, 379–406. doi:10.1080/01639620701233308

Brewer, D. D., Dudek, J. A., Potterat, J. J., Muth, S. Q., Roberts, J. M., Jr., & Woodhouse, D. E. (2006). Extent, trends, and perpetrators of prostitution-related homicide in the United States. *Journal of Forensic Science, 51*(5), 1101–1108. doi:10.1111/j.1556-4029.2006.00206.x

Buke, E, Sitter, K, & Boggan, N. (2018). Sex work and social media: Online advocacy strategies. *Cultural and Pedagogical Inquiry, 10*(1), 49–61.
Burnette, M. L., Lucas, E., Ilgen, M., Frayne, S. M., Mayo, J., & Weitlauf, J. C. (2008). Prevalence and health correlates of prostitution among patients entering treatment for substance use disorders. *Archives of General Psychiatry, 65*(3), 337–344. doi:10.1001/archpsyc.65.3.337
Campbell, J., Webster, D., & Glass, N. E. (2009). The danger assessment: Validation of a lethality risk assessment instrument for intimate partner femicide. *Journal of Interpersonal Violence, 24*, 653–674. doi:10.1177/0886260508317180
Cimino, A. N. (2012). A predictive theory of intentions to exit street-level prostitution. *Violence against Women, 18*(10), 1235-1252.
Cimino, A. N. (2013). *Developing and testing a theory of intentions to exit street-level prostitution: A mixed methods study.* Arizona State University.
Cimino, A. N. (2018). *Sex work and adult prostitution: From entry to exit.* In M. Bourke and V. Van Hasselt (Eds.), Handbook of Behavioral Criminology: Contemporary Strategies and Issues. New York, NY: Springer Publishing.
Cimino, A.N. (in press). Uncovering Intentions to Exit Prostitution: Findings from a Qualitative Study. **THIS REFERENCE IS BEING PUBLISHED IN THE SAME SPECIAL ISSUE AS THE CURRENT MANUSCRIPT. CAN YOU PLEASE ADD THE DATE AND JOURNAL INFO?
Clawson, H. J., Salomon, A., & Grace, L. G. (2008). *Treating the hidden wounds: Trauma treatment and mental health recovery for victims of human trafficking.* Washington, DC: U.S. Department of Health and Human Services.
Cobbina, J. E., & Oselin, S. S. (2011). It's not only for the money: An analysis of adolescent versus adult entry into street prostitution. *Sociological Inquiry, 81*, 310–332. doi:10.1111/j.1475-682X.2011.00375.x
Cronley, C, Cimino, A. N, Hohn, K, Davis, J, & Madden, E. (2016). Entering sex work in adolescence: youth homelessness predicts earlier entryinto prostitution. *Journal of Aggression, Maltreatment and Trauma, 25*(9), 893-908. doi: 10.1080/10926771.2016.1223246
Cusick, L. (2006). Widening the harm reduction agenda: From drug use to sex work. *International Journal of Drug Policy, 17*(1), 3–11. doi:10.1016/j.drugpo.2005.12.002
Dalla, R. L. (2006). *Exposing the "pretty woman" myth: A qualitative investigation of street-level prostituted women.* Oxford, UK: Lexington Books.
DeLateaur, M. (2016). From craigslist to Backpage.com: Conspiracy as a strategy to prosecute third-party websites for sex trafficking. *Santa Clara Law Review, 56*, 531.
Denzin, N. K. (1989). *Interpretive interactionism.* Newbury Park, CA: Sage Publications.
Edwards, J. M., Halpern, C. T., & Wechsberg, W. (2006). Correlates of exchanging sex for drugs among women who use crack cocaine. *AIDS Education & Prevention, 18*(5), 420–429. doi:10.1521/aeap.2006.18.5.420
Elliott, R., & Timulak, L. (2005). Descriptive and interpretive approaches to qualitative research. *A Handbook of Research Methods for Clinical and Health Psychology, 1*(7), 147–159.
Farley, M., Cotton, A., Lynne, J., Zumbeck, S., Spiwak, F., Reyes, M. E., … Sezgin, U. (2003). Prostitution and trafficking in nine countries: Update on violence and posttraumatic stress disorder. *The Journal of Trauma and Practice, 2*(3/4), 33–74. doi:10.1300/J189v02n03_03
Finn, M., & Stalans, L. (2016). How targeted enforcement shapes marketing decisions of pimps: Evidence of displacement and innovation. *Victims & Offenders, 11*(4), 578–599. doi:10.1080/15564886.2016.1187694
Gow, G. A., Barlott, T., Quinn, K., Linder, J., Soler, A., Edwards, G., & Hossain, S. (2015). Project backpage: Using text messaging to initiate outreach support for victims of human trafficking and sexual exploitation. *Journal of Human Trafficking, 1*(4), 259–274. doi:10.1080/23322705.2015.1016769
Harding, S. (2004). *The feminist standpoint theory reader: Intellectual and political controversies.* New York, NY: Routledge.
Heil, E., & Nichols, A. (2014). Hot spot trafficking: A theoretical discussion of the potential problems associated with targeted policing and the eradication of sex trafficking in the United States. *Contemporary Justice Review, 17*(4), 421–433. doi:10.1080/10282580.2014.980966

Higgins, A. (2019, April 11). One year ago, a bill targeting online sex trafficking took effect. Sex working say the consequences have been devastating. *The Lily*. Retrieved from https://www.lily.com

Hirschi, T. (2017). On the compatibility of rational choice and social control theories of crime. In D. B. Cornish & R. V. Clarke (Eds.), *The reasoning criminal* (pp. 105–118). New York, NY: Routledge.

Hughes, D. M. (2004). Prostitution online. *Journal of Trauma Practice*, *2*(3–4), 115–131. doi:10.1300/J189v02n03_06

Hunt, M. R. (2009). Strengths and challenges in the use of interpretive description: Reflections arising from a study of the moral experience of health professionals in humanitarian work. *Qualitative Health Research*, *19*(9), 1284–1292. doi:10.1177/1049732309344612

Jackson, C., & Heineman, J. (2018). Repeal FOSTA and decriminalize sex work. *Contexts*, *17*(3), 74–75. doi:10.1177/1536504218792534

Jeal, N., & Salisbury, C. (2004). A health needs assessment of street-based prostitutes: Cross-sectional survey. *Journal of Public Health*, *26*(2), 147–151. doi:10.1093/pubmed/fdh124

Kerrigan, D., Wirtz, A., Baral, S., Decker, M., Murray, L., & Beyrer, C. (2012). *The global HIV epidemics among sex workers*. Washington, DC: The World Bank.

Koken, J. A. (2012). Independent female escort's strategies for coping with sex work related stigma. *Sexuality and Culture*, *16*(3), 209–229. doi:10.1007/s12119-011-9120-3

Lazarus, L., Deering, K. N., Nabess, R., Gibson, K., Tyndall, M. W., & Shannon, K. (2012). Occupational stigma as a primary barrier to health care for street-based sex workers in Canada. *Culture, Health & Sexuality*, *14*(2), 139–150. Retrieved from http://www.tandfonline.com/doi/abs/10.1080/13691058.2011.628411

Lever, J., & Dolnick, D. (2000). Clients and call girls: Seeking sex and intimacy. In R. Weitzer (Ed.), *Sex for sale: Prostitution, pornography, and the sex industry* (pp. 85–100). New York, NY: Routledge.

Lincoln, Y., & Guba, E. (1985). *Naturalistic inquiry*. Beverly Hills, CA: Sage.

Manopaiboon, C., Bunnell, R. E., Kilmarx, P. H., Chaikummao, S., Limpakarnjanarat, K., Supawitkul, S., … Mastro, T. D. (2003). Leaving sex work: Barriers, facilitating factors and consequences for female sex workers in northern Thailand. *AIDS Care*, *15*(1), 39–52. doi:10.1080012021000039743

Månsson, S. A., & Hedin, U. C. (1999). Breaking the matthew effect on women leaving prostitution. *International Journal of Social Welfare*, *8*, 67–77. doi:10.1111/1468-2397.00063

Maxwell, J. A. (2010). Using numbers in qualitative research. *Qualitative Inquiry*, *16*(6), 475–482. doi:10.1177/1077800410364740

Moustakas, C. (1994). *Phenomenological research methods*. Thousand Oaks, CA: Sage.

Mueller, D. (2012). Treatment Courts and Court-Affiliated Diversion Projects for Prostitution in the United States: A report from the Prostitution Alternatives Round Table (PART) of the Chicago Coalition for the Homeless (CCH). Chicago Coalition for the Homeless.

Musheno, M., & Seeley, K. (1987). Prostitution policy and the women's movement: Historical analysis of feminist thought and organization. *Contemporary Crises*, *1*(3), 237–255. doi:10.1007/BF00729120

NVivo qualitative data analysis software. (2012). *QSR International Pty Ltd*. Version 10. Doncaster Victoria, Australia: QSR International Pty, Ltd.

Oselin, S. S. (2010). Weighing the consequences of a deviant career: Factors leading to an exit from prostitution. *Sociological Perspectives*, *53*(4), 527–549. doi:10.1525/sop.2010.53.4.527

Parmigiani, C. (2013). Curbing prostitution by arresting streetwalkers: The unequal treatment of sex workers in crime enforcement. *Law School Student Scholarship*, *384*. Retrieved from https://scholarship.shu.edu/student_scholarship/384

Patton, M. Q. (1990). Qualitative evaluation and research methods. SAGE Publications, inc.

Patton, M. Q. (1999). Enhancing the quality and credibility of qualitative analysis. *Health Services Research*, *34*, 1189–1208. doi:10.4135/9781412985727

Patton, M. Q. (2010). *Developmental evaluation: applying complexity concepts to enhance innovation and use*. Guilford Press.
Plumbridge, E, & Abel, G. (2001). A 'segmented'sex industry in new zealand: Sexual and personal safety of female sex workers. *Australian and New Zealand Journal of Public Health, 25*(1), 78–83.
Potterat, J. J., Brewer, D. D., Muth, S. Q., Rothenberg, R. B., Woodhouse, D. E., Muth, J. B., ... Brody, S. (2004). Mortality in a long-term open cohort of prostitute women. *American Journal of Epidemiology, 159*(8), 778–785. doi:10.1093/aje/kwh110
Preble, K. M. (2015). Creating trust among the distrustful: a phenomenological examination of supportive services for former sex workers.. *Journal of Aggression, Maltreatment & Trauma, 24* (4), 433–453.
Preble, K. M. (2019). Under their "control" Perceptions of Traffickers' Power and Coercion among International Female Trafficking Survivors during Exploitation. *Victims & Offenders*, 1–23.
Preble, K. M, & Black, B. M. (2019). Influence of survivors' entrapment factors and traffickers' characteristics on perceptions of interpersonal social power during exit. *Violence against women*. doi:10.1177/1077801219826742
Pyett, P. M., & Warr, D. J. (1997). Vulnerability on the streets: Female sex workers and HIV risk. *AIDS Care, 9*, 539–547. doi:10.1080/713613193
Raphael, J., & Shapiro, D. L. (2004). Violence in indoor and outdoor prostitution venues. *Violence Against Women, 10*(2), 126–139. doi:10.1177/1077801203260529
Razack, S. (1998). Race, space, and prostitution: the making of the bourgeois subject. *Can. J. Women & L., 10*, 338.
Reinharz, S. (1992). *Feminist methods in social research*. New York, NY: Oxford University Press.
Rekart, M. (2005). Sex-work harm reduction. *The Lancet, 366*, 2123–2134. doi:10.1016/S0140-6736(05)67732-X
Roe-Sepowitz, D. E., Gallagher, J., Hickle, K. E., Pérez Loubert, M., & Tutelman, J. (2014). Project ROSE: An arrest alternative for victims of sex trafficking and prostitution. *Journal of Offender Rehabilitation, 53*(1), 57–74. doi:10.1080/10509674.2013.861323
Sallmann, J. (2010). Living with stigma: Women's experiences of prostitution and substance use. *Affilia: Journal of Women and Social Work, 25*(2), 146–159. doi:10.1177/0886109910364362
Sanders, T. (2004). A continuum of risk? The management of health, physical and emotional risks by female sex workers. *Sociology of Health & Illness, 26*(5), 557–574. doi:10.1111/shil.2004.26.issue-5
Sanders, T. (2005). Researching the online sex work community. In C. Hine (Ed.), *Virtual methods* (pp. 67–79). London, UK: Berg.
Sanders, T. (2007). Becoming an ex-sex worker: Making transitions out of a deviant career. *Feminist Criminology, 2*, 74–95. doi:10.1177/1557085106294845
Sanders, T., Cunningham, S., Platt, L., Grenfell, P., & Macioti, P. G. (2017, July). *Reviewing the occupational risks of sex workers in comparison to other "risky" professions*. Wellcome Trust: University of Leicester. Retrieved from https://www2.le.ac.uk/departments/criminology/people/teela-sanders/sex-work-and-homicide
Sanders, T., O'Neill, M., & Pitcher, J. (2009). *Prostitution: Sex work, policy & politics*. Thousand Oaks, CA: Sage.
Sausa, L., Keatley, J., & Operario, D. (2007). Perceived risks and benefits of sex work among transgender women of color in San Francisco. *Archive of Sexual Behavior, 36*(6), 768–777. doi:10.1007/s10508-007-9210-3
Seib, C., Fischer, J., & Najman, J. M. (2009). The health of female sex workers from three industry sectors in Queensland, Australia. *Social Science and Medicine, 68*, 473–478. doi:10.1016/j.socscimed.2008.10.024
Smolak, A. (2013). White slavery, whorehouse riots, venereal disease, and saving women: Historical context of prostitution interventions and harm reduction in New York City during the Progressive Era. *Social Work Public Health, 28*(5), 486–508. doi:10.1080/19371918.2011.592083
Thorne, S., Kirkham, S. R., & O'Flynn-Magee, K. (2004). The analytic challenge in interpretive description. *International Journal of Qualitative Methods, 3*(1), 1–11. doi:10.1177/160940690400300101

Wahab, S., & Panichelli, M. (2013). Ethical and human rights issues in coercive interventions with sex workers. *Affilia, 28*, 344–349. doi:10.1177/0886109913505043

Weitzer, R. (1991). Prostitutes' rights in the United States: The failure of a movement. *Sociological Quarterly, 32*(1), 23–41. doi:10.1111/j.1533-8525.1991.tb00343.x

Weitzer, R. (1999). Prostitution control in america: rethinking public policy. crime. *Law and Social Change, 32*(1), 83.

Weitzer, R. (2005). New directions in research on prostitution. *Crime, Law & Social Change, 43*, 211–235. doi:10.1007/s10611-005-1735-6

Weitzer, R. (2007). Prostitution: Facts and fictions. *Contexts, 6*(4), 28–33. doi:10.1525/ctx.2007.6.4.28

Weitzer, R. (2009). Sociology of sex work. *Annual Review Of Sociology, 35*, 213-234.

Weitzer, R. (2010). *Sex for sale* (2nd ed.). New York, NY: Routledge.

Wertz, F. J. (1983). From everyday to psychological description: Analyzing the moments of a qualitative data analysis. *Journal of Phenomenological Psychology, 14*, 197–241. doi:10.1163/156916283X00108

Williamson, C., & Folaron, G. (2003). Understanding the experiences of street level prostitutes. *Qualitative Social Work, 2*(3), 271–287. doi:10.1177/14733250030023004

Self-Narratives of Persistent Pimps and Those Anticipating Desistance: Emotions, Conventional Work, and Moral Profitability Calculus

Loretta J. Stalans and Mary A. Finn

ABSTRACT

Identity, values, and emotional processes underlying desistance and persistence in the illicit sex trade have received little empirical attention. An analysis of qualitative interviews of 49 active pimps or drivers managing sex workers showed that persisting pimps and those leading double lives assigned different meanings to their participation in legitimate employment. Persisters valued legitimate work as a strategy to evade arrest, whereas pimps with "double lives" emphasized legitimate work as providing long-term financial security and enhanced social identity. Analysis yielded contextualized understanding of their self-narratives (e.g.) that underlie reflections upon who they are and who they want to become, and the moral contemplations and emotional processes involved in stigma management.

Pimps in popular culture are depicted as committed to a long-term illegal career of profiting from the management of sex workers and as adhering to deviant values that support amassing financial wealth through the exploitation of their workers. The scant empirical research also has found long careers of illegal pimping, but this research has interviewed a limited market segment of managers from disadvantaged neighborhoods who have sex workers soliciting on the street (e.g., Davis, 2017; Milner & Milner, 1973) or in massage or escort businesses (e.g., May, Harocopos, & Hough, 2000). Most research has excluded segments of the illicit sex market wherein sex workers recruit managers and establish a partnership (e.g., Morselli & Savoie-Gargiso, 2014). Moreover, some research has documented the existence of part-time pimps (Marcus, Horning, Curtis, Sanson, & Thompson, 2014), but little is known about how or why pimps reduce or terminate their involvement in illicit sex markets.

Our research begins to address this lack of empirical data, through examining pimps' perspectives on desisting or persisting in pimping. Desistance is a gradual process whereby cognitive, identity, and motivational processes change to support reduced involvement and eventual cessation of criminal activity (e.g., Paternoster & Bushway, 2009). Most research on desistance defines active desisters as those who have stopped committing offenses for one year (Maruna, 2001) or two years (e.g., Campbell & Hansen, 2012; Giordano, Cernkovich, & Rudolph, 2002); however, Giordano, Schroeder, and Cernkovich (2007) categorized those still involved in minor offenses as desisters. Focusing on more stable desisters ignores the emotional and cognitive struggles of individuals who are preparing to quit illegal behavior through continued involvement in both conventional work and in illicit markets. Research on active drug dealers living in middle class areas (Curcione, 1997; Jacques & Wright, 2015) supports that individuals can be simultaneously immersed in illicit drug markets and in conventional activities, but these studies have ignored the core identities, emotions, and values that might contribute to desistance or persistence of criminal careers or the meanings that individuals assign to conventional work activities.

Giordano et al. (2007) proposed that contemplation about self-identity and the meaning of possible external opportunities are more determinant of whether individuals persist or desist in criminal offending than simply the presence of external opportunities of legitimate work, marriage, or parenthood. Other qualitative research and theories also suggest that a change in self-narrative is critically linked to a trajectory of reduced involvement and eventual desistance from criminal activity (e.g., Maruna, 2001; Paternoster & Bushway, 2009; Presser, 2010; Sandberg, 2010). Giordano et al. (2002, 2007) argue a core self-narrative is formed through reflection about social interactions and experiences, which intertwine emotional and cognitive reactions to experiences. Individuals, for example, reflect upon and might revise their core self-narrative when significant others stigmatize their criminal activities and they feel shame, disdain for self, or guilt (Giordano et al., 2002, 2007; Vaughan, 2007). Moreover, morals, beliefs about what is right and wrong, are central concepts in self-narratives, and have their initial roots in childhood (e.g., McLean, Pasupathi, & Pals, 2007).

Theories of cognitive and emotional transformations (Giordano et al., 2002, 2007), originating from a symbolic interactionist perspective, highlight cognitive and emotional changes about one's view of self (i.e., self-identity or self-narrative) as pivotal to desistance. Conversely, life course theory of desistance (Laub & Sampson, 2003), originating from social control theories, emphasizes the constraints of external events and roles and asserts that legitimate work opportunities are "turning points" that individuals can seize to begin leading crime-free lives. Our paper analyzes the qualitative interviews of 49 pimps who were asked to present their own narratives of self-identity and their plans to persist or desist from the illicit sex trade. We compared those who identified with being a pimp[1] and were committed to a life-long career in pimping, referred to herein as self-identified persisters, and persons who plan to quit pimping, are involved in conventional work or education, have pro-social identities, and are taking cognitive and behavioral steps to quit pimping, herein referred to as preparatory desisters, or those leading double lives. Both self-identified persisters and preparatory desisters were equally likely to be involved in conventional work, but they assigned different meanings to conventional work and their pimping activity. Moreover, most symbolic interactionist research on desistance (e.g., Giordano et al., 2002, 2007; McLean et al., 2007) has focused on minors or young adults. Thus, it was crucial to assess whether pimps' views of their parental approval or disapproval of pimping were consistent with the morals in their own self-narratives, and whether these differed for self-identified persisting pimps and those in preparatory desistance.

Literature review

Individuals have multiple self-narratives, but psychological research suggests that individuals are striving to create a coherent and consistent core self-narrative (e.g., McAdams, 2013). From the viewpoint of narrative criminology (Presser & Sandberg, 2015), self-identity theory of desistance (Paternoster & Bushway, 2009) and cognitive and emotional transformation theories of desistance (Giordano et al., 2002, 2007), self-narratives of personal identity are dynamic and how individuals portray their self-identity depends in part on their audience. Moreover, social interactions also shape how people perceive themselves. Much research has suggested that self-narratives are critical in differentiating individuals who are committed to continual, persistent criminal involvement from those who are on a trajectory of reduced involvement and eventual desistance from criminal activity (e.g., Paternoster & Bushway, 2009; Sandberg, 2010). Self-narratives shape our engagement with and interpretation of events and experiences, and individuals imagine a better future self (Giordano et al., 2002; Healy, 2014) and might also contemplate their worse possible self, "a feared self" (Paternoster & Bushway, 2009). Self-narratives contain content from three functions of the self: as actor containing beliefs and representations of our social roles; as motivated agents containing emotions, hopes, goals and features; and as story-teller of stories about ourselves where reflection highlights "who the self was, is and will be as a developing person in time" (McAdams, 2013, p. 273).

Cognitive and emotional transformations

Guiding our research, Giordano et al. (2002) proposed that contemplation about self-identity and the interpreted meanings of possible external opportunities are more determinant of whether individuals persist in criminal offending or desist than the mere presence of external opportunity. Desistance involves a four stage process of cognitive transformation involving the initial stage of being open to changing one's self-narrative, then interpreting potential environmental opportunities as "hooks for change", seeing the potential role shifts of new conventional work or relationship as incompatible with the deviance, and imaging and adopting a "replacement" identity to guide behavior and interpret future experiences. Self-narratives contain our views about important priorities, patterns of behavior for certain situations, and beliefs about what is moral or wrong, which often might be connected to emotions and rationalizations. Adopting a more pro-social identity as a replacement self increases the likelihood that desistance from criminal or delinquent behavior will be sustained (Giordano et al., 2002).

Family morals on development of self-narratives

From the symbolic interactionist perspective, self-narratives influence how individuals act and sharing stories about themselves contributes to how others perceive them. "Indeed, sharing stories is the mechanism through which people become selves." (McLean et al., 2007, p. 275). Social interactions, thus, are critical for the development of deviant or conventional self-narratives, and moral content along with patterned emotional reactions and attitudes form one's self-narrative (Giordano et al., 2007; McAdams, 2013; Vaughan, 2007). Presentation of self is a performance, one often used to deflect social stigma and pass as conventional or "normal" (Goffman, 1959, 1963). Family members are an important contributor to self-narratives in childhood and parental values might also contribute to adults' self-narratives and/or emotional struggles. Drawing from the symbolic interactionist perspective, Giordano et al. (2007) proposed that emotions arise from the process of role-taking and our childhood experiences within the family shape our presentation of emotional selves. They analyzed qualitative and quantitative longitudinal data from interviews conducted in 1982, 1995 and 2003 found those with an angry self-narrative or a depressed self-narrative were more likely to be persisters than desisters, after controlling for adolescents' delinquency, race, gender, poverty, marital happiness and occupational prestige. Thus, self-narratives had independent effects on desistence beyond structural environmental conditions.

Morals, beliefs about what is right and wrong, are central concepts in self-narrative, and have their initial roots in childhood (e.g., McLean et al., 2007). Anderson (1999) conducted ethnographic research in disadvantaged Black communities in Philadelphia and depicted the co-existence of two value systems in these communities, which the residents labeled as "street code" and "decency." "Street code" is an oppositional subcultural value system in which respect is obtained through displaying physical aggression when challenged or disrespected, and the commission of crime is encouraged to obtain the status symbols of the middle class. Some children are born into "street code" families, with parents who are involved in criminal activity, such as drug dealing or prostitution, and who often encourage their children to participate (Anderson, 1999). "Decency" represents the conventional values of obtaining status through working hard at school and at legitimate jobs, obeying a religious moral code and the criminal law, and resorting only to physical fights for self-protection. Decent parents reinforce to their children that "street code" is not an appropriate lifestyle. Furthermore, longitudinal research has found that "street code" support is primarily stable from childhood through the mid-twenties, though 12.6% of the sample in one study showed a declining trend in support of "street code" mentality (Moule, Burt, Stewart, & Simons, 2015).

Prior research suggests that "street code" values include beliefs in a hostile and unfair world and the desire to obtain immediate gratification through illegal means if necessary; this belief system is used to interpret and ascribe meanings to conventional opportunities and experiences (Simons & Burt, 2011). Moreover, disadvantaged neighborhoods with greater crimes, parental socialization, and repeated coercive, violent, or degrading experiences were more likely to develop a "street code" belief system (Simons & Burt, 2011; Stewart, 2010). Thus, "street code" belief systems occur through social learning, and emphasize enhancing profits without regard to the effects on other people (Simons & Burt, 2011); individuals with low self-control are more likely to hold a "street code" belief system, but the personality trait of self-control is a distinct concept from the "street code" or "decency" belief systems (Intravia et al., 2018). Pimps also focus on maximizing profits and often hold a degrading view of sex workers; this finding is found in qualitative interviews with 85 pimps in Harlem (Horning & Sriken, 2017), with 10 managers of massage parlors used as fronts for illicit prostitution (May et al., 2000), with 25 pimps of street-soliciting sex workers (Raphael & Myers-Powell, 2010) and with 71 pimps of online-soliciting sex workers (Finn & Stalans, 2017).

Conventional work and desistance

Life course theory of desistance (Laub & Sampson, 2003) suggests that opportunities for conventional work, especially quality jobs, will promote desistance, as all people, irrespective of their belief systems, are assumed to interpret conventional work as promoting stability and enhancing social status. However, research has produced conflicting findings on whether obtaining legitimate employment reduces criminal offending (see for reviews Uggen & Wakefield, 2008; Van Der Geest, Bijleveld, & Blokland, 2011). Moreover, cognitive and emotional transformation theory (Giordano et al., 2002, 2007) suggests that individuals must be open to seeing the potential of conventional work being incompatible with their pimping activities. The perception of incompatibility will depend in part on whether the social networks formed at pimps' conventional jobs facilitate and condone the illicit sex trade, and the functions pimps assign to conventional work. Point in fact, Uggen and Shannon (2014) found that offenders assigned to the supported work program compared to the control group significantly reduced their economic-motivated offending, but maintained their use of cocaine and heroin, as their coworkers in restaurants reportedly used drugs and facilitated connections to drug sellers.

Most prior interview studies have not asked pimps about their legitimate employment, and the function that conventional employment serves. Pimps who identify with the deviant illicit sex trade might seek conventional jobs as a way of "passing" as a pro-social law-abiding person (Goffman, 1959, 1963) whereas pimps who identify with pro-social values and are committed to desistance might see conventional work as providing the long-term financial security and reputational capital to transition away from pimping. Recently, Loughran, Nagin, and Nguyen (2017) in the Pathways of Desistance study found that involvement in legal employment and desistance from crime was a gradual process, and nearly one quarter to one third of their sample simultaneously participated in legitimate work and crime. Moreover, as the periods of engagement in only legitimate work increased across time, the probability of being in a crime-free state increased.

Current research questions

Drawing from Giordano et al. (2002, 2007) symbolic interactionist perspective on the cognitive and emotional transformation underlying desistance, we sought to understand the earlier stages of the desistance process through studying pimps who were leading "double lives." These pimps have realistic plans to quit pimping, have taken preparatory steps, such as holding a conventional job or attending college, and have reduced their involvement in the illicit sex trade. We refer to the pimps leading "double lives" as engaged in "preparatory desistance". Healy (2014) studied five "liminal desisters," a term applied to those poised on the threshold between two social worlds who have constructed a new conventional identity but had not fully achieved their new conventional identity. We conducted qualitative and quantitative analyses[2] of the themes that were associated with pimps' self-narratives about their persistence or reduction in involvement in the illicit sex trade. Three questions are addressed in the current study: To what extent are moral qualms or anticipated stigma from conventional family or friends mentioned in pimps' narratives about continual or reduced involvement in the illicit sex trade, and how are these balanced with economic considerations? Do pimps vary in their interpretation of the roles of employee in conventional work such that these roles can foster either persistence or reduced involvement in illicit activities? If qualitative research finds differences in interpretations of conventional work, do childhood socialization through "street code" or "decency" values in childhood neighborhoods and parental values and also college educational opportunities, current conventional work, and entry in pimping relate to their persistence or leading double lives?

Method

Sample characteristics

The sample consisted of 49 men of which 42 actively managed sex workers in their own business, and 7 provided transportation and protection for sex workers who were self-employed or employed by a different manager. The age at the time of interview ranged from 18 to 65, with a mean age of 40.4 years. The age at which the men began pimping or driving ranged from 12 to 51 years old (mean = 26). Half had been pimping or driving 8.5 years or longer, and the range was 1 to 40 years. Educational achievement was diverse: 17 college graduates, 10 high school graduates with some college education, 17 high school graduates/GED, and 5 high school drop-outs. Racial identity was also diverse: 24 Caucasians, 18 African-Americans, 2 Asians, 3 Latinos, and 2 of mixed race. The percentage of sex workers' earnings acquired by pimps varied with half taking 50% or more, and the range was 20 to 100%. The median annual income from illicit pimping or driving was $70,100, with a range from $1,500 to $780,000.

Sampling

Recruitment occurred through advertisements on the survey, escort, and massage sections of Backpage, and referrals from selected pimps or a former prostitute. Three interviewees, a White driver involved in a sex trafficking operation, a Black pimp who entered through family socialization, and a Latino pimp who was a gang member, each received $40 for referring two additional interviewees. In addition, a former Black sex worker in the business for 25 years referred three Black pimps. The advertisement stated: "Research team seeks to interview men 18 years or older about their experiences as managers in the erotic industry. *Confidential* in-person interviews last approximately one hour. Convenient Chicago location* Will pay $60 for completed interviews. For more information, to see if you qualify, call … or email." The first author provided a number and email address specifically for this project. She then prescreened potential interviewees to determine eligibility. The interviews took place between April through June of 2013 and 2014 in a public tea establishment in Chicago. Interviewees preferred tables away from other patrons where discreet communication could occur.

Interviews

The first author's university internal review board approved the research protocol. All interviewees provided verbal consent, were instructed to refrain from providing identifying information such as employment sites, website addresses or real names of those in their social network, signed for their $60 in compensation using a false name, and were informed that an individual's identifying data would not be provided to law enforcement or others. The interviewer never knew their legal name, which decreased the risk of legal consequences for participants. Interviewees were motivated, in part, by the chance to provide information about aspects of their lives that might be part of academic publications, and to help the researcher understand how they managed workers in an illicit sex trade. Additionally, the researcher learned that meet and greet conversations were used by pimps to solicit workers, and occasionally was propositioned after the interview, as the pimps did not believe that the interview was solely for research purposes. Of course, such propositions were soundly, but politely rejected. Interviewees consented to audio recording the interviews, which were transcribed and checked for accuracy.

Interviews were conducted as informal conversations, lasting about one hour, with some general open-ended questions used to discuss their business in the illicit sex trade and their life before and after entering the sex trade. Interview questions focused on their views about who they were; how they became managers of sex workers; their business rules, strategies, and organizational structure; their current and prior roles in the sex industry, such as client, prostitute, and driver; their plans to expand or exit the illicit sex trade; and the circumstances around when sex workers were fired or left the business. Participants also had opportunities to narrate their life story beyond their illicit activities, including "self-defining moments" where they learned something about themselves. The interviewer often used simple phrases that were consistent with interviewee's language to keep the conversation going, including "right", "okay", "mmm", or repeating a key phrase, or asking for a clarification on the meaning of a key phrase. Direct questions were asked about their neighborhood and familial background including gang affiliation, visibility of prostitution in the neighborhood, family's involvement in the sex trade and approval of their involvement, and their disclosure to friends and family about what they do. Respondents were asked their current age, relationship status, educational achievement, if these were not mentioned. The open-ended conversation and the anonymity of the interview allowed rapport to be established and participants to interject what they considered to be relevant information about their lives and their illicit activities; these interviewing techniques bolstered the credibility, rich details and authenticity of the qualitative data (Sandberg, 2010).

Coding of demographic information and socialization

Information about whether college educated, holding a current conventional job were taken from questions or explicit responses; these variables were dummy-coded for Table one. Similarly, whether respondents entered pimping through family socialization or work connections was transparent in interviewees' responses, and thus these measures were dummy-coded for Table one.

Coding of parental values

Anderson's concept of whether parents instilled or supported "street code" or attempted to instill or support "decency," was coded from a set of specific questions about parental approval or facilitation. Thus, for this coding, we had a developed code sheet based on Anderson's concept. Two coders searched for relevant questions, and then extracted the information in a Word document; the three disagreements in coding were discussed, and a consensus was reached. During the training, the first author taught the research assistant to not make assumptions and to code an "affirmation" of a category only if the information was explicit. The responses were coded into three categories: a) "decency" parental values where respondents reported parental disapproval for pimping or criminal activity; b) "street code" parental values approving their criminal activity or whether their parents disapproved or would disapprove if informed; or c) parental values were not mentioned. Of the respondents coded as having parents who supported "decency", 17 of the 18 respondents directly reported that parents would express disapproval if they knew, or had expressed strong disapproval when they were informed, of any criminal activity. These selected quotes illustrate parental disapproval: "think they would just do as any other parents would do and try to encourage me not to do it and try to tell me the degree is what it is" (ID = 30); "they'd probably disown me" (ID = 42); "I would lie through my teeth. (Ok and why?) Come on, no one wants to be the mom or dad of a pimp." (ID = 47). One interviewee was coded as having a "decent" upbringing based on three indicators of conventional values: Parents have a legitimate job, go to church, and encourage the pimp/ driver to do well in school. Respondents were coded as having parent(s) that supported "street code" if the parental figure mentored their entry into the illicit prostitution or drug trade or encouraged gang affiliation. If respondents became gang members at a young age and their parent(s) did not disapprove or stop them, they were also coded as supporting "street code." Two respondents who indicated that their fathers approved but their mothers did not and had left due to domestic violence or expressed disapproval, were coded as parent supported "street code." This coding is consistent with Anderson (1999) who noted the importance of "old male heads" serving as role models. From this coding scheme, a dummy-coded variable was created: socialized in "decency" was coded as zero (n = 31, 63.7%), and parents supported "street code" (n = 18, 36.7%) was coded as one.

Coding of core self-identities: pro-social or criminal identity

A research assistant and the first author coded whether individuals perceived their criminal activity as part of their core self-identity through reading the transcriptions and examining what identities were asserted. The grouping of deviant compared to prosocial occurred after coding whether interviewees mentioned specific identities. Individuals were coded as having a self-identified criminal identity if they either reported spontaneously or when asked how they saw themselves, identified themselves as pimps (N = 13), gang members (N = 8), or drug dealer (N = 1). Indicators of self-identified pimps included the following quotes: "I was kinda like born a natural, I guess natural pimp anyways. (ID 29)"; "I got pimp lady on this arm with a money sign." (ID 35). When asked to describe a memory that was high point that brought joy, ID 44 exclaimed: "Back when I was about 35 I got nominated and came in like 2nd, you know, for a Players' Ball. ... And uh, just to place second, you know among the peers or whatever, was a good feeling." ID 41 when asked do you call yourself a pimp, responded, "Yes, yeah that's right, that's the correct term." One interviewee was not asked and did not spontaneously indicate a self-identity; he was coded as a criminal identity due to his blunt descriptions of coercive and violent acts and involvement of minors in his sex trafficking organization. The 27 interviewees categorized as having core prosocial identities were those who, without prompting, noted that they worked as a manager or in a legitimate business as well, referred to themselves as a business person, taxi driver, broker, or manager when asked what do you see yourself as, or interjected their religious or moral beliefs into the conversation, projecting self-images as ethical persons.

Qualitative coding of persisting or preparatory desisting

The first author and a research assistant read through transcribed interviews at least twice to capture information about reduction or expansion in pimping/driving, plans to exit, and non-disclosures to family and friends; only two disagreements occurred and were resolved through discussion. A short synopsis of each participant's entry and expansion or reduction in pimping or driving was written to capture the self-narrated life course of the offender. Persisting in pimping or driving was defined as a continuation of the same level of pimping activities evident at entry, with any reductions attributed to market demands or a need to readjust marketing (e.g., learning online solicitation or an expansion of sex workers, areas, or clientele). Consistent with Giordano et al. (2002) coding of cognitive transformations, those persisting in pimping had given little thought about exiting whereas those coded as preparatory desisters had taken substantial steps to reduce their involvement, held pro-social identities, were involved in conventional work, and perceived their pimping as secondary income rather than as part of their identity. For example, when asked, "Do you plan on continuing to do this for the next 5 years, 10 years, 15?" ID 51 was coded as persisting and stated: "Um, probably say, I don't know, maybe like another 5 at the most, probably. … And I'm not even sure, I don't have like a timeline or like a goal. … Like oh, I wanna save this much in this or you know this is where I wanna get with business. No, it's just right now it's more income, that's it. You know there's no goal, no plan, No agenda." Other examples of desistance are discussed in the results sections.

Results

Preparatory desisting or leading double lives defined pimps who expressed attitudes consistent with conventional society, were taking concrete steps to fully immerse back into conventional society such as participating in conventional work or education, and either expressed a desire to exit the business or exited the business for periods over one year. Those leading double lives had saved money, invested in legitimate businesses that were for purposes other than laundering money or serving as fronts, and talked about reconciling their "double lives." Three participants, at the time of the interview, had desisted for over two years from protecting or driving sex workers, and were immersed in conventional relationships and legitimate jobs (IDs 47, 54, 57); they were included in the group categorized as preparatory desisters, leading to 13 preparatory desisters emerging from the data as we did not expect that pimps would be leading "double lives".

In the results section, we describe our findings that emerged from the qualitative analysis on how preparatory desisters' self-narratives described conventional values, guilt, and emotional stress from hiding their pimping activities from conventional others whereas persisters showed an absence of guilt. Preparatory desisters and persisters also ascribed different meanings to work, although these groups did not differ on the likelihood of holding conventional jobs. After examining their self-narratives on desisting and persisting in pimping, we compare the preparatory desisters who all had prosocial identities (n = 13) to the persisters with prosocial identities (n = 14) and the self-identified pimps with street code values (n = 22) on childhood background, such as parental values and disadvantaged neighborhoods, familial socialization into the illicit sex trade, and structural opportunities of conventional work and college education. This comparison informed us as to whether persisters and preparatory desisters had different structural opportunities and socialization experiences and how their self-identities framed their interpretations of their illicit and licit work.

Self-narratives of preparatory desisters: morals and guilt overshadow profits of pimping

Desistance research suggests that a change from a deviant self-identity to a pro-social identity is a crucial transformation for persistent offenders to desist from criminal behavior (Giordano et al., 2002, 2007; Maruna, 2001; Paternoster & Bushway, 2009). However, 63% of the pimps in our study noted that they were raised with conventional values and their parents would express disapproval if they found out. Almost all (12 of the 13) interviewees leading double lives mentioned that their parents emphasized conventional values and would disapprove of their pimping. Most preparatory desisters had a pro-social self-identity at the time of pimping, which was neutralized. Eventually, their conventional upbringing and pro-social self-narrative created an emotional toll that reduced the appeal of pimping. Preparatory desisters often were concerned about what their children or women family members would think of them. For example, ID 55 responded that his biggest fear was:

> "Exposing myself, people know what, what, what I really am. That's really important cause … that's not who I am, that's what I do. … I have ambition and things in society as well. It's a double life in a way."

Their narratives contained struggles with guilt, embarrassment, and neutralizations to reconcile their simultaneous participation in the illicit sex trade and in the legal formal economy. Consistent with Vaughan's (2007, p. 393) argument, emotions often stimulated reflection about the self and modifications of their future self-narrative. ID 50 exemplified this embarrassment and non-disclosure: "It's sort of like embarrassing to tell them (ex-wife and daughter) about it (pimping). I don't really tell people about what I do, other than people that are in the business." Similarly, ID 62, who both managed and provided services, noted that disclosure to conventional persons is unsatisfying:

> "When you're in this business, … I guess you sorta isolate yourself. … It's just nicer to talk to other people in the business because you know you can't really talk with anyone else. You feel like they disapprove plus they don't understand, you know what it's like. I mean it's a job. … (I: Why would you anticipate stopping?) Cause I won't have school to pay anymore."

Preparatory desisters struggled emotionally with the moral qualms and the need to hide their activities from their conventional family and friends. Six of the thirteen preparatory desisters made explicit statements expressing their moral qualms about prostitution and did not support legalization. ID 42 articulated well his struggle of balancing aspirations for economic prosperity with his conscience:

> "Well, you know sometimes I get depressed about it, you know I got to find something else legitimate. I have to lie to my friends about what I do. Uh it's just very uh stressful and taxing on myself mentally and emotionally. It makes me feel uh very immoral about myself. Uh, I consider myself of high character with morals. Uh, also I grew up in a Christian household so I have a lot of guilt because of that. Uh, I know what I'm doing is wrong, but uh, it's uh, unfortunately it's, it's uh, again this sounds like an excuse but I'm just being honest, uh, people kind of get used to uh (I: A certain level of living) Yeah, and that's the problem and uh, I know I can't do this forever."

Childhood socialization in families that provided discussions about morals contributed to the emotional struggles of pimps leading double lives. ID 19 also expressed guilt and, due to his shame, hid his involvement from his family and girlfriend. He, moreover, explicitly noted that if the amount of money were reduced, he would not have agreed to take over his uncle's illicit prostitution business while he was in China. ID 19 explained:

> "I'm not gonna lie, it's, if, if the profit margin was a lot lower, like maybe even half, it wouldn't be worth it … because I could go to jail. And, I have a clean record. I don't know what the charge would be. I don't even know; I'm not a lawyer, but it's a felony and you know, I'm still relatively young. It, it would totally ruin my life. And I'd be in the paper; it'd just be horrible. So, you know, the fact that I'm making about $4,000, you know is good, but if it cut down to two then I wouldn't do it anymore."

Those that articulated periods of decreasing or stopping their pimping discussed the morality of making earnings from sex workers and their familial relationships with women. For example, ID 54 who had desisted from pimping and being a gang member at the end of 2012 explained his decision to go only the conventional route:

> I wanted uh, to go straight and make an earning, a legit, a legit earning, living. I guess like backed up off the gang. … It's very time consuming and I just, I just got tired of the lifestyle. Like I said I got tired of like living off of women. … And the things that they were doing were immoral. I knew that, but the money was good. (I: Oh, you think it is immoral?) Yeah, yeah. (I: Ok.) And I have sisters so, and then I also have a daughter so all of that came into play when I, I wanted to stop, when I wasn't messing with ladies and decided to stop. (I: Alright. Did your family know you were doing this?) No. … . (I: Ok, so do you think you're going to get back into the game?) Uh, it's, it's crossed my mind a couple of times, but things haven't really got like tight and like they were before, when I first got in, they never got tight like that. Cause now I'm in a relationship. (I: So both of you are living together?) Yes, and you know she's not gonna let me be in the streets like that. (I: Ok.) Yeah, she's kinda, kinda firm on that. (So, she's more conventional?) Yes, yes. (I: And does she have a job as well?) Yes, she, she works.

Similarly, ID 57 and ID 55 struggled with their conscience as they were concerned that their reputation would be damaged and would not reflect their true selves as prosocial persons. ID 57 moved away from his kids to hide his illicit activities and stopped selling drugs and driving sex workers when his kids were around 12 years of age. He noted: "It was like that's part of my life I wanted to put behind me cause I didn't want my nieces, nephews and my kids … to have that vision of me." ID 55 who sells electronics expressed how identity and conscience were central to his emotional struggles:

> "I think I'd like to wrap this business, you know I'm thinking about a current transition just trying to find what else, it's not something I'm comfortable really doing. … You grow up and you start to you know form values and stuff like that and I'm realizing that I don't think I wanna keep a family, yeah. I'm sad, I'm not really proud of what I'm doing."

These quotes highlight that the process of desistance centered around being perceived as a good and prosocial person and believing that they were persons of moral character who were participating in an immoral enterprise. Pro-social self-identities were center stage, as well as their conventional upbringing and continual interactions with others who held prosocial identities. Those with prosocial identities leading a double life underscored the mental toll that the upfront stage work (Goffman, 1959, 1963) required to maintain a legitimate social identity and hide the stigmatizing involvement in the illicit sex trade.

However, two preparatory desisters had no moral issues with prostitution, and exhibited a sequential process of participating in either legitimate work or involvement in the illicit sex trade. The lack of moral reflection might have contributed to these relapses (Vaughan, 2007); for example, ID 27 who also worked in a legitimate business described his involvement in the illicit sex trade as: "I was in for a good, two or three years, out for about four years, back in for about three years." He hid his involvement from conventional relationships and turned back to pimping when he lost his legitimate job.

Persisting pimps focus on profits and avoid deep reflection

Self-identified pimps (N = 14) were defined as those who spontaneously labeled and identified themselves as pimps, indicating it was an important part of their self-identity. In addition, eight interviewees identified as gang members and drug dealers, and their pimping occurred in conjunction with their other crimes. Almost all, except two, were deeply immersed in the illicit sex trade without plans to exit. Of these 14 self-identified pimps, 86% of their parents approved of their pimping. Eight self-identified pimps learned their illicit trade from family members, and fellow gang members taught the other three. The other three self-identified pimps sought tutelage from pimps and sex workers that they befriended in the illicit sex trade. Fathers, uncles, brothers, a couple of mothers and other workers in the illicit sex trade exposed, taught, and provided the necessary opportunities to learn pimping. In addition, family members often provided validation that the activities were not immoral. A white pimp, (ID 45), who is 46 years old was socialized by his brother and emotionally close to his mother described his mother's approval and encouragement:

> Mom knew and she just always said, use your head, use your eyes, use your ears, use your mind, if something doesn't seem right, you know you don't need it, so walk away, whereas my brother, he never can walk away. … (I: She didn't have any moral qualms about it?) No, no it was a way of making a living. I was much better at it than my brother and she couldn't understand why I wouldn't expand. … I wanted the girls to care about what they did and the services that were provided.

Most self-identified pimps deflected some responsibility to external circumstances in discussing how they began pimping. ID 29 minimized his agency for pimping and for using violence on sex workers, suggesting that he was complying with the desires and expectations of his sex workers:

> I was kinda like born a natural, I guess natural pimp anyways. … My first girl, she kind of led the way in the beginning; she uh had grabbed a couple more uh, ladies and brought to the stable. … I just went with the flow. … I tried to be a smooth pimp. I didn't try to be a violent

> pimp you know, but sometimes … . They don't respect you if you don't do certain things. (I: Right). Then, they uh, you know physically attack you if you don't.

Some pimps had conflicting messages and acknowledged their choice between a legitimate pathway and a criminal pathway. Some, however, illustrated agency in choosing whether to become a pimp as they received conflicting messages from their mother and father. ID 13 who is 18 years old described how he learned through role modeling his father and rejected his mother's attempts to instill more conventional values:

> Really it was my father's business, I kinda picked it up after him, when I was late 15. … . I went to military school, 16. Around the time uh, started, started 15, late 15 I dropped out of school, so early 16, you know, working on the business. Early 16 working on the business, mid 16 um, went to military school. My mom's idea. (I: Tried to get you out of the business?) Yeah. I mean she doesn't really know about the business but she knows, you know, my dad's up to no good. She could tell, she could tell I'm kinda not on the best track. So, she knows a little bit but not really what we're doin.

ID 13 was aware of his mother's disapproval, describes later that his father started talking to him when he was 15 about pimps, facilitated his first sexual experience with a sex worker, and did not reject his desire to join the business. He did graduate from military school, but during military school was still pimping. His mother who had two younger children left his father, and ID 13 continues to live with his father. When asked what would make him leave the business, ID 13 responded:

> My father leaving. That's it. (I: So you, you stay in the business now because?) My father, yeah. (I: Out of respect, or fear, or what?) I mean, I have no problem doing it. I, I see, I mean of course I know it's wrong, but it makes us money and it helps us eat; so I have no wrong doing it. And as long as my dad's doin it, I'm gonna do it. My dad stops, I feel like it's a reason my dad's stopping, so I'll stop. But if my dad doesn't stop, there's no reason to stop.

Persistent pimps who were socialized by family members often espoused a pride about pimping in their self-narratives as the above quotes suggest.

This pride was coupled with a belief that prostitution and pimping were a legitimate way to earn a living. Most persisting pimps generally espoused the importance of accumulating wealth without considering conventional norms as they believed that their activities were not legally or ethically wrong. A focus on money motivated persisters to enter the illicit sex trade and then expand or continue their pimping. ID 21 exclaimed: "No matter what, it all breaks down to money. (I: What wouldn't you do for money?) I won't do anything homosexual and I won't kill nobody." Further buttressing the focus on profits, ID 15 explained:

> The initial motivator was money and really was the idea of pleasing other people that were lacking something and then I just took a reasonable percentage cause I still have another gig, that now is more of a side gig, then was the original job that I had. (I: So you have a legitimate job as well?) Yeah. (I: How many, uh, uh, sexual providers did you, start with?) Initially I had four, now I have 15 that I work with.

Of those persisting who had prosocial self-narratives, ten expressed that the sex trade should be legal and regulated. Four persisters who projected prosocial self-narratives also noted that it was morally wrong to be involve in the illicit sex trade, but had no plans to quit. These persisters prioritized money over morals. For example, ID 51 illustrates their focus on money over morals:

> You know good morals; I know right and wrong and I know what I get myself into. … Like in my case, I know I don't like to be doing this. I said I've always been money hungry and I always like providing the best for you know my son. … (I: Do you plan on continuing to do this for the next 5 years 10 years, 15?) … I'm not even sure, I don't have like a timeline or like a goal.

ID 51 demonstrates that avoiding deep reflection is one way to keep the focus on profitability and ignore one's conscience. When asked about legalizing prostitution, ID 63 who does not date sex workers articulated well how to ignore any feelings of guilt:

> I don't think it should be legalized. (I: Why?) The example they're gonna show to society. … Everyone's gonna start saying like, ok this is an easy way to make money and instead of seeing more, how can I say it, appropriate people, you're gonna see messed up people. … It's not an appropriate activity. … (I: Do you then feel any guilt or shame around what you do?) Sometimes, I do but you can't mix your feelings with the business, if not then everything's gonna go down. … whenever … I'm starting to think uh, like that, I just forget about it and start doing something else.

Thus, persisters either had reconciled their pimping activity with the belief that the illicit sex trade should be legal or prioritized their pimping and suppressed any thoughts that would make salient the dissonance between their actions and their beliefs.

Persisters and desisters attribute different meanings to conventional jobs

How persisters and "preparatory desisters" interpreted opportunities for and the role of their conventional and legal work also supports the cognitive transformation theory of desistance (Giordano et al., 2002, 2007) and challenges the assumption that all people perceive legal work as providing stability and social status as social control theories would suggest (Laub & Sampson, 2003). Congruent with their salient prosocial identities, the "preparatory desisters" adopted a prosocial conventional view of the function of work, and noted the benefits of a stable income, less stress due to compliance with the law, and a more respectable social status. For example, ID 47 worked full-time as a pimp for ten years from age 24 to 34 while he was in college trying to become a pro-wrestler. He simultaneously worked as a bouncer at an upscale nightclub and referred girls to celebrities as well as drove/protected sex workers for a fee. He earned two college degrees, had a stable job selling hearing aids, and had reduced his work as a bouncer/door host because it was connected to referring girls and drugs and was not a secure income. He disclosed only doing two to three referrals a month. He indicated an unstable pattern of stopping and relapsing across time due to desire for money, but eventually saw marriage as stopping all referrals.

ID 47 described the benefits of legitimate work that prompted his reduced involvement in the illicit sex trade:

> "(I: alright so you started since last year to ease your way out of it?) Yeah, yeah, I had to get a legitimate gig. … I got a call to interview for the job I have now and then I was like you know what, they started me out at like $11 an hour, which for retail is not bad … after a certain amount of time, I mean I have health insurance, I have a 401k, I have you know

> I pay $32 a month for my health and dental and vision. (I: Right, so you have to pay for that stability, that feeling of) Right. But then I, here's my thing, I'm like well, I work Tuesday through Saturday. I don't have to get up on Sunday, I could probably work Saturday nights. You know and like last Saturday I had a bad weekend, I made $60 on Saturday night. The weekend before that I made $450. … (I: Now, you don't really plan on stopping that sorta) The bar? (I: The bar.) It would be tough. (I: The referrals?) At some point it's gonna stop, I mean you know, you get married.

ID 47 highlights his agency for obtaining a legitimate job and reducing referrals (he no longer drives), but sees marriage as the final piece of respectable identity. Another preparatory desister (ID 43) spoke about the need to switch permanently to conventional work for stability, but suffered from depression:

> "I'm seeing a therapist and have been telling her about what I do and telling her that I need to change my life … . She's trying to help me do that and I have a problem with depression. So I don't know, I was thinking about going back to school, for my MBA or Law School or something. I'm kind of stuck, I need to get back, I need to get a job. I can't just do that and not because then I still need income so I have to get a job, or it's gonna force me to doing this."

Preparatory desisters focused on the stability of the conventional work, the steady income, and the reduced stress from not worrying about police detection. ID 23, college educated, had a conventional job and gave this advice to those thinking about pimping: "keep it small, keep it simple, um, don't get greedy and um, above all, just stay smart … and don't stay in it too long, cause you get too jumpy."

Persisting pimps were motivated to seek legitimate work because it facilitated deceiving law enforcement or conventional persons in their social network. Eight interviewees simultaneously worked legitimate jobs, but were embedded in a deviant lifestyle, involving current or prior commission of other crimes such as drug dealing. Consistent with Goffman's (1963) concept of passing, persisters had legitimate jobs to justify the proceeds made from the illicit sex or drug trade or to launder money. For example, ID 46 noted that legitimate jobs provided good justifications for having large sums of cash when police officers stopped him. He asserted:

> When the police pull up on you, you got $2,000 in your pocket, and they say where you work at? I don't have a job, that's shit right there. … But you pull up on me, I got $2,000. How you get? I drive a truck. (I: Ok.) I can have $2,000. (I: Right, so that's why you also have conventional jobs?) Always, and everybody's that's worked with us, all of us, we had [legitimate jobs]. When they busted us, they busted a stand of us, they said we had the biggest distribution of heroin in the City. (I: Were you distributing?) We were distributing. We were doing everything … because the girls came along because of the drugs.

Legitimate businesses also aided pimps as a means to launder money to avoid suspicion. Five pimps owned massage parlors or legal escort services for the purposes of deceiving law enforcement and avoiding sanctions. The fringe businesses of massage parlors, strip clubs, and legal escort services provided further ambiguity about whether prostitution should be criminalized or managed as a legitimate business. Individuals understood that these fringe businesses were fertile places to learn how to manage sex workers, and four pimps sought mentoring from those who worked in these fringe businesses as they entered or expanded their business.

Beyond these fringe businesses, pimps who were employed at nightclubs or in the entertainment industry were more likely to see their involvement in the illicit sex trade as an extension of their legitimate work. Four interviewees described how their work as a manager, DJ or bouncer at conventional and upscale nightclubs facilitated their pimping activity. Nine other interviewees noted that the bars provided connections to clients, potential sex workers, and illicit drugs. For example, ID 49, a persister, started legitimate work after being released from juvenile detention at 18 and vowed to never go back to jail. He explained the function of legitimate work:

> "I started DJing. ... (I: So how long did you DJ?) I think for about 20 years on and off. ... . I'm smart. I've held a legitimate career; you know what I mean (I: Right.) And I still do stuff, you know and I still have a side company cause you gotta justify the money. (I: Right.) ... That's how they catch you. They can't get you for nothing else."

Those who entered through night clubs or entertainment businesses learned normative approval of the party lifestyle embraced in these legitimate businesses. Interviewees also noted that working legitimately in upscale night clubs provided access to clients who held powerful positions and social status in society. Other forms of legitimate work provided the connections to clients and potential sex workers. Interviewees who held construction jobs, truck driving jobs, and management positions in corporations or smaller businesses also discussed the role that the legitimate work played in facilitating their immersion into pimping or driving.

Do persisters and preparatory desisters have similar environmental backgrounds and opportunities?

Thus far, our analysis suggests that the meanings ascribed to conventional work or other environmental opportunities to take on conventional roles are more important than the structural opportunities. However, our analysis has primarily focused on conventional work, and has not considered pimps' childhood upbringing or their structural opportunity to attend college. To assess whether preparatory desisters had similar childhood structural opportunities and similar current opportunities, Table one presents a comparison of self-identified pimps, persistent pimps with pro-social identity, and preparatory desisters on being raised in disadvantaged neighborhood with visible prostitution, parental values, current conventional work, college education, and entry into pimping.

Are persisters and "preparatory desisters" equally likely to hold conventional work? As shown in Table 1, the three groups (self-identified pimps, persisters with pro-social identities, and those leading double lives) were equally likely to hold a current job and across these groups twenty pimps held a current conventional job. Among the 20 pimps with conventional jobs, eight considered their conventional work to be a part-time job (none of the "double lives" by nature of coding), nine considered their pimping activity to be part-time, and three leading "double lives" had transitioned from simultaneous participation in legal employment and in illicit sex trade to exclusively holding a conventional job. Four individuals owned massage parlors or other small businesses that primarily were used to hide their illicit activities and were not coded as having a current conventional job and as "persisters." Of those with current legal work, half also described other conventional jobs held over the course of their lives. In addition, 14 of the 29 interviewees who

Table 1. Persistent self-identified pimps, pro-social persistent pimps, and pimps leading double life: Comparison on childhood socialization and structural opportunities.

	Persisting, Self-Identified Pimp (N = 22)	Persisting Pimp Pro-Social Identity (N = 14)	Leading Double Life (N = 13)
Neighborhood[1]			
Disadvantaged	81.8% (N = 18)	35.7% (N = 5)	38.5% (N = 5)
Middle Class	18.2% (N = 4)	64.3% (N = 9)	61.5% (N = 8)
Parental Values[2]			
Street values or not mentioned	68.2% (N = 15)	14.3% (N = 2)	7.7% (N = 1)
Middle class values	31.8% (N = 7)	85.7% (N = 12)	92.3% (N = 12)
Participant's Education[3]			
No college degree	86.4% (N = 19)	71.4% (N = 10)	23.1% (N = 3)
College degree	13.6% (N = 3)	28.6% (N = 4)	76.9% (N = 10)
Current Legitimate Work[4]			
No	68.2% (N = 15)	57.1% (N = 8)	46.2% (N = 6)
Yes	31.8% (N = 7)	42.9% (N = 6)	53.8% (N = 7)
Is Currently Immersed in Other Crime[5]			
No	22.7% (N = 5)	78.6% (N = 11)	76.9% (N = 10)
Yes	77.3% (N = 17)	21.4% (N = 3)	23.1% (N = 3)
Socialized Into Pimping Through Family[6]			
No	54.5% (N = 12)	78.6% (N = 11)	92.3% (N = 12)
Yes	45.5% (N = 10)	21.4% (N = 3)	15.4% (N = 1)
Entered Pimping Through Job[7]			
No	95.5% (N = 21)	21.4% (N = 3)	53.8% (N = 7)
Yes	4.5% (N = 1)	78.6% (N = 11)	46.2% (N = 6)

Note. Chi-square tests: [1]$X^2(2) = 9.94$, $p < .007$, Cramer's V = .45; [2]$X^2(2) = 17.11$, $p < .0001$, Cramer's V = .59; [3] $X^2(2) = 14.77$, $p < .001$, Cramer's V = .55; [4] $\times^2(2) = 1.62$, $p < .43$, Cramer's V = .19, $p. < .47$; [5] $X^2(2) = 14.75$, $p < .001$, Cramer's V = .55; [6] $X^2(2) = 6.20$, $p < .05$, Cramer's V = .36; [7] $X^2(2) = 20.84$, $p < .0001$, Cramer's V = .65.

were not currently holding a legal job described past conventional employment. Current and previous legitimate work included: managers in shoe stores, apartments, or businesses; business consultant; chief executive officer; truck driver; bus driver; barber; DJ; pro-wrestler; professional boxer; bouncer; sewage worker; iron worker; chef; salesperson in medical supply companies; construction worker; computer programmer; and owner of construction or towing businesses. The similarity of working conventional jobs, in connection with the different reasons offered for seeking conventional jobs, supports that conclusion that the meaning assigned to the job is crucial in supporting desistance from pimping. As shown in Table 1, double live pimps and persisters with a pro-social identity were more likely to enter pimping through having lost a conventional job or through social networking within a conventional job, suggesting that social networking within these jobs also contributed to entry into the illicit sex trade. In contrast, self-identified pimps were more likely to enter pimping through socialization from family members.

Supporting the qualitative analysis of the role of conventional family and friends in supporting desistance, Table one shows that almost all "double lives" pimps and persisters with a pro-social identity reported that their parents would disapprove of their pimping (held "decency" values) whereas only about one-third of self-identified pimps reported that their parents would disapprove. Parental approval or disapproval alone is not a one-to -one correspondence with the pimps' self-narratives, but individuals who have "street code" parents were more likely to incorporate being a pimp as part of their self-identity and were motivated to persist in their pimping activities. Furthermore, about three-quarters of the double live pimps and persisters with a prosocial identity were not involved in other crimes whereas only a little over 20% of self-identified pimps were not involved in other criminal activity. Thus, how their parents communicated their own values and socialized them during childhood is related to their involvement in other criminal activity.

Although preparatory desisters and persisters did not differ on involvement in conventional work, a little over three-quarters of preparatory desisters had a college degree whereas 13.6% of the self-identified pimps and 28.6% of persisters with a pro-social identity had earned a college degree. A logistic regression revealed that pimps with a college education or with parents who disapproved were over 11 times more likely to be in the group of preparatory desisters than were those without these characteristics, $p < .006$. These findings suggest that preparatory desistance is more likely with a college education, due to increased options for conventional jobs that yielded higher earnings. The meaning attributed to conventional work matters, but a college education often allows conventional work to become part of one's self-identity and provides greater opportunities for conventional jobs that offer more pay and more autonomy.

Discussion

Pimping has often been construed as a lifetime career (e.g., Davis, 2017), and an exploration of pimps' perspectives on the desisting and persisting process is a relatively new area of inquiry. Our research highlights that "hooks for change" such as legitimate employment can be interpreted to support persisting or desisting in the illicit sex trade. Our qualitative analysis suggests that engaging in legitimate employment is not simply an external event but it unfolds through social interactions and reflections on the meaning of these roles shape one's core self-identity. Consistent with the cognitive and emotional transformation theory (Giordano et al., 2002, 2007), offenders actively constructed their self-identities, values, and attitudes about the illicit sex trade from their parental values and their social networks of co-workers, family and friends. Those leading double lives, drawing from their childhood conventional values, focused on serving as role models of good character and having long-term security in legitimate work that avoided stigmatization and supported a reputable social identity. Persisters sought out conventional jobs to hide their illegal activities and avoid official sanctions.

The meaning of work and preparatory desistance

Life-course theory (Laub & Sampson, 2003), derived from social control theories, assumes that roles serve purposes consistent with conventional values and conformity to criminal laws. Our qualitative research findings challenge that assumption, and highlight that individuals attributed meaning to their participation in social roles of legitimate work that supported their persistence or reduced involvement in the illicit sex trade. Likewise, social ties to conventional others and fulfillment of traditional social roles of father, husband, and son served either to motivate continued involvement in criminal behavior or to reduce involvement to avoid repute from conventional family and friends. The interviews highlighted that decisions about persisting or desisting were made within social relationships and contexts, which were actively constructed through hiding illicit activities from conventional others. Embarrassment and guilt of those leading double lives often coincided with deeper reflection about plans to exit the illicit sex trade, as avoiding stigma was a critical concern.

Legitimate work is connected to masculinity ideologies that allow individuals to attribute meanings that might foster persistence in illicit activities (Bruckert, 2018; Stalans & Finn, 2018). Consistent with prior quantitative research (e.g., Loughran et al., 2017), our findings supported that transitions to conventional work were not enough to stimulate desistance and demonstrated that how offenders actively construed these transitions were related to their continual or reduced involvement in pimping. Pimps who adopted a deviant self-identity or persisted in pimping sought legitimate work to hide their illicit activities. Those leading double lives sought legitimate work for its long-term security and ability to enhance social status, emphasizing the importance of serving as a role model for their children if they were fathers, and maintaining relationships with conventional others by not disclosing their pimping activities. Thus, legitimate work in and of itself is not an assurance that desistance will begin, echoing the conflicting findings of the relationship between employment and reductions in criminal activity (Uggen & Wakefield, 2008). Work programs that foster prosocial values through allowing positive generative contributions to the community might foster transformations from a deviant to a prosocial core self.

The narratives also suggest that it might matter as much with whom one associates with at work as the quality of the work itself. The social networks obtained in legitimate work environments facilitated entry and continual involvement in the illicit sex trade for those in the entertainment, construction, corporate finance and trucking driving sectors. Highlighting the cultural and social aspects of work supports prior research that has found legitimate restaurant work contributed to continual use of illicit drugs (e.g., Uggen & Shannon, 2014). Recent quantitative research on young adult offenders (Loughran et al., 2017) has found that many active offenders participate in both legitimate employment and illicit activities. The relationship between legitimate work and desistance is a complicated one. Given that we examined individuals involved in the illicit sex industry, an industry that often thrives and is supported by fringe businesses that are legitimate and lucrative, one might expect that the transition to only legitimate work might be easier. However, legitimate work in entertainment, construction, corporations, and skilled trades also tolerated the broader cultural misogynistic frames, and the informal socializing with co-workers facilitated an underground illicit sex trade within legitimate business settings (Bruckert, 2018; Stalans & Finn, 2018). There was no sharp demarcation between legitimate work and illicit sex work in some employment settings. Our findings suggest that norms and values are an important part of conversations among acquaintances and friends in social and work settings. Thus, "hook-up" sexual cultures that are part of the norms of bars and college life raise questions about the broader societal views on the wrongfulness of prostitution and its prohibition. From these subcultural norms that pimping is not harmful, persisting offenders can frame their activities as a service to sex workers rather than an exploitation of sex workers.

Importance of morals and guilt

The emotional and moral content of self-narratives were central to preparatory desisters' reasons for transitioning or to exit from pimping. This finding reinforces the psychological research on self-identity (McAdams, 2013) and the importance of moral or emotional dilemmas in self-narratives of decisions to transition away from illegal activity (e.g., Vaughan, 2007). Davis' (2017) interviews with nine retired Black pimps who had been pimping for 15 to 25 years before retiring still expressed their self-narratives around pimping. Preparatory desisters in our study expressed both guilt and conventional values as the reason why pimping's fast-paced lifestyle was becoming undesirable and allowed them to frame conventional work and relationships as providing desired stability and less questionable respectability.

Directions for future research and policy implications

Our purposive sample is diverse, containing pimps and drivers involved in high-end as well as low-end sex industry sectors. Interviewees came from diverse educational, racial, and socio-economic backgrounds. Individuals with legitimate jobs and those without legitimate jobs did not differ on background characteristics, suggesting selection effects could not explain who held legitimate jobs, though those with legitimate jobs were older when they entered and had fewer years of involvement in the illicit sex trade. It, however, was clear that those who were leading double lives came from families that emphasized conventional values, whereas self-identified persisting pimps were from families that were embedded in deviant subcultures and disadvantaged neighborhoods. This purposive sample and the grounded theory approach are not intended to generalize to a wider population of third-party facilitators. These self-narratives contained thick detailed stories that articulated the self-identities, values, social pressures, and economic and social status rewards contributing to their past and anticipated future involvement in the illicit sex trade. Many of the interviewees naturally told stories about their past that they believed were important for the interviewer to understand how, when, and why they became involved in pimping and driving, and their anticipated continuation or desisting from these activities. These detailed stories about specific situations and detailed information about how they did their work provide more confidence that interviewees were pimping, even though we were unable to observe pimps managing their sex workers (see Scott, 2008). Moreover, these stories are socially constructed but convey pimps' and drivers' views of the roles that conventional work, fatherhood, and social relationships serve in their decisions about involvement in the illicit sex trade (for methodological discussion on narratives see Sandberg, 2010). While we were unable to observe pimps actually managing work, we took other precautions to assess whether they were involved in pimping by obtaining specific details about their work and the natural stories that unfolded provide some confidence that they were engaged in pimping. Further research needs to explore how individuals reconcile parallel lives of participating in conventional roles such as legitimate employment and conventional relationships with their participation in deviant subcultures such as illicit sex or drug markets. How the social context and their self-identities shape what narratives pimps and drivers shared with others and whether such storytelling contributes to desistance are questions for future research.

Pimping is often regarded as a crime motivated primarily by economic profit, and thus increased certainty and severity of sanctioning is often recommended as the most effective strategy. Pimps leading double lives were raised in homes that emphasized conventional values and disapproval of illegal activities. Some pimps who were in the process of reducing their participation in the illicit sex trade articulated qualms with the immorality of prostitution and considered the amount of economic gain in relationship to their conscience; these pimps were in it for the short-term to accumulate sufficient income to become fully legitimate. Programs in several jurisdictions in the U.S. have attempted to send the message of the immoral nature of buying or facilitating the sale of sex to counter normative messages approving of the illicit sex trade. These efforts convey that the community does not support treating sex as a commodity, and by implication buyers and third-party facilitators are perpetuating a harm on the community as their willingness to purchase or profit from the sale of sex may involve the exploitation of women and minors. The pimps and drivers who expressed moral qualms about the exploitation of women might have drawn from these wider cultural frames, which stimulated their embarrassment and guilt. These media campaigns provide narratives that counter the no harm and profitability messages, which might provide frames for those leading "double lives" to discontinue their involvement in the illicit sex trade. Self-identified pimps or "hobbyists", however, might discount the normative and deterrent messages of these campaigns. Deterrence campaigns, even with normative messages, often will be ineffective for those who cannot pursue college educations or have adopted a deviant self-narrative from familial socialization. Pimps who have the trappings of conventional work and college education often can pass as complying, but pimps professing pro-social self-narratives, especially if they interact with primarily conventional others, will be more likely to desist from the illicit sex trade.

Notes

1. Pimp, in this paper, is not used as a pejorative term, but a legal term, and is not based on the self-identity of the interviewees. The term, pimp, is consistent with state crimes of pandering, pimping, or promotion of prostitution.
2. Our research is informed through a mixed method approach. As Brent and Kraska (2010) noted, "This approach requires that our field abandon the incompatibility thesis and dismissive thinking. Our research objectives, and not methodological preference, should guide method selection – whether qualitative, quantitative, or both." (p. 427). Pragmatism is the typical philosophy of science associated with mixed methods, and it challenges the beliefs that qualitative and quantitative are incompatible. In the current research, the qualitative description of non-coercive pimps provides the needed contextual details to understand the strategies they employed and their background, and to have more confidence in their reports. The statistical tools allowed a more systematic way to see the patterns among the socialization concepts and coercion. In this study, we utilized conversational open-ended qualitative interviews to avoid making assumptions about how pimps run their business, and informed participants that we would ask follow-up questions so that we fully understood their perspective. The researchers had no prior or current experience in the illicit sex trade, and had or have no firm opinions about the appropriate policies for the illicit sex trade. As interdisciplinary researchers in the fields of criminal justice and social psychology who appreciate both qualitative and quantitative research, we wanted to learn as much as possible about the pimps' views, life history, and their business from their perspective.

Disclosure statement

No potential conflict of interest was reported by the authors.

References

Anderson, E. (1999). *Code of the street: Decency, violence, and the moral life of the inner city.* New York, NY: W. W. Norton & Company.

Brent, J., & Kraska, P. B. (2010). Moving beyond our methodological default: A case for mixed methods. *Journal of Criminal Justice Education, 21*(4), 412–430. doi:10.1080/10511253.2010.516562

Bruckert, C. (2018). Who are third parties? Pathways in and out of third party work. In C. Bruckert & C. Parent (Eds.), *Getting past the Pimp: Management in the sex industry* (pp. 36–55). Toronto, Canada: University of Toronto Press.

Campbell, H., & Hansen, T. (2012). Getting out of the game: Desistance from drug trafficking. *International Journal of Drug Policy, 23*(6), 481–487. doi:10.1016/j.drugpo.2012.04.002

Curcione, N. (1997). Suburban snowmen: Facilitating factors in the careers of middle-class coke dealers. *Deviant Behavior, 18*, 233–253. doi:10.1080/01639625.1997.9968057

Davis, H. (2017). Exit from the game: Ex-pimps and desistance in the U.S.A. In A. Horning & A. Marcus (Eds.), *Third party sex work and pimps in the age of anti-trafficking* (pp. 111–129). Gewerbestrasse, Switzerland: Springer International Publishing.

Finn, M. A., & Stalans, L. J. (2017). The influence of managers' rules on health and safety on economic success in illicit sex market. In A. Horning & A. Marcus (Eds.), *Third party sex work and pimps in the age of anti-trafficking* (pp. 89–110). New York, NY: Springer.

Giordano, P. C., Cernkovich, S. A., & Rudolph, J. L. (2002). Gender, crime, and desistance: Toward a theory of cognitive transformation. *American Journal of Sociology, 107*(4), 990–1064. doi:10.1086/343191

Giordano, P. C., Schroeder, R. D., & Cernkovich, S. A. (2007). Emotions and crime over the life course: A neo-median perspective on criminal continuity and change. *American Journal of Sociology, 112*(6), 1603–1661. doi:10.1086/512710

Goffman, E. (1959). *The presentation of self in everyday life.* New York, NY: Doubleday.

Goffman, E. (1963). *Stigma: Notes on the management of spoiled identity.* Englewood Cliffs, NJ: Prentice Hall.

Healy, D. (2014). Becoming a desister: Exploring the role of agency, coping and imagination in the construction of a new self. *British Journal of Criminology, 54*(5), 873–891. doi:10.1093/bjc/azu048

Horning, A., & Sriken, J. (2017). Pimps, bottoms, and the nexus of caring and cash in a Harlem sex market. In A. Horning & A. Marcus (Eds.), *Third party sex work and pimps in the age of anti-trafficking* (pp. 71–88). Springer Publications.

Intravia, J., Gibbs, B. R., Wolff, K. T., Paez, R., Berheimer, A., & Piquero, A. R. (2018). The mediating role of street code attitudes on the self-control and crime relationship. *Deviant Behavior, 39*(10), 1305–1321. doi:10.1080/01639625.2017.1410611

Jacques, S., & Wright, R. (2015). *Code of the Suburb: Inside the world of young middle-class drug dealers.* Chicago, IL: University of Chicago Press.

Laub, J. H., & Sampson, R. J. (2003). *Shared beginnings, divergent lives: Delinquent boys to age 70.* Cambridge, MA: Harvard University Press.

Loughran, T. A., Nagin, D. S., & Nguyen, H. (2017). Crime and legal work: A Markovian model of the desistance process. *Social Problems, 64*(1), 30–52. doi:10.1093/socpro/spw027

Marcus, A., Horning, A., Curtis, R., Sanson, J., & Thompson, E. (2014). Conflict and agency among sex workers and pimps: A closer look at domestic minor sex trafficking. *The ANNALS of the American Academy of Political and Social Science, 653*(1), 225–246. doi:10.1177/002716214521993

Maruna, S. (2001). *Making Good: How ex-convicts reform and rebuild their lives.* Washington, DC: American Psychological Association Publication.

May, T., Harocopos, A., & Hough, M. (2000). *For love of money: Pimps and the management of sex work* (Police Research Series, 134). London: Home Office, Policing and Reducing Crime Unit, Research, Development and Statistics Directorate. Clive House, Petty France. London, UK, SW1H 9HD.

McAdams, D. P. (2013). The psychological self as actor, agent and author. *Perspectives on Psychological Science, 8*(3), 272–295. doi:10.1177/1745691612464657

McLean, K. C., Pasupathi, M., & Pals, J. L. (2007). Selves creating stories creating selves: A process model of self-development. *Personality and Social Psychology Review*, *11*, 262–278. doi:10.1177/1088868307301034

Milner, C., & Milner, R. (1973). *Black players: The secret world of black pimps*. New York, NY: Bantam.

Morselli, C., & Savoie-Gargiso, I. (2014). Coercion, control, and cooperation in a prostitution ring. *The ANNALS of the American Academy of Political and Social Science*, *653*(1), 247–265. doi:10.1177/0002716214521995

Moule, R. K., Burt, C. H., Stewart, E. A., & Simons, R. L. (2015). Developmental trajectories of individuals' code of the street beliefs through emerging adulthood. *Journal of Research in Crime and Delinquency*, *52*(3), 342–372. doi:10.1177/0022427814565904

Paternoster, R., & Bushway, S. (2009). Desistance and the feared self: Toward an identity theory of criminal desistance. *The Journal of Criminal Law and Criminology*, *99*(4), 1103–1156.

Presser, L. (2010). Collecting and analyzing the stories of offenders. *Journal of Criminal Justice Education*, *21*(4), 431–446. doi:10.1080/10511253.2010.516563

Presser, L., & Sandberg, L. (2015). Conclusion. In L. Presser & S. Sandberg (Eds.), *Narrative criminology: Understanding stories of crime* (pp. 287–299). New York: New York University Press.

Raphael, J., & Myers-Powell, B. (2010). *From victims to victimizers: Interviews with 25 ex-pimps in Chicago*. Chicago, IL: DePaul University College of Law.

Sandberg, S. (2010). What can "lies" tell us about life? Notes towards a framework of narrative criminology. *Journal of Criminal Justice Education*, *21*(4), 447–465. doi:10.1080/10511253.2010.516564

Scott, G. (2008). "They got their program, and I got mine": A cautionary tale concerning the ethical implications of using respondent-driven sampling to study injection drug users. *International Journal of Drug Policy*, *19*, 42–51.

Simons, R. L., & Burt, C. H. (2011). Learning to be bad: Adverse social conditions, social schemas, and crime. *Criminology*, *49*(2), 553–597. doi:10.1111/j.1745-9125.2011.00231.x

Stalans, L. J., & Finn, M. A. (2018). Pimps' perspectives on good and bad sex workers. In S. Brown & O. Sefiha (Eds.), *Handbook of deviance* (pp. 257–271). New York, NY: Routledge.

Stewart, E. A. (2010). Race, Code of the Street, and Violent Delinquency: A multilevel investigation of neighborhood street culture and individual norms of violence. *Criminology*, *48*(2), 569–605. doi:10.1111/j.1745-9125.2010.00196.x

Uggen, C., & Wakefield, S. (2008). What have we learned from longitudinal studies of work and crime?. In A. M. Liberman (Ed.), *The long view of crime: A synthesis of longitudinal research* (pp. 191–219). New York, NY: Springer.

Uggen, C., & Shannon, S. K. S. (2014). Productive addicts and harm reduction: How work reduces crime – But not drug use. *Social Problems*, *61*(1), 105–130. doi:10.1525/sp.2013.11225

Van Der Geest, V. R., Bijleveld, C. C. J. H., & Blokland, A. A. J. (2011). The effects of employment on longitudinal trajectories of offending: A follow-up of high-risk youth from 18 to 32 years of age. *Criminology*, *49*(4), 1195–1234. doi:10.1111/j.1745-9125.2011.00247.x

Vaughan, B. (2007). The internal narrative of desistance. *British Journal of Criminology*, *47*, 390–404. doi:10.1093/bjc/azl083

Index